Sir Perceval of Galles

and

Ywain and Gawain

Middle English Texts

General Editor

Russell A. Peck
University of Rochester

Advisory Board

Rita Copeland
University of Minnesota

Thomas G. Hahn
University of Rochester

Lisa Kiser
Ohio State University

Alan Lupack
University of Rochester

Thomas Seiler
Western Michigan University

R. A. Shoaf
University of Florida

Bonnie Wheeler
Southern Methodist University

The Middle English Texts Series is designed for classroom use. Its goal is to make available to teachers and students texts which occupy an important place in the literary and cultural canon but which have not been readily available in student editions. The series does not include those authors such as Chaucer, Langland, the Pearl-poet, or Malory, whose English works are normally in print in good student editions. The focus is, instead, upon Middle English literature adjacent to those authors that teachers need in compiling the syllabuses they wish to teach. The editions maintain the linguistic integrity of the original work but within the parameters of modern reading conventions. The texts are printed in the modern alphabet and follow the practices of modern capitalization and punctuation. Manuscript abbreviations are expanded, and u/v and j/i spellings are regularized according to modern orthography. Hard words, difficult phrases, and unusual idioms are glossed on the page, either in the right margin or at the foot of the page. Textual notes appear at the end of the text, along with a glossary. The editions include short introductions on the history of the work, its merits and points of topical interest, and also include briefly annotated bibliographies.

Sir Perceval of Galles
and
Ywain and Gawain

Edited by
Mary Flowers Braswell

Published for TEAMS
(The Consortium for the Teaching of the Middle Ages)
in Association with the University of Rochester

by

Medieval Institute Publications

WESTERN MICHIGAN UNIVERSITY

Kalamazoo, Michigan — 1995

for Mary

Library of Congress Cataloging-in-Publication Data

Sir Perceval of Galles.
   Sir Perceval of Galles ; and, Ywain and Gawain / edited by Mary
Flowers Braswell.
      p.   cm. -- (Middle English texts)
   Text in Middle English; notes in English.
   Includes bibliographical references.
   ISBN 1-879288-60-5
   1. Perceval (Legendary character)--Romances. 2. English poetry-
-Middle English, 1100-1500. 3. Gawain (Legendary character)-
-Romances. 4. Ywain (Legendary character)--Romances. 5. Arthurian
romances. 6. Romances, English. I. Braswell, Mary Flowers, 1943-
. II. Consortium for the Teaching of the Middle Ages. III. Ywain
and Gawain. IV. Title. V. Series: Middle English texts (Kalamazoo,
Mich.)
   PR2065 .P4 1995
   821'.030801--dc20   95-31669
                                                            CIP

ISBN 1-879288-60-5

Copyright 1995 by the Board of The Medieval Institute
Second Printing 2003

Cover design by Elizabeth King

Printed in the United States of America

Contents

Preface

For assistance in preparing this edition I am grateful to the Graduate School of the University of Alabama in Birmingham for awarding me a Faculty Research Grant in the Summer of 1989 that enabled me to visit London and Lincoln and to view the relevant manuscripts. My thanks to the British Library for permission to edit *Ywain and Gawain* from the Cotton MS Galba E IX and to the Lincoln Cathedral Library for access to the Thornton Manuscript, Lincoln Cathedral MS 91, containing *Sir Perceval of Galles*. I wish also to thank Theodore M. Benditt, Dean of the School of Arts and Humanities, for providing me with funds to attend Columbia University during the summers of 1989 and 1990, where I studied Paleography and Codicology; Ms. Denise Parker for clerical assistance during the earlier stages of this project; and the National Endowment for the Humanities, for providing assistance to the University of Rochester for the production of this volume. I am indebted most of all to Russell A. Peck, General Editor of the Middle English Texts Series, for his patience and careful reading of my text, and to Alan Lupack, who reviewed the manuscript in its final stages. Lee Dongchoon read my work against microfilms and facsimiles of the original manuscripts as well as subsequent modern editions, thereby discovering several errors in my work and in the editions of others. I am likewise grateful to Karen Saupe, Eve Salisbury, and Jennifer Church for their assistance in proofreading, tracking down references, making corrections, and formatting the volume. All remaining errors are, of course, my own. Finally, I wish to thank the National Endowment for the Humanities for their support in the production of this edition.

Mary Flowers Braswell
Birmingham, Alabama
January 15, 1995

Sir Perceval of Galles

Introduction

The unique copy of *Sir Perceval of Galles* is contained in the Thornton Manuscript, preserved in Lincoln Cathedral as MS 91. The 322-page manuscript contains sixty-four pieces in all, ranging from saints' lives to medical treatises, and including seven additional romances: the *Alliterative Morte Arthure*, *The Romance of Octovyane*, *The Romance of Sir Ysambrace*, *The Romance of Dyoclicyane*, *Sir Degrevante*, *Sir Eglamour*, and *The Awentyrs of Arthure at the Terne Wathelyne*. The contents are all written in one hand, a variable mid-fifteenth-century *Anglicana Formata*, and the dialect — which may not be the original — is northern, reflecting the North Riding Yorkshire district of the scribe. Decorations are confined to initials outlined in black with tinted sprays and foliage, red initials flourished in black or violet, and various touches of red, marking headings and paragraphs. The manuscript is written on paper and is in generally good condition, although certain of its pages have been damaged with loss of text. Worm holes occasionally obscure the writing; ink blots and water stains appear throughout. The original binding, probably the "thick oaken boards, covered with white leather, and fastened with a clasp," referred to by Madden, has been replaced by later oak boards covered with a pig-skin leather.

The scribe was one Robert Thornton of East Newton, Yorkshire, whose own name (and that of various family members) appears several times throughout the work. The British Library Additional Manuscript 31042, containing the unique copy of *Wynnere and Wastoure*, was apparently also copied by Thornton who appears to have been an educated amateur. A manor lord who died between 1456 and 1465, Thornton likely copied his texts over the years as materials became available to him. At his death, his library passed on to his family where it remained for several generations. In the late seventeenth century, Thomas Comber, husband of Alice Thornton, either gave or sold the manuscript to Daniel Brevint, Dean of Lincoln, and the work has remained in the possession of the Cathedral Library since that time.

Sandwiched between *Awentyrs of Arthure* and *Three Charms for Toothache*, *Sir Perceval of Galles* is the first (and besides Malory, the only) English rendering of the naive and bungling knight made popular in Chrétien de Troyes' twelfth-century *Conte del Graal*. The young Perceval, his father killed in battle, is raised in the forest by his

1

mother, who abhors chivalry and the courtly world. He wears goatskins, hunts animals with his spear, and, after his first introduction to civilization, rides a pregnant mare that he thinks is a stallion. Encountering three knights in the woods one day, he determines to become like them, and, despite his mother's reluctance to let him go, he sets off for Arthur's court wearing his mother's ring. Coming upon a lady sleeping in a tent, he exchanges his ring for her (unknown to him) magic one, a ring which has the ability to protect its wearer from harm. He then follows adventures familiar to readers of romance where a "childe" triumphs over seemingly insurmountable odds. Young Perceval defeats successively the Red Knight, the Black Knight, the Sudan, and the giant Gollerothirame. He liberates Lady Lufamore, marries her, and becomes a king. He then decides to restore his mother. On his return to the woods of his origin he rescues the "tent lady" and restores to her her rightful ring; and he finds his mother in time to release her from the insanity she suffered at believing her son was dead. Finally, Perceval leaves for the Holy Land where he wins many cities before he is killed. And "thusgate," notes the poet, "endis hee."

Despite its persistent liveliness, *Sir Perceval* has until recent years suffered at the hands of those critics who judged it "uninteresting," "wretched," and "crude." The poet, who probably operated in the north-east Midlands during the first half of the fourteenth century, has been denounced for not understanding his original source and for having little or no poetic "flair." It is true that the grammatical constructions are sometimes loose and that the diction is occasionally labored. Moreover, the poetic line lacks that density and texture one finds in Chaucer and the *Gawain*-poet, and the kind of "machinery" — such courtly trappings as forest naps, the *locus amoenus*, catalogues of birds, spices, and food — we have come to associate with the more sophisticated romances is not to be found in this poem. But it is ultimately the comparison to Chrétien's romance — which the English poet might or might not have known — that has worked most to the latter poet's detriment. And Chaucer's supposedly snide reference in *Sir Thopas* to "sire Percevell" drinking water of the well has added to the poem's stigmatization. Recent criticism, however, views the poem in a more favorable light.

The poet of *Sir Perceval* was no mere hack writer. Certain scenes, for example, are clearly and effectively parodic of the romance genre, as when the country lad wearing goatskins and carrying a dart rides his pregnant mare into Arthur's court to be made a knight. Chaucer's Thopas, pricking through the forest on a sweaty horse, carrying a too-light launcegay and searching for any available elf-queen, fits nicely into Perceval's cortege, leading one to suspect that the poem provided an impetus as well as an object for Chaucer's satire. Moreover, the crude but successful young hero who knows so little of "nurtour" becomes a foil to the effete and courtly Arthur, thus suggesting the disenchantment with the noble ideal that accelerated as the Middle

Introduction

Ages waned. This attitude seems also to be reflected in the poem's black humor that should not be mistaken for crudity. When Perceval tosses the Red Knight's witch-mother into the fire, for example, he remarks casually that she might "lie still and sweat," and when the knight severs the foot of Gollerothirame, he notes that although the giant might have trouble in walking, he should take pleasure in leaping! In addition to tonal sophistication, the poet has taken some care to integrate the various aspects of his plot. By and large, events are not superfluous; characters are introduced and then returned to; loose ends are effectively sewn together. The maiden in the tent, for example, is not merely a formulaic device to be used and discarded, but instead a crucial factor that allows for the events to follow and assists in securing a conclusion that Chrétien never attained. Nor is the grieving mother left simply to wander in the woods forever (Chrétien allows her to die). Instead she is ultimately sought out and cared for by a more concerned, more considerate son who has now deferentially shed his knightly garb for his familiar goatskins. There is a hint of regeneration as the story comes full circle; the "wilde gerys" [behavior] of Perceval have been tamed.

The poem employs a tail-rhyme stanza of sixteen lines, rhyming (sometimes roughly) *aaabcccbdddbeeeb*. Key words in the final "b" line are repeated in the first line of the following stanza. Such a rhyme scheme is often found in the so-called "minstrel romances" flourishing in East Anglia in the fourteenth century. Other copies of the manuscript (including the one known to Chaucer) have been lost, although the dissemination of the poem from its supposed north-east Midlands origins to the London area and then to the north presupposes that there were at one time multiple copies.

This edition is based on the Thornton MS. I have regularized *u/v* and *i/j* usage according to modern spelling conventions and have ignored *ff* spellings where modern orthography would write *f*. All emendations are acknowledged in the end-notes, along with variant readings in other modern printed editions.

Select Bibliography

Manuscript

Lincoln Cathedral MS 91 (Thornton, c. 1440), fols. 161r–176r.

Facsimile

The Thornton Manuscript (Lincoln Cathedral MS 91). Introduction by D. S. Brewer and A. E. B. Owen. London: The Scolar Press, 1977.

Editions

Baldwin, Dean Richard, ed. *Sir Perceval of Galles: An Edition*. Dissertation, Ohio State University, 1973.

Campion, J., and F. Holthausen, eds. *Sir Perceval of Gales*. Alt- und Mittelenglische Texte 5. Heidelberg: Carl Winter, 1913.

Ellis, F. S., ed. *Syr Perecyvelle of Gales*. Hammersmith: Kelmscott, 1895.

French, Walter Hoyt, and Charles Brockway Hale, eds. *Middle English Metrical Romances*. Vol. 2. New York: Prentice-Hall, 1930. Rpt. New York: Russell & Russell, 1964. Pp. 529–604.

Griffiths, J. J., ed. *Sir Percevell of Gales*. Masters Thesis, University College of North Wales, 1977.

Halliwell [-Phillipps], James Orchard, ed. *The Thornton Romances: The Early English Metrical Romances of Perceval, Isumbras, Eglamour, and Degrevant*. Camden Society 30. London: J.B. Nichols and Son for the Camden Society, 1844.

Mills, Maldwyn, ed. *Ywain and Gawain, Sir Percyvell of Gales, The Anturs of Arther*. London: Everyman's Library, 1992.

Catalogues and Studies of the Manuscript

Keiser, George. "The Nineteenth-Century Discovery of the Thornton Manuscript (Lincoln Cathedral Library MS 91)." *Papers of the Bibliographical Society of America* 77 (1983), 167–90.

Thompson, R. M., ed. *Catalogue of the Manuscripts of Lincoln Cathedral Chapter Library*. Cambridge: Boydell and Brewer, 1989.

Introduction

Bibliographies

Newstead, Helaine. "Arthurian Legends." In *A Manual of the Writings in Middle English*, ed. J. Burke Severs. Vol. 1. New Haven: Connecticut Academy of Arts and Sciences, 1967. P. 250.

Rice, Joanne A. *Middle English Romance: An Annotated Bibliography, 1955–1985*. New York: Garland Publishing, Inc., 1987. Pp. 503–06.

Selected Critical Studies

Baron, F. Xavier. "Mother and Son in *Sir Perceval of Galles*." *Papers on Language and Literature* 8 (1972), 3–14. [Argues that the sensitive handling of the relationship between Perceval and Acheflour is unique in the traditional Perceval story.]

Busby, Keith. "Chrétien de Troyes English'd." *Neophilologus* 71 (1987), 596–613. [Examines how the English poet changes characters, shortens passages, adds supernatural figures in his adaptation of Chrétien's work.]

Brown, Arthur C. L. "The Grail and the English *Sir Perceval*." *Modern Philology* 16 (1918–19), 553–68; 17 (1919–20), 361–82; 18 (1920–21), 201–28 and 661–73; 22 (1924–25), 79–98 and 113–32. [Claims that the English *Perceval* is at least partially independent of Chrétien's *Conte del Graal*, being influenced by motifs drawn from fairy tales and Irish history.]

Fowler, David C. "*Le Conte du Graal* and *Sir Perceval of Galles*." *Comparative Literature Studies* 12 (1975), 5–20. [Claims that the author of *Sir Perceval* did indeed know Chrétien's work but that he purposefully omitted references to the Grail while retaining the serious theme.]

Griffith, Reginald Harvey. *Sir Perceval of Galles: A Study of the Sources of the Legend*. Chicago: University of Chicago Press, 1911. [Sees multi-stage development of the English poet's work with which Chrétien had little or no influence.]

Hood, Edna Sue. *Sir Perceval of Galles: Medieval Fiction*. Dissertation, University of Wisconsin, 1966. [Compares *Sir Perceval* to the "Fair Unknown" stories; discusses the work as a romance and as narrative fiction.]

Eckhardt, Caroline D. "Arthurian Comedy: The Simpleton-Hero in *Sir Perceval of Galles*." *Chaucer Review* 8 (1974), 205–20. [Argues for the merits of the poem, including its skillful integration of narrative details, its effective characterization, and its sustained comic tone.]

Speirs, John. *Medieval English Poetry: The Non-Chaucerian Tradition*. London: Faber and Faber, 1957. Pp. 122–38. [Discusses the mythological aspects of *Sir Perceval*.]

Veldhoen, N. H. G. E. "'I Haffe Spedde Better Þan I Wend': Some Notes of the Middle English *Sir Perceval of Galles*." *Dutch Quarterly Review* 11 (1981), 279–86. [Stresses the tightness of the poet's structure and the relationships among the various characters.]

Wilson, Anne. *The Magical Quest: The Use of Magic in Arthurian Romance*. Manchester: Manchester University Press, 1988. See Chapter Three: "Sir Perceval of Galles," pp. 143–48. [Claims that the omission of the Grail castle episode in the English poet's work can be explained by that author's desire to move in a different direction — from the relationship of Perceval to the king (as in Chrétien) to the guilty, incestuous relationship of Perceval with his mother.]

Here Begynnes the Romance of Sir Percyvell of Gales

Lef, lythes to me	*Everyone; listen*
Two wordes or thre,	
Of one that was faire and fre	
And felle in his fighte.	*fierce; fighting*
His righte name was Percyvell,	
He was fosterde in the felle,	*brought up; moors*
He dranke water of the welle,	
And yitt was he wyghte.	*yet; strong*
His fadir was a noble man;	
Fro the tyme that he began,	
Miche wirchippe he wan	*Much honor*
When he was made knyghte	
In Kyng Arthures haulle.	*palace*
Beste byluffede of alle,	*beloved*
Percyvell thay gan hym calle,	*did call him*
Whoso redis ryghte.	*reads correctly*
Who that righte can rede,	
He was doughty of dede,	*bold*
A styffe body on a stede	*powerful; war horse*
Wapynes to welde;	*Weapons; wield*
Tharefore Kyng Arthoure	
Dide hym mekill honoure:	*much*
He gaffe hym his syster Acheflour,	*gave*
To have and to holde	
Fro thethyn till his lyves ende,	*thence*
With brode londes to spende,	*have the use of*
For he the knyght wele kende.	*well knew*
He bytaughte hir to welde,	*entrusted, govern*
With grete gyftes to fulfill;	
He gaffe his sister hym till	*to him*
To the knyght, at ther bothers will,	*both their*
With robes in folde.	*luxurious*

Line numbers: 5, 10, 15, 20, 25, 30

	He gaffe hym robes in folde,	*luxurious*
	Brode londes in wolde,	*in his possession*
35	Mony mobles untolde,	*possessions*
	His syster to take.	
	To the kirke the knyghte yode	*church; went*
	For to wedde that frely fode,	*gentle creature*
	For the gyftes that ware gude	
40	And for hir ownn sake.	
	Sythen, withowtten any bade,	*Since that time; delay*
	A grete brydale thay made,	*wedding feast*
	For hir sake that hym hade	
	Chosen to hir make;	*mate*
45	And after, withowtten any lett,	*delay*
	A grete justyng ther was sett;	*jousting*
	Of all the kempes that he mett	*contestants*
	Wolde he none forsake.	*cease [from fighting]*

	Wolde he none forsake,	
50	The Rede Knyghte ne the Blake,	*Black*
	Ne none that wolde to hym take	*come*
	With schafte ne with schelde;	*lance; shield*
	He dose als a noble knyghte,	*does as*
	Wele haldes that he highte;	*Ever faithful [to his] promises*
55	Faste preves he his myghte:	*proves*
	Deres hym none elde.	*Injures; older [knight]*
	Sexty schaftes, I say,	
	Sir Percyvell brake that ilke day,	*same*
	And ever that riche lady lay	
60	One walle and byhelde.	*On*
	Thofe the Rede Knyghte hade sworne,	*Though*
	Oute of his sadill is he borne	
	And almoste his lyfe forlorne,	*destroyed*
	And lygges in the felde.	*lies*

65	There he lygges in the felde —	
	Many men one hym byhelde —	*on*
	Thurgh his armour and his schelde	*Throughout*
	Stoneyde that tyde.	*Stunned; time*
	That arghede all that ther ware,	*made fainthearted*
70	Bothe the lesse and the mare,	*common; noble*

	That noble Percyvell so wele dare	*able*
	Syche dynttys habyde.	*blows to suffer*
	Was ther nowthir more ne lasse	
	Of all those that ther was	
75	That durste mete hym one the grasse,	*dared; on; grassy plot*
	Agaynes hym to ryde.	
	Thay gaffe Sir Percyvell the gree:	*victory*
	Beste worthy was he;	
	And hamewardes than rode he,	
80	And blythe was his bryde.	*happy*

	And thofe the bryde blythe be	*though*
	That Percyvell hase wone the gree,	*victory*
	Yete the Rede Knyghte es he	
	Hurte of his honde;	
85	And therfore gyffes he a gyfte	*he makes a pledge*
	That if he ever covere myghte	*return (recover)*
	Owthir by day or by nyghte,	
	In felde for to stonde,	
	That he scholde qwyte hym that dynt	*repay; blow*
90	That he of his handes hynte;	*from; received*
	Sall never this travell be tynt,	*Shall; effort be in vain*
	Ne tolde in the londe	
	That Percyvell in the felde	
	Schulde hym schende thus undire schelde,	*defeat; under*
95	Bot he scholde agayne it yelde,	*Unless*
	If that he were leveande.	*living*

	Now than are thay leveande bathe;	*both alive*
	Was noghte the Rede Knyghte so rathe	*impatient*
	For to wayte hym with skathe.	*afflict; injury*
100	Er ther the harmes felle,	*Before; calamity*
	Ne befelle ther no stryffe,	
	Till Percyvell had in his lyffe	*Until*
	A son by his yonge wyffe,	
	Aftir hym to duelle.	
105	When the childe was borne,	
	He made calle it one the morne	*on*
	Als his fadir highte byforne —	*was named*
	Yonge Percyvell.	

	The knyghte was fayne a feste made	*eager [to have]*
110	For knave-childe that he hade;	*boy*
	And sythen, withowtten any bade	*then; further ado*
	Offe justynges they telle.	*Of joustings*

	Now of justynges they tell:	
	They sayne that Sir Percyvell	
115	That he will in the felde duelle,	*dwell*
	Als he hase are done.	*previously*
	A grete justynge was ther sett	
	Of all the kempes that ther mett,	*contestants*
	For he wolde his son were gette	*trained*
120	In the same wonne.	*manner*
	Theroff the Rede Knyghte was blythe,	
	When he herde of that justynge kythe,	*jousting news*
	And graythed hym armour ful swythe,	*prepared for himself; at once*
	And rode thedir righte sone;	
125	Agayne Percyvell he rade,	*Against*
	With schafte and with schelde brade,	*broad*
	To holde his heste that he made,	*keep his vow*
	Of maistres to mone.	*Because of injuries remembered*

	Now of maistres to mone,	*conquests worth mention*
130	Percyvell hase wele done,	
	For the love of his yonge sone,	
	One the firste day.	
	Ere the Rede Knyghte was bownn,	*Before; ready [to enter the lists]*
	Percyvell hase borne downn	
135	Knyght, duke, erle, and baroun,	
	And vencusede the play.	*vanquished the field*
	Right als he hade done this honour,	*As soon as*
	So come the Rede Knyghte to the stowre.	*battle*
	Bot "Wo worthe wykkyde armour!"	*A curse on bad equipment!*
140	Percyvell may say.	
	For ther was Sir Percyvell slayne,	
	And the Rede Knyghte fayne —	*joyful*
	In herte is noghte for to layne —	*conceal*
	When he went on his way.	

145	When he went on his way,	
	Durste ther no man to hym say,	
	Nowther in erneste ne in play,	
	To byd hym habyde;	*command; stay*
	For he had slayne righte thare	
150	The beste body at thare ware,	*person that there was*
	Sir Percyvell, with woundes sare,	*deadly*
	And stonayed that tyde.	*stunned; time (see note)*
	And than thay couthe no better rede	*knew; plan*
	Bot put hym in a prevee stede,	*sequestered (private) place*
155	Als that men dose with the dede,	*dead*
	In erthe for to hyde.	
	Scho that was his lady	*She*
	Mighte be full sary,	*sorry*
	That lorne hade siche a body:	*lost*
160	Hir aylede no pryde.	*(i.e., She felt)*
	And now is Percyvell the wighte	*creature*
	Slayne in batelle and in fyghte,	
	And the lady hase gyffen a gyfte,	*made a pledge*
	Holde if scho may,	*Keep it*
165	That scho schall never mare wone	*she; dwell*
	In stede, with hir yonge sone,	*[any] place*
	Ther dedes of armes schall be done,	*Where*
	By nyghte ne be daye.	
	Bot in the wodde schall he be:	*wilderness*
170	Sall he no thyng see	*Shall*
	Bot the leves of the tree	
	And the greves graye;	*groves*
	Schall he nowther take tent	*pay attention*
	To justes ne to tournament,	
175	Bot in the wilde wodde went,	*go*
	With bestes to playe.	*animals*
	With wilde bestes for to playe,	
	Scho tuke hir leve and went hir waye,	*She*
	Bothe at baron and at raye,	*from the nobility; king*
180	And went to the wodde.	
	Byhynde scho leved boure and haulle;	*left bower; hall*
	A mayden scho tuke hir withalle,	

That scho myghte appon calle
 When that hir nede stode.   *(i.e., she needed service)*
185 Other gudes wolde scho nonne nayte,   *goods; require*
Bot with hir tuke a tryppe of gayte,   *flock of goats*
With mylke of tham for to bayte   *drink*
 To hir lyves fode.   *For*
Off all hir lordes faire gere,
190 Wolde scho noghte with hir bere
Bot a lyttill Scottes spere,   *Except*
 Agayne hir son yode.   *In anticipation of her son's learning to walk*

And when hir yong son yode,   *walked about*
Scho bade hym walke in the wodde,
195 Tuke hym the Scottes spere gude,   *Presented*
 And gaffe hym in hande.
"Swete modir," sayde he,
"What manere of thyng may this bee
That ye nowe hafe taken mee?   *given to*
200 What calle yee this wande?"   *stick*
Than byspakke the lady:
"Son," scho sayde, "sekerly,   *truly*
It es a dart doghty;   *is; worthy*
 In the wodde I it fande."
205 The childe es payed, of his parte,   *pleased*
His modir hafe gyffen hym that darte;
Therwith made he many marte   *slain beast*
 In that wodde-lande.

Thus he welke in the lande,   *walks*
210 With hys darte in his hande;
Under the wilde wodde-wande   *branches*
 He wexe and wele thrafe.   *grew; throve*
He wolde schote with his spere
Bestes and other gere,   *things*
215 As many als he myghte bere.   *carry*
 He was a gude knave!   *boy*
Smalle birdes wolde he slo,   *slay*
Hertys, hyndes also;   *Male and female deer*
Broghte his moder of thoo: *those*

220	Thurte hir none crave. [1]	
	So wele he lernede hym to schote,	
	Ther was no beste that welke one fote	*walked*
	To fle fro hym was it no bote.	*useless*
	When that he wolde hym have,	
225	Even when he wolde hym have.	*Even then*
	Thus he wexe and wele thrave,	*throve*
	And was reghte a gude knave	*truly; boy*
	Within a fewe yere.	
	Fyftene wynter and mare	
230	He duellede in those holtes hare;	*gray woods*
	Nowther nurture ne lare	*courtesy; learning*
	Scho wolde hym none lere.	*teach*
	Till it byfelle, on a day,	
	The lady till hir son gun say,	*to; did*
235	"Swete childe, I rede thou praye	*counsel*
	To Goddes Sone dere,	
	That he wolde helpe the —	
	Lorde, for His poustee —	*power*
	A gude man for to bee,	
240	And longe to duelle here."	
	"Swete moder," sayde he,	
	"Whatkyns a godd may that be	*What kind of*
	That ye nowe bydd mee	
	That I schall to pray?"	
245	Then byspakke the lady even:	*directly*
	"It es the grete Godd of heven:	
	This worlde made He within seven,	
	Appon the sexte day."	
	"By grete Godd," sayde he than,	
250	"And I may mete with that man,	*If*
	With alle the crafte that I kan,	
	Reghte so schall I pray!"	
	There he levede in a tayte	*left with eagerness*
	Bothe his modir and his gayte,	*goats*

---

[1] *She need not even ask for them (the slaughtered animals)*

13

255 The grete Godd for to layte,   *seek*
       Fynde hym when he may.

      And as he welke in holtes hare,   *walked; gray woods*
      He sawe a gate, as it ware;   *path*
      With thre knyghtis mett he thare
260   Off Arthrus in.   *household*
      One was Ewayne fytz Asoure,
      Another was Gawayne with honour,
      And Kay, the bolde baratour,   *warrior*
          And all were of his kyn.
265 In riche robes thay ryde;
      The childe hadd no thyng that tyde   *time*
      That he myghte in his bones hyde,
          Bot a gaytes skynn.   *goat's*
      He was a burely of body, and therto right brade;   *broad*
270 One ayther halfe a skynn he hade;   *On both sides*
      The hode was of the same made,   *hood*
          Juste to the chynn.

      His hode was juste to his chyn,   *hood*
      The flesche halfe tourned within.
275 The childes witt was full thyn
          When he scholde say oughte.   *speak properly*
      Thay were clothede all in grene;
      Siche hade he never sene: *Such*
      Wele he wened that thay had bene   *assumed*
280   The Godd that he soghte.
      He said, "Wilke of yow alle three   *Which*
      May the grete Godd bee
      That my moder tolde mee,
          That all this werlde wroghte?"
285 Bot than ansuerde Sir Gawayne
      Faire and curtaisely agayne,
      "Son, so Criste mote me sayne,   *must me save*
          For swilke are we noghte."   *such*

      Than saide the fole one the filde,   *naif in the field*
290 Was comen oute of the woddes wilde,
      To Gawayne that was meke and mylde

	And softe to ansuare,	
	"I sall sla yow all three	*slay*
	Bot ye smertly now telle mee	*Unless*
295	Whatkyns thynges that ye bee,	
	Sen ye no goddes are."	
	Then ansuerde Sir Kay,	
	"Who solde we than say	*should*
	That hade slayne us to-day	
300	In this holtis hare?"	*gray woods*
	At Kayes wordes wexe he tene:	*grew; angry*
	Bot he a grete bukke had bene,	*As if*
	Ne hadd he stonde tham bytwene,[1]	
	He hade hym slayne thare.	*He [Percyvell] would have*

305	Bot than said Gawayn to Kay,	
	"Thi prowde wordes pares ay;	*do harm always*
	I scholde wyn this childe with play,	*in a softer manner*
	And thou wolde holde the still.	*If*
	Swete son," than said he,	
310	"We are knyghtis all thre;	
	With Kyng Arthoure duelle wee,	
	That hovyn es on hyll."	*Who has remained on*
	Then said Percyvell the lyghte,	
	In gayte-skynnes that was dyghte,	*dressed*
315	"Will Kyng Arthoure make me knyghte,	
	And I come hym till?"	*If*
	Than saide Sir Gawayne righte thare,	
	"I kane gyffe the nane ansuare;	
	Bot to the Kynge I rede thou fare,	*advise; go*
320	To wete his awenn will!"	*know; own*

	To wete than the Kynges will	
	Thare thay hoven yitt still;	*remain*
	The childe hase taken hym till	
	For to wende hame.	*home*
325	And als he welke in the wodde,	
	He sawe a full faire stode	*corral*
	Offe coltes and of meres gude,	*mares*

---

[1] *Regardless of whoever had stood between them*

15

	Bot never one was tame;	
	And sone saide he, "Bi Seyne John,	*Saint*
330	Swilke thynges as are yone	*Such; yonder*
	Rade the knyghtes apone;	*Rode*
	Knewe I thaire name,	
	Als ever mote I thryffe or thee,	*prosper; thrive*
	The moste of yone that I see	*largest; yonder*
335	Smertly schall bere mee	
	Till I come to my dame."	*mother*

He saide, "When I come to my dame,
And I fynde hir at hame, — *home*
Scho will telle the name
340   Off this ilke thynge." — *aforementioned*
The moste mere he thare see — *largest mare*
Smertly overrynnes he, — *runs down*
And saide, "Thou sall bere me — *shall*
To-morne to the Kynge."
345 Kepes he no sadill-gere, — *He puts no store in*
Bot stert up on the mere: — *leaps upon*
Hamewarde scho gun hym bere,
Withowtten faylynge.
The lady was never more sore bygone. — *sorely overwhelmed*
350 Scho wiste never whare to wonne, — *knew; what to do*
When scho wiste hir yonge sonne
Horse hame brynge. — *home*

Scho saw hym horse hame brynge;
Scho wiste wele, by that thynge, — *knew*
355 That the kynde wolde oute sprynge — *natural course*
For thynge that be moughte. — *would prevail*
Than als sone saide the lady,
"That ever solde I sorowe dry, — *should; endure*
For love of thi body,
360   That I hafe dere boghte!
Dere son," saide scho hym to,
"Thou wirkeste thiselfe mekill unroo, — *work; unrest*
What will thou with this mere do,
That thou hase hame broghte?"
365 Bot the boye was never so blythe

16

Als when he herde the name kythe		*made known*
Of the stode-mere stythe.		*stud-mare strong*
Of na thyng than he roghte.		*had he concern*

Now he calles hir a mere,
370 Als his moder dide ere; *before*
He wened all other horses were *assumed*
And hade bene callede soo.
"Moder, at yonder hill hafe I bene;
Thare hafe I thre knyghtes sene,
375 And I hafe spoken with tham, I wene,
Wordes in throo; *anger*
I have highte tham all thre *promised*
Before thaire Kyng for to be:
Siche on schall he make me *Such a one*
380 As is one of tho!" *those*
He sware by grete Goddes myghte,
"I schall holde that I hafe highte; *promised*
Bot-if the Kyng make me knyghte, *Unless*
To-morne I sall hym sloo!" *slay*

385 Bot than byspakke the lady,
That for hir son was sary — *Who; grieved*
Hir thoghte wele that scho myght dy *die*
And knelyde one hir knee: *on*
"Sone, thou has takyn thi rede, *plan*
390 To do thiselfe to the dede! *death*
In everilke a strange stede, *every foreign place*
Doo als I bydde the: *command*
To-morne es forthirmaste Yole-day, *first*
And thou says thou will away
395 To make the knyghte, if thou may,
Als thou tolde mee.
Lyttill thou can of nurtoure: *know; courtesy*
Luke thou be of mesure *moderation*
Bothe in haulle and in boure, *chamber*
400 And fonde to be fre." *try to be well-mannered*

Than saide the lady so brighte,
"There thou meteste with a knyghte,

17

Do thi hode off, I highte, *hood; bid*
  And haylse hym in hy." *greet; right away*
405 "Swete moder," sayd he then,
"I saw never yit no men;
If I solde a knyghte ken, *recognize*
  Telles me wharby." *Tell me how I'll know him*
Scho schewede hym the menevaire — *showed; ermine*
410 Scho had robes in payre. *in sets*
"Sone, ther thou sees this fare *where; handsome fur*
  In thaire hodes lye." *hoods*
"Bi grete God," sayd he,
"Where that I a knyghte see, *Wherever*
415 Moder, as ye bidd me,
  Righte so schall I."

All that nyghte till it was day,
The childe by the modir lay,
Till on the morne he wolde away,
420   For thyng that myghte betyde. *Despite anything; happen*
Brydill hase he righte nane; *none*
Seese he no better wane, *Sees; means*
Bot a wythe hase he tane, *withy (pliable branch); taken*
  And kevylles his stede. *bridles*
425 His moder gaffe hym a ryng,
And bad he solde agayne it bryng;
"Sonne, this sall be oure takynnyng, *sign (token)*
  For here I sall the byde." *await you*
He tase the rynge and the spere, *takes*
430 Stirttes up appon the mere: *Leaps*
Fro the moder that hym bere,
  Forthe gan he ryde.

One his way as he gan ryde,
He fande an haulle ther besyde; *castle*
435 He saide, "For oghte that may betyde,
  Thedir in will I."
He went in withowtten lett; *hindrance*
He fande a brade borde sett, *broad dining table*
A bryghte fire, wele bett, *kindled*
440   Brynnande therby. *Burning*

18

	A mawnger ther he fande,	*manger; found*
	Corne therin lyggande;	*lying*
	Therto his mere he bande	*bound*
	With the withy.	*branch*
445	He saide, "My modir bad me	*told*
	That I solde of mesure bee	*should; moderation*
	Halfe that I here see	
	Styll sall it ly."	*shall*
	The corne he pertis in two,	*divides*
450	Gaffe his mere the tone of thoo,	*one of those*
	And to the borde gan he goo,	
	Certayne that tyde.	
	He fande a lofe of brede fyne	
	And a pychere with wyne,	
455	A mese of the kechyne,	*dinner; kitchen*
	A knyfe ther besyde.	
	The mete ther that he fande,	
	He dalte it even with his hande,	*divided*
	Lefte the halfe lyggande	
460	A felawe to byde.	*Another person to sustain*
	The tother halfe ete he;	*The other*
	How myghte he more of mesure be?	*moderation*
	Faste he fonded to be free,	*Eagerly; sought; courteous*
	Thofe he were of no pryde.	*Although*
465	Thofe he were of no pryde,	
	Forthyrmore gan he glyde	*move*
	Till a chambir ther besyde,	*To*
	Moo sellys to see.	*More marvels*
	Riche clothes fande he sprede,	
470	A lady slepande on a bedde;	
	He said, "Forsothe, a tokyn to wedde	*sign as a pledge*
	Sall thou lefe with mee."	*Shall; leave*
	Ther he kyste that swete thynge;	
	Of hir fynger he tuke a rynge;	*From*
475	His awenn modir takynnynge	*own mother's token*
	He lefte with that fre.	*noble [woman]*
	He went forthe to his mere,	
	Tuke with hym his schorte spere,	

19

88888888888

888888888888

| | Lepe on lofte, as he was ere; | *Jumped upon [his mare]* |
| 480 | His way rydes he. | |

	Now on his way rydes he,	
	Moo selles to see;	*More marvels*
	A knyghte wolde he nedis bee,	
	Withowtten any bade.	*further ado*
485	He came ther the Kyng was,	*where*
	Servede of the firste mese.	*course*
	To hym was the maste has	*To [address] him (the King); primary goal*
	That the childe hade;	
	And thare made he no lett	*permitted no hindrance*
490	At gate, dore, ne wykett,	
	Bot in graythely he gett —	*readily*
	Syche maistres he made.	*So powerfully he acted*
	At his firste in-comynge,	
	His mere, withowtten faylynge,	
495	Kyste the forhevede of the Kynge —	*forehead*
	So nerehande he rade!	*close up; rode*

	The Kyng had ferly thaa,	*pulled back in surprise then*
	And up his hande gan he taa	*take*
	And putt it forthir hym fraa,	
500	The mouthe of the mere.	
	He saide, "Faire childe and free,	
	Stonde still besyde mee,	
	And tell me wythen that thou bee,	*from whence*
	And what thou will here."	*desire*
505	Than said the fole of the filde,	*fool; field*
	"I ame myn awnn modirs childe,	*own*
	Comen fro the woddes wylde	
	Till Arthure the dere.	*Unto; great*
	Yisterday saw I knyghtis three:	
510	Siche on sall thou make mee	*Such a one*
	On this mere byfor the,	
	Thi mete or thou schere!"	*ere; cut*

	Bot than spak Sir Gawayne,	
	Was the Kynges trenchepayne,	*[Who] was; bread server*
515	Said, "Forsothe, is noghte to layne,	*[he]; lying*

20

I am one of thaa. — *those*
Childe, hafe thou my blyssyng — *have*
For thi feres folowynge! — *following thy fellows*
Here hase thou fonden the Kynge
520   That kan the knyghte maa." — *thee; make*
Than sayde Peceyvell the free,
"And this Arthure the Kyng bee, — *If*
Luke he a knyghte make mee: — *See to it*
   I rede at it be swaa!" — *demand; so*
525   Thofe he unborely were dyghte, — *meanly; dressed*
He sware by mekill Goddes myghte:
"Bot if the Kyng make me knyghte, — *Unless*
   I sall hym here slaa!" — *slay*

All that ther weren, olde and yynge,
530   Hadden ferly of the Kyng, — *wonder*
That he wolde suffre siche a thyng
   Of that foull wyghte — *person*
On horse hovande hym by. — *waiting*
The Kyng byholdes hym on hy;
535   Than wexe he sone sory
   When he sawe that syghte.
The teres oute of his eghne glade, — *eyes flowed*
Never one another habade. — *one waiting for the other*
"Allas," he sayde, "that I was made,
540   Be day or by nyghte,
One lyve I scholde after hym bee
That me thynke lyke the:[1]
Thou arte so semely to see,
   And thou were wele dighte!" — *If; dressed*

545   He saide, "And thou were wele dighte,
Thou were lyke to a knyghte
That I lovede with all my myghte
   Whills he was one lyve. — *alive*
So wele wroghte he my will
550   In all manere of skill,

---

[1] *That I should continue living after the one / Who, it seems to me, looked like you (i.e., Perceval's father)*

21

I gaffe my syster hym till,
  For to be his wyfe.
He es moste in my mane: *remembrance*
Fiftene yere es it gane,   *have gone by*
555   Sen a theffe hade hym slane   *Since a thief*
  Abowte a littill stryffe!   *disagreement*
Sythen hafe I ever bene his fo,   *Since that time; foe*
For to wayte hym with wo.   *afflict*
Bot I myghte hym never slo,   *slay*
560   His craftes are so ryfe."   *numerous*

He sayse, "His craftes are so ryfe,
Ther is no man apon lyfe,
With swerde, spere, ne with knyfe
  May stroye hym allan,   *destroy; alone*
565   Bot if it were Sir Percyvell son.   *Unless*
Whoso wiste where he ware done!   *put*
The bokes says that he mon
  Venge his fader bane."   *Avenge; father's destroyer*
The childe thoghte he longe bade   *waited too long*
570   That he ne ware a knyghte made,
For he wiste never that he hade
  A fader to be slayne;
The lesse was his menynge.   *understanding*
He saide sone to the Kynge,
575   "Sir, late be thi jangleynge!   *stop; chattering*
  Of this kepe I nane."   *care*

He sais, "I kepe not to stande
With thi jangleyns to lange.   *too long*
Make me knyghte with thi hande,
580   If it sall be done!"
Than the Kyng hym hendly highte   *eagerly promised*
That he schold dub hym to knyghte,
With thi that he wolde doun lighte   *Provided that*
  And ete with hym at none.   *at that time*
585   The Kyng biholdes the vesage free, *noble countenance*
And ever more trowed hee   *believed*
That the childe scholde bee
  Sir Percyvell son:

22

	It ran in the Kynges mode,	*mind*
590	His syster Acheflour the gude —	
	How scho went into the wodde	
	With hym for to wonn.	*dwell*
	The childe hadde wonnede in the wodde;	*lived*
	He knewe nother evyll ne gude;	*wrong nor right*
595	The Kynge hymselfe understode	
	He was a wilde man.	
	So faire he spakke hym withall,	*(i.e., Arthur)*
	He lyghtes doun in the haulle,	*(i.e., Perceval)*
	Bonde his mere amonge tham alle	*mare*
600	And to the borde wann.	*turned*
	Bot are he myghte bygynn	*before*
	To the mete for to wynn,	*enjoy*
	So commes the Rede Knyghte in	
	Emanges tham righte than,	*Among*
605	Prekande one a rede stede;	*Riding rapidly*
	Blode-rede was his wede.	*clothing*
	He made tham gammen full gnede,	*full sorry sport*
	With craftes that he can.	*knew*
	With his craftes gan he calle,	
610	And callede tham recrayhandes all,	*cowards*
	Kynge, knyghtes inwith walle,	
	At the bordes ther thay bade.	
	Full felly the coupe he fett,	*fiercely; cup; took*
	Bifore the Kynge that was sett.	
615	Ther was no man that durste hym lett,	*oppose*
	Thofe that he were fadde.	*Even though; eager for battle*
	The couppe was filled full of wyne;	*cup*
	He dranke of that that was therinn.	
	All of rede golde fyne	
620	Was the couppe made.	
	He tuke it up in his hande,	
	The coupe that he there fande,	*found*
	And lefte tham all sittande,	
	And fro tham he rade.	*rode away*

23

625	Now from tham he rade,	
	Als he says that this made.	*(i.e., the author of the poem)*
	The sorowe that the Kynge hade	
	Mighte no tonge tell.	
	"A! dere God," said the Kyng than,	
630	"That all this wyde werlde wan,	*Who; won*
	Whethir I sall ever hafe that man	
	May make yone fende duelle?	*fiend desist*
	Fyve yeres hase he thus gane,	
	And my coupes fro me tane,	*taken from me*
635	And my gude knyghte slayne,	
	Men calde Sir Percyvell;	
	Sythen taken hase he three,	*Since then*
	And ay awaye will he bee,	*always*
	Or I may harnayse me	*Before; arm myself*
640	In felde hym to felle."	*kill*

	"Petir!" quod Percyvell the yonge,	
	"Hym than will I down dynge	*strike*
	And the coupe agayne brynge,	
	And thou will make me knyghte."	*If*
645	"Als I am trewe kyng," said he,	
	"A knyghte sall I make the,	
	Forthi thou will brynge mee	
	The coupe of golde bryghte."	
	Up ryses Sir Arthoure,	
650	Went to a chamboure	
	To feche doun armoure,	
	The childe in to dyghte;	*arm*
	Bot are it was doun caste,	*before; taken down*
	Ere was Percyvell paste,	*gone*
655	And on his way folowed faste,	
	That he solde with fyghte.	*That [knight]; should*

	With his foo for to fighte,	*enemy*
	None othergates was he dighte,	*otherwise; prepared*
	Bot in thre gayt-skynnes righte,	*goat*
660	A fole als he ware.	

He cryed, "How, man on thi mere!   *You! (interjection); mare*
Bryng agayne the Kynges gere,   *goods*
Or with my dart I sall the fere   *terrify*
   And make the unfere!"   *infirm*
665 And after the Rede Knyghte he rade,
Baldely, withowtten bade: *hesitation*
Sayd, "A knyght I sall be made
   For som of thi gere."   *With; equipment*
He sware by mekill Goddes payne,   *great*
670 "Bot if thou brynge the coupe agayne,   *Unless*
With my dart thou sall be slayne
   And slongen of thi mere."   *thrown off; mare*
The kynghte byhaldes hym in throo,   *anger*
Calde hym fole that was hys foo,   *fool; foe*
675 For he named hym soo —   *Because he called his horse a mare*
   The stede that hym bere.

And for to see hym with syghte,
He putt his umbrere on highte,   *visor*
To byhalde how he was dyghte,   *armed*
680   That so till hym spake.   *The one who spoke so to him*
He sayde, "Come I to the, appert fole;   *impudent fool*
I sall caste the in the pole,   *marsh*
For all the heghe days of Yole,   *Despite*
   Als ane olde sakke."   *As; sack*
685 Than sayd Percyvell the free,   *noble*
"Be I fole, or whatte I bee,
Now sone of that sall wee see   *soon*
   Whose browes schall blakke."   *turn pale*
Of schottyng was the childe slee: *skillful*
690 At the knyghte lete he flee,
Smote hym in at the eghe   *eye*
   And oute at the nakke.   *neck*

For the dynt that he tuke,   *took*
Oute of sadill he schoke,   *was shaken*
695 Whoso the sothe will luke,
   And ther was he slayne.
He falles down one the hill;
His stede rynnes whare he will.

Than saide Percyvell hym till,

700   "Thou art a lethir swayne."   *feeble knave*

Then saide the childe in that tyde,

"And thou woldeste me here byde,   *If; wait here for me*

After thi mere scholde I ryde

   And brynge hir agayne;

705 Then myghte we bothe with myghte

Menskfully togedir fyghte,   *Honorably*

Ayther of us, as he were a knyghte,

   Till tyme the tone ware slayne."   *one*

Now es the Rede Knyghte slayne,

710 Lefte dede in the playne.

The childe gon his mere mayne   *direct*

   After the stede.

The stede was swifter than the mere,

For he hade no thynge to bere

715 Bot his sadill and his gere,

   Fro hym thofe he yede.   *though; went*

The mere was bagged with fole;   *heavy; foal*

And hirselfe a grete bole;   *swelled up [animal]*

For to rynne scho myghte not thole,   *run; suffer*

720 Ne folowe hym no spede.

The childe saw that it was soo,

And till his fete he gan hym too;   *to; take himself*

The gates that he scholde goo   *steps (gaits)*

   Made he full gnede.   *stingy (i.e., no extra steps)*

725 The gates made he full gnede   *stingy*

In the waye ther he yede;   *where; went*

With strenght tuke he the stede

   And broghte to the knyghte.

"Me thynke," he sayde, "thou arte fele   *trustworthy*

730 That thou ne will away stele;   *sneak away*

Now I houppe that thou will dele   *hope; deal*

   Strokes appon hyghte.   *high (horseback)*

I hafe broghte to the thi mere   *you your mare*

And mekill of thyn other gere;   *much*

735 Lepe on hir, as thou was ere,   *before*

   And thou will more fighte!"

	The knyghte lay still in the stede:	*in that place*
	What sulde he say, when he was dede?	*should; dead*
	The childe couthe no better rede,	*knew; advice*
740	Bot down gun he lyghte.	

	Now es Percyvell lyghte	*off his horse*
	To unspoyle the Rede Knyghte,	*strip of his armour*
	Bot he ne couthe never fynd righte	
	The lacynge of his wede.	*fastenings; armor*
745	He was armede so wele	
	In gude iryn and in stele,	
	He couthe no gett of a dele,	*off; piece*
	For nonkyns nede.	*No matter what*
	He sayd, "My moder bad me,	*taught*
750	When my dart solde broken be,	
	Owte of the iren bren the tree:	*burn; wood*
	Now es me fyre gnede."	*lacking*
	Now he getis hym flynt,	
	His fyre-iren he hent,	*steel; seizes*
755	And then, withowtten any stynt,	*delay*
	He kyndilt a glede.	*spark*

	Now he kyndils a glede,	
	Amonge the buskes he yede	*woods; went*
	And gedirs, full gude spede,	*gathers; quickly*
760	Wodde, a fyre to make.	
	A grete fyre made he than,	
	The Rede Knyghte in to bren,	*burn*
	For he ne couthe nott ken	*figure out how*
	His gere off to take.	
765	Be than was Sir Gawayne dyght,	*prepared*
	Folowede after the fyghte	
	Betwene hym and the Rede Knyghte,	
	For the childes sake.	
	He fande the Rede Knyght lyggand,	*lying*
770	Slayne of Percyvell hande,	
	Besyde a fyre brynnande	*burning*
	Off byrke and of akke.	*birch; oak*

	Ther brent of birke and of ake	*birch; oak*
	Gret brandes and blake.	*flames; smoke*
775	"What wylt thou with this fyre make?"	
	Sayd Gawayne hym till.	
	"Petir!" quod Percyvell then,	*By Saint Peter!*
	"And I myghte hym thus ken,	*see*
	Out of his iren I wolde hym bren	
780	Righte here on this hill."	
	Bot then sayd Sir Gawayne,	
	"The Rede Knyghte for thou has slayne,	
	I sall unarme hym agayne,	
	And thou will holde the still."	*If*
785	Than Sir Gawayn doun lyghte,	
	Unlacede the Rede Knyghte;	
	The childe in his armour dight	*dressed*
	At his awnn will.	
	When he was dighte in his atire,	*dressed*
790	He tase the knyghte bi the swire,	*takes; neck*
	Keste hym reghte in the fyre,	
	The brandes to balde.	*flames; increase*
	Bot then said Percyvell on bost,	*boast*
	"Ly still therin now and roste!	*roast*
795	I kepe nothynge of thi coste,	*care; distressed condition*
	Ne noghte of thi spalde!"	*limbs*
	The knyghte lygges ther on brede;	*sprawling*
	The childe es dighte in his wede,	*equipped; arms*
	And lepe up apon his stede,	
800	Als hymselfe wolde.	
	He luked doun to his fete,	
	Saw his gere faire and mete:	*becoming*
	"For a knyghte I may be lete	*allowed to pass*
	And myghte be calde."	*called [one]*
805	Then sayd Sir Gawayn hym till,	
	"Goo we faste fro this hill!	
	Thou hase done what thou will;	
	It neghes nere nyghte."	*nears*
	"What! trowes thou," quod Percyvell the yonge,	*do you believe*
810	"That I will agayn brynge	

Untill Arthoure the Kynge
  The golde that es bryghte?
Nay, so mote I thryfe or thee,   *thrive; prosper*
I am als grete a lorde als he;
815   To-day ne schall he make me
  None other gates knyghte.   *otherwise [than a] knight*
Take the coupe in thy hande
And mak thiselfe the presande,   *present*
For I will forthire into the lande,
820   Are I doun lyghte."   *Before*

Nowther wolde he doun lyghte,
Ne he wolde wende with the knyght,
Bot rydes forthe all the nyghte,
  So prowde was he than.
825   Till on the morne at forthe dayes,   *late in the morning*
He mett a wyche, as men says.   *witch*
His horse and his harnays
  Couthe scho wele ken.   *recognize*
Scho wende that it hade bene   *assumed*
830   The Rede Knyghte that scho hade sene,
Was wonnt in those armes to bene,   *accustomed; be*
  To gerre the stede rynne.   *equip; [to] run*
In haste scho come hym agayne,
Sayde, "It is not to layne,
835   Men tolde me that thou was slayne
  With Arthours men.

Ther come one of my men,
Till yonder hill he gan me kenne,   *led me to understand*
There thou sees the fyre brene,   *Where*
840   And sayde that thou was thare."
Ever satt Percyvell stone-still,
And spakke no thynge hir till
Till scho hade sayde all hir will,
  And spakke lesse ne mare.   *neither less nor more*
845   "At yondere hill hafe I bene:
Nothynge hafe I there sene
Bot gayte-skynnes, I wene.
  Siche ill-farande fare!"   *wretched stuff*

29

"Mi sone, and thou ware thare slayne   *if*

850 And thyn armes of drawen,   *carried away*

I couthe hele the agayne   *could heal you*

   Als wele als thou was are."   *before*

Than wist Percyvell by thatt,   *knew*

It servede hym of somwhatt,

855 The wylde fyre that he gatt

   When the knyghte was slayne;

And righte so wolde he, thare   *he wanted*

That the olde wiche ware.

Oppon his spere he hir bare

860   To the fyre agayne;

In ill wrethe and in grete,   *wrath; anger*

He keste the wiche in the hete;   *cast; flames*

He sayde, "Ly still and swete   *sweat*

   Bi thi son, that lyther swayne!"   *wicked*

865 Thus he leves thaym twoo,

And on his gates gan he goo: *way*

Siche dedis to do moo   *more*

   Was the childe fayne.   *eager*

Als he come by a wodd-syde,

870 He sawe ten men ryde;

He said, "For oughte that may betyde,

   To tham will I me."   *I myself will [go] to them*

When those ten saw hym thare,

Thay wende the Rede Knyghte it ware,   *thought*

875 That wolde tham all forfare,   *destroy*

   And faste gan thay flee;

For he was sogates cledde,   *Since; thus clad*

Alle belyffe fro hym thay fledde;   *quickly*

And ever the faster that thay spedde,

880   The swiftlyere sewed hee,   *followed*

Till he was warre of a knyghte,

And of the menevaire he had syght;   *ermine*

He put up his umbrere on hight,   *visor*

   And said, "Sir, God luke thee!"   *May God watch over you!*

885	The childe sayde, "God luke the!"	
	The knyght said, "Now wele the be!	
	A, lorde Godd, now wele es mee	
	That ever was I made!"	
	For by the vesage hym thoghte	*countenance*
890	The Rede Knyghte was it noghte,	
	That hade them all bysoughte;	*searched for*
	And baldely he bade.	*fearlessly; commanded*
	It semede wele bi the syghte	
	That he had slayne the Rede Knyght:	
895	In his armes was he dighte,	*dressed*
	And on his stede rade.	*rode*
	"Son," sayde the knyghte tho,	*then*
	And thankede the childe full thro,	*eagerly*
	"Thou hase slayne the moste foo	*greatest*
900	That ever yitt I hade."	
	Then sayde Percyvell the free,	
	"Wherefore fledde yee	
	Lange are, when ye sawe mee	*Earlier*
	Come rydande yow by?"	*riding*
905	Bot than spake the olde knyghte,	
	That was paste out of myghte	*passed (i.e., too old)*
	With any man for to fyghte:	
	He ansuerde in hy;	
	He sayde, "Theis children nyne,	*These*
910	All are thay sonnes myne.	
	For ferde or I solde tham tyne,	*fear that; should; lose*
	Therfore fledd I.	
	We wende wele that it had bene	*thought indeed*
	The Rede Knyghte that we hade sene;	
915	He walde hafe slayne us bydene,	*altogether*
	Withowtten mercy.	
	Withowtten any mercy	
	He wolde hafe slayne us in hy;	*haste*
	To my sonnes he hade envy	*Of*
920	Moste of any men.	
	Fiftene yeres es it gane	
	Syn he my brodire hade slane;	*brother*

31

	Now hadde the theefe undirtane	undertaken
	To sla us all then:	
925	He was ferde lesse my sonnes sold hym slo	afraid lest; should; slay
	When thay ware eldare and moo,	older; more [capable]
	And that thay solde take hym for thaire foo	
	Where thay myghte hym ken;	see
	Hade I bene in the stede	place
930	Ther he was done to the dede,	death
	I solde never hafe etyn brede	
	Are I hade sene hym bren."	Until; burn
	"Petir!" quod Percyvell, "he es brende!	burned
	I haffe spedde better than I wend	been more successful; thought
935	Ever at the laste ende."	
	The blythere wexe the knyghte;	The more happy became
	By his haulle thaire gates felle,	castle their way passed
	And yerne he prayed Percyvell	eagerly
	That he solde ther with hym duelle	
940	And be ther all that nyghte.	
	Full wele he couthe a geste calle.	invite
	He broghte the childe into the haulle;	
	So faire he spake hym withalle	
	That he es doun lyghte;	
945	His stede es in stable sett	
	And hymselfe to the haulle fett,	fetched
	And than, withowtten any lett,	delay
	To the mette thay tham dighte.	food; prepared themselves
	Mete and drynke was ther dighte,	
950	And men to serve tham full ryghte;	
	The childe that come with the knyghte,	
	Enoghe ther he fande.	
	At the mete as thay beste satte,	At the height of the feast
	Come the portere fro the gate,	
955	Saide a man was theratte	
	Of the Maydenlande;	
	Saide, "Sir, he prayes the	
	Off mete and drynke, for charyté;	
	For a messagere es he	
960	And may nott lange stande."	

32

The knyght badde late hym inn,
"For," he sayde, "it es no synn,
The man that may the mete wynn *who enjoys food*
   To gyffe the travellande." *To give to the traveler*

965 Now the travellande man
The portere lete in than;
He haylsede the knyghte as he can, *greeted*
   Als he satt on dese. *As; dais*
The knyghte askede hym thare
970 Whase man that he ware, *Whose*
And how ferre that he walde so fare, *far; travel*
   Withowtten any lese. *lies*
He saide, "I come fro the Lady Lufamour,
That sendes me to Kyng Arthoure,
975 And prayes hym, for his honoure,
   Hir sorowes for to sesse. *put an end to*
Up resyn es a Sowdane: *Uprisen*
Alle hir landes hase he tane; *taken*
So byseges he that woman
980   That scho may hafe no pese." *peace*

He sayse that scho may have no pese,
The lady, for hir fayrenes, *despite; beauty*
And for hir mekill reches. *great wealth*
   "He wirkes hir full woo; *causes; woe*
985 He dose hir sorow all hir sythe, *causes; days*
And all he slaes doun rythe; *slays straight away*
He wolde have hir to wyfe,
   And scho will noghte soo.
Now hase that ilke Sowdane *same*
990 Hir fadir and hir eme slane, *uncle slain*
And hir brethir ilkane, *each one of her brothers*
   And is hir moste foo. *greatest enemy*
So nere he hase hir now soughte *closely; pursued*
That till a castelle es scho broghte,
995 And fro the walles will he noghte,
   Ere that he may hir too. *Until; take*

	The Sowdane sayse he will hir ta;	*take*
	The lady will hirselfe sla	*slay*
	Are he, that es hir maste fa,	*Ere; foe*
1000	Solde wedde hir to wyfe.	
	Now es the Sowdan so wyghte,	*strong*
	Alle he slaes doun ryghte:	
	Ther may no man with hym fyghte,	
	Bot he were kempe ryfe."	*renowned warrior*
1005	Than sayde Percyvell, "I the praye,	
	That thou wolde teche me the waye	*show*
	Thedir, als the gates laye,	*Thither; roads lie*
	Withowtten any stryfe;	
	Mighte I mete with that Sowdan	
1010	That so dose to that woman,	
	Alsone he solde be slane,	*Instantly*
	And I myghte hafe the lyfe!"	*If I have life [to do it]*

	The messangere prayed hym mare	*rather*
	That he wolde duell still thare:	
1015	"For I will to the Kynge fare,	
	Myne erandes for to say.	
	For then mekill sorowe me betyde,	
	And I lenger here habyde,	*If*
	Bot ryghte now will I ryde,	
1020	Als so faste als I may."	
	The knyghte herde hym say so;	
	Yerne he prayes hym to too	*Eagerly; take*
	His nyne sonnes, with hym to goo.	
	He nykkes hym with nay.	*[Perceval] refuses*
1025	Bot so faire spekes he	
	That he takes of tham three,	
	In his felawchipe to be —	
	The blythere were thay.	*happier*

	Thay ware blythe of ther bade,	*these tidings*
1030	Busked tham and forthe rade;	*Made themselves ready*
	Mekill myrthes thay made:	*Much glee*
	Bot lyttill it amende.	*remedied*
	He was paste bot a while —	*[Perceval]; gone*
	The montenance of a myle —	*distance*

34

1035	He was bythoghte of a gyle	*trick*
	Wele werse than thay wende.	*imagined*
	Thofe thay ware of thaire fare fayne,	*journey joyful*
	Forthwarde was thaire cheftayne;	*Ahead*
	Ever he sende on agayne	*one back*
1040	At ilke a myle ende,	*each*
	Untill thay ware alle gane;	
	Than he rydes hym allane	
	Als he ware sprongen of a stane,	*issued; stone*
	Thare na man hym kende,	*tells him what to do*
1045	For he walde none sold hym ken.	*instruct*
	Forthe rydes he then,	
	Amanges uncouthe men	*foreign*
	His maystres to make.	*wonders; perform*
	Now hase Percyvell in throo	*haste*
1050	Spoken with his emes twoo,	*uncles*
	Bot never one of thoo	*those*
	Took his knawlage.	*Recognized his plan*
	Now in his way es he sett	
	That may hym lede, withowtten lett,	*hindrance*
1055	Thare he and the Sowdan sall mete,	
	His browes to blake.	*turn pale*
	Late we Percyvell the yynge	*Leave; young*
	Fare in Goddes blyssynge,	*To fare*
	And untill Arthoure the Kynge	*unto*
1060	Will we agayne take.	
	The gates agayne we will tane:	*different direction; take*
	The Kyng to care-bedd es gane;	
	For mournynge es his maste mane.	*main moan*
	He syghes full sore.	
1065	His wo es wansome to wreke,	*woe; [so] miserable; avenge*
	His hert es bownn for to breke,	
	For he wend never to speke	
	With Percyvell no more.	
	Als he was layde for to ly,	*put to bed*
1070	Come the messangere on hy	*in haste*
	With lettres fro the lady,	
	And schewes tham righte thare.	

	Afote myghte the Kyng noght stande,	*On his feet*
	Bot rede tham thare lyggande,	*But advise; lying there*
1075	And sayde, "Of thyne erande	
	Thou hase thyn answare."	
	He sayde, "Thou wote thyne ansuare:	*know*
	The mane that es seke and sare,	*man; sick; sore*
	He may full ill ferre fare	*hardly travel far*
1080	In felde for to fyghte."	
	The messangere made his mone:	
	Saide, "Wo worthe wikkede wone!	*Woe befall wicked conduct*
	Why ne hade I tournede and gone	
	Agayne with the knyghte?"	
1085	"What knyghte es that," said the Kyng,	
	"That thou mase of thy menynge?	*speak about*
	In my londe wot I no lordyng	
	Es worthy to be a knyghte."	*know*
	The messangere ansuerd agayne,	
1090	"Wete ye, his name es for to layne,	*Know; conceal*
	The whethir I wolde hafe weten fayne	*Although; known*
	What the childe highte.	*was called*
	Thus mekill gatt I of that knyght:	*much learned*
	His dame sonne, he said, he hight.	*mother's; is called*
1095	One what maner that he was dight	*called*
	Now I sall yow telle:	
	He was wighte and worthly,	*manly; fine*
	His body bolde and borely,	*goodly*
	His armour bryghte and blody —	
1100	Hade bene late in batell;	
	Blode-rede was his stede,	
	His akton, and his other wede;	*jacket; clothing*
	His cote of the same hede	*quality*
	That till a knyghte felle."	*to; was befitting*
1105	Than comanded the Kyng	
	Horse and armes for to brynge:	
	"If I kan trow thi talkynge,	*believe*
	That ilke was Percyvell."	*same person*

	For the luffe of Percyvell,	
1110	To horse and armes thay felle;	
	Thay wolde no lengare ther duelle:	
	To fare ware thay fayne.	
	Faste forthe gan thay fare;	
	Thay were aferde full sare,	
1115	Ere thay come whare he ware,	
	The childe wolde be slayne.	
	The Kyng tase with hym knyghtis thre:	*takes*
	The ferthe wolde hymselfe be;	
	Now so faste rydes hee,	
1120	May folowe hym no swayne.	
	The Kyng es now in his waye;	
	Lete hym come when he maye!	
	And I will forthir in my playe	
	To Percyvell agayne.	

1125	Go we to Percyvell agayne.	
	The childe paste oute on the playne,	*journeyed across*
	Over more and mountayne,	*moor*
	To the Maydenlande;	
	Till agayne the even-tyde,	
1130	Bolde bodys sawe he byde,	*men*
	Pavelouns mekill and unryde	*large; numerous*
	Aboute a cyté stonde.	
	On huntyng was the Sowdane;	*Out*
	He lefte men many ane,	*a one*
1135	Twenty score that wele kan:	
	Be the gates yemande —	*guarding*
	Elleven score one the nyghte,	
	And ten one the daye-lighte —	
	Wele armyde at alle righte,	*particulars*
1140	With wapyns in hande.	

	With thaire wapyns in thaire hande,	
	There will thay fight ther thay stande,	
	Sittande and lyggande,	
	Elleven score of men.	
1145	In he rydes one a rase,	*in a rush*
	Or that he wiste where he was,	*Before; knew*

37

Into the thikkeste of the prese   *crowd*
   Amanges tham thanne.
And up stirt one that was bolde,
1150 Bygane his brydill to holde,
And askede whedire that he wolde   *where*
   Make his horse to rynne.
He said, "I ame hedir come
For to see a Sowdane;
1155 In faythe, righte sone he sall be slane,
   And I myghte hym ken.   *If only; see*

If I hym oghte ken may,
To-morne, when it es lighte daye
Than sall we togedir playe
1160   With wapyns unryde."   *cruel*
They herde that he had undirtane
For to sle thaire Sowdane.
Thay felle aboute hym, everilkane,   *everyone*
   To make that bolde habyde.   *brave one remain [for battle]*
1165 The childe sawe that he was fade,   *eager for battle*
The body that his bridill hade: *person; held*
Even over hym he rade,
   In gate there bisyde.
He stayred about hym with his spere;   *thrust*
1170 Many thurgh gane he bere: *pierce*
Ther was none that myght hym dere,   *oppose*
   Percevell, that tyde.

Tide in townne who will telle,   *What happened*
Folkes undir his fete felle;
1175 The bolde body Percevelle,
   He sped tham to spill.   *hastened*
Hym thoghte no spede at his spere: *rest for*
Many thurgh gane he bere,
Fonde folke in the here,   *Foolish people of the enemy*
1180   Feghtyng to fill.   *(i.e., they get their fill of fighting)*
Fro that it was mydnyghte
Till it was even at daye-lighte,
Were thay never so wilde ne wighte,
   He wroghte at his will.

1185	Thus he dalt with his brande,	*dealt blows; sword*
	There was none that myght hym stande	*withstand*
	Halfe a dynt of his hande	
	That he stroke till.	*struck*
	Now he strykes for the nonys,	*strongly*
1190	Made the Sarazenes hede-bones	
	Hoppe als dose hayle-stones	
	Abowtte one the gres;	*grass*
	Thus he dalt them on rawe	*in turn*
	Till the daye gun dawe:	*dawn*
1195	He layd thaire lyves full law,	*low*
	Als many als there was.	
	When he hade slayne so many men,	
	He was so wery by then,	
	I tell yow for certen,	
1200	He roghte wele the lesse	*cared scarcely at all*
	Awther of lyfe or of dede;	*death*
	To medis that he were in a stede	*In the midst of that place*
	Thar he myghte riste hym in thede	*he would rest himself there*
	A stownde in sekirnes.	*moment; safety*
1205	Now fonde he no sekirnes,	*safety*
	Bot under the walle ther he was,	*Except*
	A faire place he hym chese,	*chose for himself*
	And down there he lighte.	
	He laide hym doun in that tyde;	
1210	His stede stode hym besyde:	
	The fole was fayne for to byde —	*glad; abide*
	Was wery for the fyght	
	Till one the morne that it was day.	
	The wayte appon the walle lay:	*sentinel*
1215	He sawe an uggly play	*fearful performance*
	In the place dighte;	*provided*
	Yitt was ther more ferly:	*marvel*
	Ther was no qwyk man left therby!	*living*
	Thay called up the lady	
1220	For to see that sighte.	

Now commes the lady to that sight,
The Lady Lufamour, the brighte;
Scho clambe up to the walle on hight
    Full faste to beholde;
1225 Hedes and helmys ther was
    (I tell yow withowtten lese),   *lie*
    Many layde one the gresse,   *grass*
       And many schelde brode.
    Grete ferly thaym thoghte   *wonder*
1230 Who that wondir had wroghte,
    That had tham to dede broghte,   *death*
       That folke in the felde,
    And wold come none innermare   *no further inside*
    For to kythe what he ware,   *make known*
1235 And wist the lady was thare,
       Thaire warysoune to yelde.   *reward; claim*

Scho wold thaire warysone yelde: *their reward pay*
    Full faste forthe thay bihelde
    If thay myghte fynde in the felde
1240   Who hade done that dede;
    Thay luked undir thair hande,   *just below*
    Sawe a mekill horse stande,   *mighty*
    A blody knyghte liggande
       By a rede stede.
1245 Then said the lady so brighte,
    "Yondir ligges a knyghte
    That hase bene in the fighte,
       If I kane righte rede;
    Owthir es yone man slane,
1250 Or he slepis hym allane,
    Or he in batelle es tane,
       For blody are his wede."   *clothes*

Scho says, "Blody are his wede,
    And so es his riche stede;
1255 Siche a knyght in this thede   *country*
       Saw I never nane.
    What so he es, and he maye ryse,
    He es large there he lyse,

	And wele made in alle wyse,	
1260	Ther als man sall be tane."	*judged*
	Scho calde appon hir chaymbirlayne,	
	Was called hende Hatlayne —	
	The curtasye of Wawayne	*manners*
	He weldis in wane;	
1265	Scho badd hym, "Wende and see	*Go*
	Yif yon man on lyfe be.	*yonder; alive*
	Bid hym com and speke with me,	
	And pray hym als thou kane."	*can*
	Now to pray hym als he kane,	
1270	Undir the wallis he wane;	*goes*
	Warly wakend he that mane:	*Cautiously awakened; man*
	The horse stode still.	
	Als it was tolde unto me,	
	He knelid down on his kne;	
1275	Hendely hailsed he that fre,	*Courteously greeted; nobleman*
	And sone said hym till,	
	"My lady, lele Lufamour,	*fair*
	Habyddis the in hir chambour,	*Awaits you*
	Prayes the, for thyn honour,	
1280	To come, yif ye will."	
	So kyndly takes he that kyth	*request*
	That up he rose and went hym wyth,	
	The man that was of myche pyth	*strength*
	Hir prayer to fulfill.	
1285	Now hir prayer to fulfill,	
	He folowed the gentilmans will,	
	And so he went hir untill,	
	Forthe to that lady.	
	Full blythe was that birde brighte	*fair lady*
1290	When scho sawe hym with syghte,	
	For scho trowed that he was wighte,	*manly*
	And askede hym in hy:	*questioned*
	At that fre gan scho frayne,	*noble one; ask*
	Thoghe he were lefe for to layne,	*eager to hide the facts*
1295	If he wiste who had tham slayne —	
	Thase folkes of envy.	

	He sayd, "I soghte none of tho;	*those*
	I come the Sowdane to slo,	*slay*
	And thay ne wolde noghte late me go;	
1300	Thaire lyfes there refte I."	

	He sayd, "Belyfe thay solde aby."	*Happily; abide*
	And Lufamour, that lele lady,	*fair*
	Wist ful wele therby	*Knew*
	The childe was full wighte.	*powerful*
1305	The birde was blythe of that bade	*noble lady; news*
	That scho siche and helpe hade;	*such a helper*
	Agayne the Sowdane was fade	*Against; [he] was determined*
	With alle for to fighte.	
	Faste the lady hym byhelde:	*Earnestly*
1310	Scho thoght hym worthi to welde,	*govern*
	And he myghte wyn hir in felde,	*field of battle*
	With maystry and myghte.	
	His stede thay in stabill set	
	And hymselfe to haulle was fet,	*hall; brought*
1315	And than, withowtten any let,	*delay*
	To dyne gun thay dighte.	*prepare*

	The childe was sett on the dese,	*high table*
	And served with reches —	*dainties*
	I tell yow withowtten lese —	*lie*
1320	That gaynely was get,	*handsomely was served*
	In a chayere of golde	
	Bifore the fayrest, to byholde	
	The myldeste mayden one molde,	*on earth*
	At mete als scho satt.	
1325	Scho made hym semblande so gude,	*friendly welcome*
	Als thay felle to thaire fude,	
	The mayden mengede his mode	*roused his spirits*
	With myrthes at the mete,	
	That for hir sake righte tha	*then*
1330	Sone he gane undirta	*undertake*
	The sory Sowdane to sla,	
	Withowtten any lett.	*delay*

He sayd, withowtten any lett,

"When the Sowdane and I bene mett,

1335 A sadde stroke I sall one hym sett,   *solemn*

    His pride for to spyll."

Then said the lady so free,

"Who that may his bon be   *death (bane)*

Sall hafe this kyngdome and me,

1340   To welde at his will."

He ne hade dyned bot smalle   *a little*

When worde come into the haulle

That many men withalle

    Were hernyste one the hill;   *armed*

1345 For tene thaire felawes were slayne,   *anger [that]*

The cité hafe thay nere tane.   *nearly taken*

The men that were within the wane   *stronghold*

    The comon-belle gun knylle.   *did knell*

Now knyllyn thay the comon-belle.

1350 Worde come to Percevell,

And he wold there no lengere duelle,

    Bot lepe fro the dese —   *high table*

Siche wilde gerys hade he mo —   *impulsive ways; plenty*

Sayd, "Kynsmen, now I go.

1355 For alle yone sall I slo

    Longe are I sese!"   *before; cease*

Scho kiste hym withowtten lett;   *delay*

The helme on his hede scho sett;

To the stabill full sone he gett,

1360   There his stede was.

There were none with hym to fare;

For no man then wolde he spare! —   *hold back*

Rydis furthe, withowtten mare,   *alone*

    Till he come to the prese.   *Sowdan's gang*

1365 When he come to the prese,

He rydes in one a rese;   *in a rush*

The folkes, that byfore hym was,

    Thaire strenght hade thay tone;   *taken*

To kepe hym than were thay ware;   *oppose; eager*

1370 Thaire dynttis deris hym no mare   *blows harm*

Then whoso hade strekyn sare   *fiercely*
   One a harde stone.
Were thay wighte, were thay woke,   *strong; weak*
Alle that he till stroke,
1375 He made thaire bodies to roke: *fall back*
   Was ther no better wone.   *fate*
I wote, he sped hym so sone
That day, by heghe none   *noon*
With all that folke hade he done:
1380   One lefe lefte noghte one.   *Alive*

When he had slayne all tho,
He loked forthir hym fro,
If he myghte fynde any mo
   With hym for to fyghte;
1385 And als that hardy bihelde,   *hardy [lad] looked about*
He sese, ferre in the felde,   *sees far*
Fowre knyghtis undir schelde
   Come rydand full righte.   *vigorously*
One was Kyng Arthour,
1390 Anothir Ewayne, the floure,   *most excellent*
The thirde Wawayne with honoure,
   And Kay, the kene knyghte.
Percevell saide, withowtten mare,
"To yondir foure will I fare;
1395 And if the Sowdane be thare,
   I sall holde that I highte."   *keep; promised*

Now to holde that he hase highte,
Agaynes thaym he rydis righte,
And ay lay the lady brighte
1400   One the walle, and byhelde   *On*
How many men that he had slane,
And sythen gane his stede mayne   *rode; powerful*
Foure kempys agayne,   *warriors to meet*
   Forthir in the felde.
1405 Then was the lady full wo
When scho sawe hym go
Agaynes foure knyghtys tho,   *To meet*
   With schafte and with schelde.

44

	They were so mekyl and unryde	*great; huge*
1410	That wele wende scho that tyde	*time*
	With bale thay solde gare hym byde	*grief; make*
	That was hir beste belde.	*protector*
	Thofe he were beste of hir belde,	*protection*
	As that lady byhelde,	
1415	He rydes forthe in the felde,	
	Even tham agayne.	*Directly against*
	Then sayd Arthoure the Kyng,	
	"I se a bolde knyghte owt spryng;	*charging*
	For to seke feghtyng,	
1420	Forthe will he frayne.	*seek battle*
	If he fare forthe to fighte	
	And we foure kempys agayne one knyght,	*warriors*
	Littill menske wold to us lighte	*honor*
	If he were sone slayne."	
1425	They fore forthward right faste,	
	And sone kevells did thay caste,	*lots*
	And evyr fell it to frayste	*try*
	Untill Sir Wawayne.	*Unto*
	When it felle to Sir Wawayne	
1430	To ryde Percevell agayne,	*against*
	Of that fare was he fayne,	*chance*
	And fro tham he rade.	
	Ever the nerre hym he drewe,	*nearer*
	Wele the better he hym knewe,	
1435	Horse and hernays of hewe,	
	That the childe hade.	
	"A, dere God!" said Wawayne the fre,	
	"How-gates may this be?	*However*
	If I sle hym, or he me,	
1440	That never yit was fade,	*his enemy*
	And we are sisters sones two,	*For*
	And aythir of us othir slo,	*If*
	He that lifes will be full wo	*lives; utterly woeful*
	That ever was he made."	

1445	Now no maistrys he made,	*menacing gestures*
	Sir Wawayne, there als he rade,	
	Bot hovyde styll and habade	*remained; stopped*
	His concell to ta.	*take*
	"Ane unwyse man," he sayd, "am I,	
1450	That puttis myselfe to siche a foly;	
	Es there no man so hardy	
	That ne anothir es alswa.	*also*
	Thogfe Percevell hase slayne the Rede Knight,	*Although*
	Yitt may another be als wyghte,	
1455	And in that gere be dyghte,	*armor; dressed*
	And taken alle hym fra.	
	If I suffire my sister sone,	*am gentle with*
	And anothir in his gere be done	*equipment*
	And gete the maystry me appon,	
1460	That wolde do me wa;	*woe*
	It wolde wirke me full wa!	
	So mote I one erthe ga,	
	It ne sall noghte betyde me swa,	
	If I may righte rede!	*be well advised*
1465	A schafte sall I one hym sett,	
	And I sall fonde firste to hitt;	*try*
	Then sall I ken be my witt	
	Who weldys that wede."	*wears that armor*
	No more carpys he that tyde,	*debates*
1470	Bot son togedyr gon thay ryde-	
	Men that bolde were to byde,	
	And styff appon stede;	
	Thaire horse were stallworthe and strange,	*strong*
	Thair scheldis were unfailande;	
1475	Thaire speris brake to thaire hande,	*splintered in*
	Als tham byhoved nede.	*As they were bound to do*
	Now es broken that are were hale,	*ere; whole*
	And than bygane Percevale	
	For to tell one a tale	
1480	That one his tonge laye.	*on*
	He sayde, "Wyde-whare hafe I gane;	*Far and wide*
	Siche anothir Sowdane	*Such*

In faythe sawe I never nane,
   By nyghte ne by daye.
1485 I hafe slayne, and I the ken,   *tell you*
Twenty score of thi men;
And of alle that I slewe then,
   Me thoghte it bot a playe
Agayne that dynt that I hafe tane;   *Compared to; blow*
1490 For siche one aughte I never nane   *possessed*
Bot I qwyte two for ane,   *Unless; repay*
   Forsothe, and I maye."

Then spake Sir Wawayne —
Certanely, is noghte to layne —   *lie*
1495 Of that fare was he fayne,   *glad*
   In felde there thay fighte:
By the wordis so wylde
At the fole one the felde,   *naïf in*
He wiste wele it was the childe,
1500   Percevell the wighte —   *strong*
He sayse, "I ame no Sowdane,
Bot I am that ilke man   *same*
That thi body bygan
   In armours to dighte.
1505 I giffe the prise to thi pyth.   *prize; strength*
Unkyndely talked thou me with:
My name es Wawayne in kythe,   *among my people*
   Whoso redys righte."

He sayes, "Who that will rede the aryghte,   *advise you*
1510 My name es Wawayne the knyghte."
And than thay sessen of thaire fighte,   *cease*
   Als gude frendes scholde.
He sayse, "Thynkes thou noghte when
That thou woldes the knyghte brene,
1515 For thou ne couthe noghte ken   *didn't know how*
   To spoyle hym alle colde?"   *plunder*
Bot then was Percevell the free
Als blythe als he myghte be,
For then wiste he wele that it was he,
1520   By takens that he tolde.   *details*

He dide then als he gane hym lere: *had been taught*
Putt up hys umbrere;   *visor*
And kyste togedir with gud chere
 Those beryns so bolde.   *warriors*

1525 Now kissede the beryns so bolde,   *warriors*
 Sythen talkede what thay wolde.
 Be then come Arthour the bolde,   *By*
  That there was knyghte and kyng
 Als his cosyns hadd done,
1530 Thankede God also sone.
 Off mekill myrthis thay mone   *reminisce*
  At thaire metyng.
 Sythen, withowtten any bade,   *delay*
 To the castelle thay rade
1535 With the childe that thay hade,
  Percevell the yynge.
 The portere was redy thare,
 Lete the knyghtis in fare;
 A blythere lady than . . .
1540 . . . .   *(see note)*

 "Mi grete socour at thou here sende,   *that*
 Off my castell me to diffende,
 Agayne the Sowdane to wende,
  That es my moste foo."   *greatest enemy*
1545 Theire stedis thay sett in the stalle.
 The Kyng wendis to haulle;   *goes*
 His knyghtis yode hym with alle,   *went*
  Als kynde was to go.   *As was the custom*
 Thaire metis was redy,   *food*
1550 And therto went thay in hy,   *quickly*
 The Kyng and the lady,
  And knyghtis also.

 Wele welcomed scho the geste
 With riche metis of the beste,
1555 Drynkes of the derreste,   *most costly*
  Dighted bydene.   *Prepared for everyone*
 Thay ete and dranke what thay wolde,

	Sythen talked and tolde	*Then*
	Off othir estres full olde,	*stories*
1560	The Kyng and the Qwene.	
	At the firste bygynnyng,	*outset*
	Scho frayned Arthour the Kyng	*questioned*
	Of childe Percevell the yyng,	*About*
	What life he had in bene.	*had formerly*
1565	Grete wondir had Lufamour	
	He was so styffe in stour	*strong; battle*
	And couthe so littill of nurtour	*knew; courtesy*
	Als scho had there sene.	
	Scho had sene with the childe	
1570	No thyng bot werkes wylde:	*acts of violence*
	Thoghte grete ferly on filde	*wonders in field*
	Of that foly fare.	*foolish behavior*
	Then said Arthour the Kyng	
	Of bold Percevell techyng,	*Perceval's upbringing*
1575	Fro the firste bygynnyng	
	Till that he come thar:	
	How his fadir was slayne,	
	And his modir to the wode gane	
	For to be there hir allane	
1580	In the holtis hare,	
	Fully feftene yere	
	To play hym with the wilde dere:	*animals*
	Littill wonder it were	
	Wilde if he ware!	
1585	When he had tolde this tale	*[Arthur]*
	To that semely in sale	*comely one; hall*
	He hade wordis at wale	*will*
	To tham ilkane.	*each of them*
	Then said Percevell the wighte,	
1590	"Yif I be noghte yitt knyghte,	
	Thou sall halde that thou highte,	*promised*
	For to make me ane."	
	Than saide the Kyng full sone,	
	"Ther sall other dedis be done,	
1595	And thou sall wynn thi schone	*[knight's] shoes*

49

	Appon the Sowdane."	*against*
	Then said Percevell the fre,	
	"Als sone als I the Sowdane see,	
	Righte so sall it sone be,	
1600	Als I hafe undirtane."	*undertaken*
	He says, "Als I hafe undirtane	
	For to sla the Sowdane,	
	So sall I wirke als I kanne,	
	That dede to bygynn."	
1605	That day was ther no more dede	*activity*
	With those worthily in wede,	
	Bot buskede tham and to bedde yede,	*prepared themselves; went*
	The more and the mynn;	*less*
	Till one the morne erely	
1610	Comes the Sowdane with a cry,	
	Fonde all his folkes hym by	
	Putt into pyn.	*torment (i.e., dead)*
	Sone asked he wha	*who*
	That so durste his men sla,	
1615	And wete hym one lyfe gaa,	*(see note)*
	The maystry to wynn.	
	Now to wynn the maystry,	
	To the castell gan he cry,	
	If any were so hardy,	
1620	The maistry to wynn:	
	"A man for ane,	*[a man]*
	Thoghe he hadd all his folke slane,	
	Here sall he fynde Golrotherame	
	To mete hym full ryghte,	
1625	Appon siche a covenande	*pact*
	That ye hefe up your hande;	*lift*
	Who that may the better stande	
	And more es of myghte	
	To bryng that other to the dede,	*death*
1630	Browke wele the londe on brede	*Possess; broad land*
	And hir that is so faire and rede,	
	Lufamour the brighte!"	

50

	Then the Kyng Arthour	
	And the Lady Lufamour	
1635	And all that were in the towre	
	Graunted therwith.	
	Thay called Percevell the wight;	
	The Kyng doubbed hym to knyghte.	
	Thofe he couthe littill insighte,	*had little wisdom*
1640	The childe was of pith.	*strong*
	He bad he solde be to prayse,	*act in a praiseworthy way*
	Therto hende and curtayse;	
	Sir Percevell the Galayse	
	Thay called hym in kythe.	*among his people*
1645	Kyng Arthour in Maydenlande	
	Dubbid hym knyghte with his hande,	
	Bad hym ther he his fo fande	
	To gyff hym no grythe.	*peace*

	Grith takes he nane:	*Peace*
1650	He rydes agayne the Sowdane	
	That highte Gollerotherame,	*was called*
	That felle was in fighte.	*cruel*
	In the felde so brade,	
	No more carpynge thay made,	
1655	Bot sone togedir thay rade,	
	Theire schaftes to righte.	*spears; raise*
	Gollerotheram, thofe he wolde wede,	*rage*
	Percevell bere hym fro his stede	*knocked him off*
	Two londis one brede,	*(see note)*
1660	With maystry and myghte.	
	At the erthe the Sowdane lay;	
	His stede gun rynn away;	
	Than said Percevell one play,	*in*
	"Thou haste that I the highte."	*what I promised you*

1665	He sayd, "I highte the a dynt,	
	And now, me thynke, thou hase it hynt.	*received*
	And I may, als I hafe mynt,	*intended*
	Thou schalt it never mende."	
	Appon the Sowdan he duelled	*pressed*
1670	To the grownde ther he was felled,	

51

And to the erthe he hym helde
  With his speres ende.
Fayne wolde he hafe hym slayne,
This uncely Sowdane,   *hapless*
1675   Bot gate couthe he get nane,   *means could*
  So ill was he kende.   *trained*
Than thynkes the childe
Of olde werkes full wylde:
"Hade I a fire now in this filde,
1680   Righte here he solde be brende."

He said, "Righte here I solde the brene,
And thou ne solde never more then
Fighte for no wymman,
  So I solde the fere!"   *terrify you*
1685   Then said Wawayne the knyghte,
"Thou myghte, and thou knewe righte,   *if*
And thou woldes of thi stede lighte,   *If; get off*
  Wynn hym one were."   *Defeat; in battle*
The childe was of gamen gnede;   *banter cautious*
1690   Now he thynkes one thede,   *on the spot*
"Lorde! whethir this be a stede   *can this; steed*
  I wende had bene a mere?"   *mare*
In stede righte there he in stode,   *place*
He ne wiste nother of evyll ne gude,
1695   Bot then chaunged his mode
  And slaked his spere.   *released*

When his spere was up tane,
Then gan this Gollerothiram,
This ilke uncely Sowdane,   *same hapless*
1700   One his fete to gete.
Than his swerde drawes he,
Strykes at Percevell the fre.
The childe hadd no powsté   *power*
  His laykes to lett.   *sword play; oppose*
1705   The stede was his awnn will: *acted on his own*
Saw the swerde come hym till,   *toward him*
Leppe up over an hill,
  Fyve stryde mett.   *measured*

52

	Als he sprent forby,	*flew past*
1710	The Sowdan keste up a cry;	
	The childe wann owt of study	*awoke; meditation*
	That he was inn sett.	*absorbed in*
	Now ther he was in sett,	*absorbed in*
	Owt of study he gett,	
1715	And lightis downn, withowtten lett,	*hesitation*
	Agaynes hym to goo.	
	He says, "Now hase thou taughte me	
	How that I sall wirke with the."	*work*
	Than his swerde drawes he	
1720	And strake to hym thro.	*assails; fiercely*
	He hitt hym even one the nekk-bane,	
	Thurgh ventale and pesane.	*chest and neck armor*
	The hede of the Sowdane	
	He strykes the body fra.	*from*
1725	Then full wightly he yode	*went*
	To his stede, there he stode;	
	The milde mayden in mode,	*spirit*
	Mirthe may scho ma!	*make*
	Many mirthes then he made;	
1730	In to the castell he rade,	
	And boldly he there habade	*dwelt*
	With that mayden brighte.	
	Fayne were thay ilkane	*each*
	That he had slane the Sowdane	
1735	And wele wonn that wymman,	
	With maystry and myghte.	
	Thay said Percevell the yyng	*young*
	Was beste worthy to be kyng,	
	For wele withowtten lesyng	
1740	He helde that he highte.	*He kept his promise*
	Ther was no more for to say,	
	Bot sythen, appon that other day,	
	He weddys Lufamour the may,	*maiden*
	This Percevell the wighte.	

1745   Now hase Percevell the wight
        Wedded Lufamour the bright,
        And is a kyng full righte
           Of alle that lande brade.   *broad*
        Than Kyng Arthour in hy
1750   Wolde no lengare ther ly:
        Toke lefe at the lady.   *leave of*
           Fro tham than he rade:
        Left Percevell the yyng
        Off all that lande to be kyng,
1755   For he had with a ryng
           The mayden that it hade. [1]
        Sythen, appon the tother day,   *the next*
        The Kyng went on his way,
        The certane sothe, als I say,
1760   Withowtten any bade.   *delay*

        Now than yong Percevell habade
        In those borowes so brade   *broad*
        For hir sake, that he hade   *whom*
           Wedd with a ryng.
1765   Wele weldede he that lande,   *ruled*
        Alle bowes to his honde;   *bow*
        The folke, that he byfore fonde,   *sought*
           Knewe hym for kyng.
        Thus he wonnes in that wone   *dwells; place*
1770   Till that the twelmonthe was gone,
        With Lufamour his lemman.   *beloved*
           He thoghte on no thyng,
        Now on his moder that was,
        How scho levyde with the gres,   *upon grass*
1775   With more drynke and lesse,
           In welles, there thay spryng.

        Drynkes of welles, ther thay spryng,
        And gresse etys, withowt lesyng!   *grass; it's no lie*
        Scho liffede with none othir thyng
1780   In the holtes hare.   *gray woods*

---

[1] *For with a ring he had / The maiden who had the land*

Till it byfelle appon a day,
Als he in his bedd lay,
Till hymselfe gun he say,
   Syghande full sare,
1785   "The laste Yole-day that was,
Wilde wayes I chese:
My modir all manles   *unprotected*
   Leved I thare."   *Left*
Than righte sone saide he,
1790   "Blythe sall I never be   *Happy*
Or I may my modir see,   *Until*
   And wete how scho fare."   *know; fares*

Now to wete how scho fare,
The knyght busked hym yare;   *made himself ready soon*
1795   He wolde no lengare duelle thare
   For noghte that myghte bee.
Up he rose in that haulle,
Tuke his lefe at tham alle,   *leave from*
Both at grete and at smalle;
1800   Fro thaym wendis he.
Faire scho prayed hym even than,   *Eloquently*
Lufamour, his lemman,
Till the heghe dayes of Yole were gane,
   With hir for to bee.
1805   Bot it served hir of no thyng:
A preste he made forthe bryng,
Hym a messe for to syng,
   And aftir rode he.

Now fro tham gun he ryde;
1810   Ther wiste no man that tyde
Whedirwarde he wolde ryde,
   His sorowes to amende.
Forthe he rydes allone;
Fro tham he wolde everichone:
1815   Mighte no man with hym gone,
   Ne whedir he wolde lende.   *arrive*
Bot forthe thus rydes he ay,
The certen sothe als I yow say,

Till he come at a way
1820   By a wode-ende.
Then herde he faste hym by   *close by*
Als it were a woman cry:
Scho prayed to mylde Mary
    Som socoure hir to sende.

1825   Scho sende hir socour full gude,
Mary, that es mylde of mode.
As he come thurgh the wode,
    A ferly he fande.   *marvel*
A birde, brighteste of ble,   *noble lady; complexion*
1830   Stode faste bonden till a tre —
I say it yow certanly —
    Bothe fote and hande.
Sone askede he who,
When he sawe hir tho,
1835   That had served hir so,
    That lady in lande.   *(see note)*
Scho said, "Sir, the Blake Knyghte
Solde be my lorde with righte;
He hase me thusgates dighte   *thusly tied*
1840   Here for to stande."

She says, "Here mon I stande
For a faute that he fande   *fault*
That sall I warande
    Is my moste mone.   *greatest moan*
1845   Now to the I sall say:
Appon my bedd I lay
Appon the laste Yole-day —
    Twelve monethes es gone —
Were he knyghte, were he king,
1850   He come one his playnge.   *sporting*
With me he chaungede a ring,   *exchanged*
    The richeste of one.   *finest of all*
The body myght I noghte see
That made that chaungyng with me,
1855   Bot what that ever he be,
    The better hase he tone!"   *taken*

56

Scho says, "The better hase he tane;
Siche a vertue es in the stane,   *stone*
In alle this werlde wote I nane   *know of none*
1860   Siche stone in a rynge;
A man that had it in were   *war*
One his body for to bere,
There scholde no dyntys hym dere,   *blows; harm*
     Ne to the dethe brynge."
1865 And then wiste Sir Percevale
Full wele by the ladys tale
That he had broghte hir in bale   *into grief*
     Thurgh his chaungyng.   *exchanging [of rings]*
Than also sone sayd he
1870 To that lady so fre,
"I sall the louse fro the tre,   *shall loosen you*
     Als I ame trewe kyng."

He was bothe kyng and knyght:
Wele he helde that he highte;   *kept; promised*
1875 He loused the lady so brighte,   *loosened*
     Stod bown to the tre.   *bound*
Down satt the lady,
And yong Percevall hir by.
Forwaked was he wery: *He was utterly weary from lack of sleep*
1880   Rist hym wolde he.   *Rest himself*
He wende wele for to ryst,
Bot it wolde nothyng laste.
Als he lay althir best,   *very comfortably*
     His hede one hir kne,
1885 Scho putt on Percevell wighte,   *awakened*
Bad hym fle with all his myghte,
"For yonder comes the Blake Knyghte;
     Dede mon ye be!"   *must*

Scho sayd, "Dede mon ye be,
1890 I say yow, sir certanly:
Yonder out comes he
     That will us bothe slee!"
The knyghte gan hir answere,
"Tolde ye me noghte lang ere   *earlier*

57

1895	Ther solde no dynttis me dere,	*blows; harm*
	Ne wirke me no woo?"	
	The helme on his hede he sett;	
	Bot or he myght to his stede get,	*ere*
	The Blak Knyght with hym mett,	
1900	His maistrys to mo.	*conquest; accomplish*
	He sayd, "How! hase thou here	
	Fonden now thi play-fere?	*playmate*
	Ye schall haby it full dere	*pay for it dearly*
	Er that I hethen go!"	*hence*

1905	He said, "Or I hethyn go,	*hence*
	I sall sle yow bothe two,	
	And all siche othir mo,	
	Thaire waryson to yelde."	*reward*
	Than sayd Percevell the fre,	
1910	"Now sone than sall we see	
	Who that es worthy to bee	
	Slayne in the felde."	
	No more speke thay that tyde,	
	Bot sone togedir gan thay ryde,	
1915	Als men that wolde were habyde,	*engage in war*
	With schafte and with schelde.	
	Than Sir Percevell the wight	
	Bare down the Blake Knyght.	
	Than was the lady so bright	
1920	His best socour in telde;	*camp*

	Scho was the beste of his belde:	*protectors*
	Bot scho had there bene his schelde,	*Unless*
	He had bene slayne in the felde,	
	Right certeyne in hy.	
1925	Ever als Percevell the kene	*Even as; brave*
	Sold the knyghtis bane hafe bene,	*Should; death*
	Ay went the lady bytwene	
	And cryed, "Mercy!"	
	Than the lady he forbere,	*spared*
1930	And made the Blak Knyghte to swere	
	Of alle evylls that there were,	
	Forgiffe the lady.	

	And Percevell made the same othe	
	That he come never undir clothe	
1935	To do that lady no lothe	*injury*
	That pendid to velany.	*pertained*
	"I did hir never no velany;	
	Bot slepande I saw hir ly:	
	Than kist I that lady —	
1940	I will it never layne.	*lie*
	I tok a ryng that I fande;	
	I left hir, I undirstande,	*believe*
	That sall I wele warande,	*guarantee*
	Anothir ther-agayne."	*as a substitute*
1945	Thofe it were for none other thyng,	*not otherwise*
	He swere by Jhesu, Heven-kyng,	
	To wete withowtten lesyng,	*lying*
	And here to be slayne;	
	"And all redy is the ryng;	
1950	And thou will myn agayne bryng,	*If*
	Here will I make the chaungyng,	*exchange*
	And of myn awnn be fayne."	*joyful*
	He saise, "Of myn I will be fayne."	*joyful*
	The Blak Knyghte ansuers agayne:	
1955	Sayd, "For sothe, it is noghte to layne,	*lie*
	Thou come over-late.	*too late*
	Als sone als I the ryng fande,	
	I toke it sone off hir hande;	
	To the lorde of this lande	
1960	I bare it one a gate.	*straight away*
	That gate with grefe hafe I gone:	*way*
	I bare it to a gude mone,	*man*
	The stalwortheste geant of one	*most stalwart giant of all*
	That any man wate.	*knows*
1965	Es it nowther knyghte ne kyng	
	That dorste aske hym that ryng,	
	That he ne wolde hym down dyng	*strike*
	With harmes full hate."	*much violence*

	"Be thay hate, be thay colde,"	*hot*
1970	Than said Percevell the bolde,	
	For the tale that he tolde	*Because of*
	He wex all tene.	*angry*
	He said, "Heghe on galous mote he hyng	*High; gallows*
	That to the here giffes any ryng,	*you here gives*
1975	Bot thou myn agayne brynge,	*[That] you have*
	Thou haste awaye geven!	
	And yif it may no nother be,	*none other*
	Righte sone than tell thou me	
	The sothe: whilke that es he	*truth*
1980	Thou knawes, that es so kene?	*know; bold*
	Ther es no more for to say,	
	Bot late me wynn it yif I may,	
	For thou hase giffen thi part of bothe away,	
	Thof thay had better bene."	*more valuable*
1985	He says, "Thofe thay had better bene."	*more valuable*
	The knyghte ansuerde in tene,	*anger*
	"Thou sall wele wete, withowtten wene,	*know; doubt*
	Wiche that es he!	*Which*
	If thou dare do als thou says,	
1990	Sir Percevell de Galays,	
	In yone heghe palays,	*lofty*
	Therin solde he be,	
	The riche ryng with that grym!	*horrid creature*
	The stane es bright and nothyng dym;	
1995	For sothe, ther sall thou fynd hym:	
	I toke it fro me;	*He*
	Owthir within or withowt,	
	Or one his play ther abowte,	
	Of the he giffes littill dowte,	*you; has no fear*
2000	And that sall thou see."	
	He says, "That sall thou see,	
	I say the full sekirly."	*tell you; surely*
	And than forthe rydis he	
	Wondirly swythe.	*swiftly*
2005	The geant stode in his holde,	*castle*
	That had those londis in wolde:	*[his] power*

Saw Percevell, that was bolde,
  One his lande dryfe;   *gallop [his horse]*
He calde one his portere:
2010   "How-gate may this fare?   *However*
I se a bolde man yare   *prepared to fight*
  On my lande ryfe.   *well-endowed*
Go reche me my playlome,   *battle weapon*
And I sall go to hym sone;
2015   Hym were better hafe bene at Rome,
  So ever mote I thryfe!"   *prosper*

Whethir he thryfe or he the,   *thrive; prosper*
Ane iryn clobe takes he;   *iron club*
Agayne Percevell the fre
2020   He went than full right.
The clobe wheyhed reghte wele   *weighed a lot*
That a freke myght it fele: *knight*
The hede was of harde stele,
  Twelve stone weghte!   *(168 pounds)*
2025   Ther was iryn in the wande,   *iron; shaft*
Ten stone of the lande,   *(140 pounds' worth)*
And one was byhynde his hande,   *(see note)*
  For holdyng was dight.   *designed*
Ther was thre and twenty in hale;   *all (i.e., 322 pounds weight)*
2030   Full evyll myght any men smale,   *poorly*
That men telles nowe in tale,
  With siche a lome fighte.   *weapon*

Now are thay bothe bown,   *armed*
Mett one a more brown,   *moor*
2035   A mile withowt any town,   *outside*
  Boldly with schelde.
Than saide the geant so wight,
Als sone als he sawe the knyght,
"Mahown, loved be thi myght!"   *Mahomet*
2040   And Percevell byhelde.
"Art thou hym, that," saide he than,
"That slew Gollerothirame?
I had no brothir bot hym ane,   *alone*
  When he was of elde."   *full grown*

2045 Than said Percevell the fre,
   "Thurgh grace of God so sall I the,   *prosper*
   And siche geantes as ye
    Sle thaym in the felde!"

   Siche metyng was seldom sene.
2050 The dales dynned thaym bytwene   *resounded*
   For dynttis that thay gaffe bydene   *to each other*
    When thay so mett.
   The gyant with his clobe-lome   *club-weapon*
   Wolde hafe strekyn Percevell sone,   *smitten*
2055 Bot he therunder wightely come,   *skillfully*
    A stroke hym to sett.
   The geant missede of his dynt;
   The clobe was harde as the flynt:
   Or he myght his staffe stynt   *Before; stop*
2060 Or his strengh lett,   *control*
   The clobe in the erthe stode:
   To the midschafte it wode.   *was embedded*
   The Percevell the gode,   *Then*
    Hys swerde owt he get.

2065 By then hys swerde owt he get,
   Strykes the geant withowtten lett,   *delay*
   Merkes even to his nekk,   *Thrusts straight*
    Reght even ther he stode;
   His honde he strykes hym fro,   *from him*
2070 His lefte fote also,
   With siche dyntis as tho.   *those*
    Nerre hym he yode.   *Nearer; went*
   Then sayd Percevell, "I undirstande
   Thou myghte with a lesse wande   *smaller stick*
2075 Hafe weledid better thi hande
    And hafe done the some gode;
   Now bese it never for ane   *is; anyone*
   The clobe of the erthe tane.   *from; to take*

I tell thi gatis alle gane, [1]

2080   Bi the gude Rode!"   *Cross*

He says, "By the gud Rode,

As evyll als thou ever yode,   *However poorly you walk hereafter*

Of thi fote thou getis no gode;

     Bot lepe if thou may!"   *hop*

2085 The geant gan the clobe lefe,   *leave*

And to Percevell a dynt he yefe;   *gave*

In the nekk with his nefe.   *fist*

     So ne neghede thay.   *near approached*

At that dynt was he tene: *outraged*

2090 He strikes off the hande als clene

Als ther hadde never none bene.

     That other was awaye.   *already chopped off*

Sythen his hede gan he off hafe;   *Then; cut off*

He was ane unhende knave   *discourteous*

2095 A geantberde so to schafe,   *shave*

     For sothe, als I say!

Now for sothe, als I say,

He lete hym ly there he lay,

And rydis forthe one his way

2100   To the heghe holde.   *high castle*

The portare saw his lorde slayne;

The kayes durste he noght layne.   *keys; withhold*

He come Percevell agayne;

     The gatis he hym yolde.   *yielded*

2105 At the firste bygynnyng,

He askede the portere of the ryng —

If he wiste of it any thyng —

     And he hym than tolde:

He taughte hym sone to the kiste   *showed; chest*

2110 Ther he alle the golde wiste,   *knew [to be]*

Bade hym take what hym liste   *desired*

     Of that he hafe wolde.

---

[1] *I say there will be no more pathways to walk (i.e., your career is ended)*

Percevell sayde, hafe it he wolde,
And schott owtt all the golde   *cast*
2115   Righte there appon the faire molde;   *the floor*
       The ryng owte glade.   *flew out*
The portare stode besyde,
Sawe the ryng owt glyde,
Sayde ofte, "Wo worthe the tyde   *Woe be the time*
2120   That ever was it made!"
Percevell answerde in hy,
And asked wherefore and why
He banned it so brothely,   *cursed; vehemently*
       Bot if he cause hade.   *Unless*
2125   Then alsone said he,
And sware by his lewté: *fealty*
"The cause sall I tell the,
       Withowten any bade."   *delay*

He says, "Withowtten any bade,
2130   The knyghte that it here hade,   *brought it here*
Theroff a presande he made,   *present*
       And hedir he it broghte.
Mi mayster tuke it in his hande,
Ressayved faire that presande: *Received*
2135   He was chefe lorde of this lande,
       Als man that mekill moghte.   *had great power*
That tyme was here fast by
Wonnande a lady,   *Dwelling*
And hir wele and lely   *goodly and loyally*
2140   He luffede, als me thoghte.
So it byfelle appon a day,
Now the sothe als I sall say,
Mi lorde went hym to play,
       And the lady bysoghte.   *importuned*

2145   Now the lady byseches he
That scho wolde his leman be;
Fast he frayned that free,   *asked; noble lady*
       For any kyns aughte.   *on any terms*
At the firste bygynnyng,
2150   He wolde hafe gyffen hir the ryng;

And when scho sawe the tokynyng,
Then was scho un-saughte.   *distraught*
Scho gret and cried in hir mone;   *wept; grief*
Sayd, 'Thefe, hase thou my sone slone   *Thief; slain*
2155 And the ryng fro hym tone,   *taken*
   That I hym bitaughte?'   *entrusted*
Hir clothes ther scho rafe hir fro,   *tore*
And to the wodd gan scho go;
Thus es the lady so wo,
2160   And this is the draghte.   *course [of fate]*

For siche draghtis als this,   *Because of; luck (draughts)*
Now es the lady wode, iwys,   *gone mad, truly*
And wilde in the wodde scho es,
   Ay sythen that ilke tyde.   *Ever since*
2165 Fayne wolde I take that free,
Bot alsone als scho sees me,   *as soon as*
Faste awaye dose scho flee:
   Will scho noghte abyde."
Then sayde Sir Percevell,
2170 "I will assaye full snelle   *attempt; quickly*
To make that lady to duelle;
   Bot I will noghte ryde:
One my fete will I ga,
That faire lady to ta.   *capture*
2175 Me aughte to bryng hir of wa: *rescue her from woe*
   I laye in hir syde."   *(i.e., "I am her son.")*

He sayse, "I laye in hir syde;
I sall never one horse ryde
Till I hafe sene hir in tyde,   *time*
2180   Spede if I may;   *Have better luck*
Ne none armoure that may be
Sall come appone me
Till I my modir may see,
   Be nyghte or by day.
2185 Bot reghte in the same wode
That I firste fro hir yode,   *went*
That sall be in my mode   *determination*
   Aftir myn other play;   *Despite anything else*

	Ne I ne sall never mare	*more*
2190	Come owt of yone holtis hare	*gray woods*
	Till I wete how scho fare,	*know; fares*
	For sothe, als I saye."	

	Now for sothe, als I say,	
	With that he helde one his way,	
2195	And one the morne, when it was day,	
	Forthe gonn he fare.	
	His armour he leved therin,	*left*
	Toke one hym a gayt-skynne,	*goatskin*
	And to the wodde gan he wyn,	
2200	Among the holtis hare.	
	A sevenyght long hase he soghte;	
	His modir ne fyndis he noghte.	
	Of mete ne drynke he ne roghte,	*cared about*
	So full he was of care.	*anxiety*
2205	Till the nynte day, byfell	*ninth*
	That he come to a welle	
	Ther he was wonte for to duelle	
	And drynk take hym thare.	

	When he had dronken that tyde,	
2210	Forthirmare gan he glyde;	*Farther; walk*
	Than was he warre, hym besyde,	*Then; aware*
	Of the lady so fre;	
	Bot when scho sawe hym thare,	
	Scho bygan for to dare,	*hide*
2215	And sone gaffe hym answare,	
	That brighte was of ble.	
	Scho bigan to call and cry:	
	Sayd, "Siche a sone hade I!"	
	His hert lightened in hy,	
2220	Blythe for to bee.	
	Be that he come hir nere	
	That scho myght hym here,	*hear*
	He said, "My modir full dere,	
	Wele byde ye me!"	

2225	Be that, so nere getis he	*With that*
	That scho myghte nangatis fle,	*in no way*
	I say yow full certeynly.	
	Hir byhoved ther to byde.	*It behooved her*
	Scho stertis appon hym in tene;	*anger*
2230	Wete ye wele, withowtten wene,	*Know; doubt*
	Had hir myghte so mekill bene,	*Had she been strong enough*
	Scho had hym slayne that tyde!	
	Bot his myghte was the mare,	*greater*
	And up he toke his modir thare;	
2235	One his bake he hir bare:	
	Pure was his pryde.	*He had no pride*
	To the castell, withowtten mare,	
	The righte way gon he fare;	
	The portare was redy yare,	*soon*
2240	And lete hym in glyde.	*walk*
	In with his modir he glade,	*walked*
	Als he sayse that it made;	
	With siche clothes als thay hade,	
	Thay happed hir forthy.	*covered; accordingly*
2245	The geant had a drynk wroghte,	
	The portere sone it forthe broghte,	
	For no man was his thoghte	
	Bot for that lady.	
	Thay wolde not lett long thon,	*did not wait long then*
2250	Bot lavede in hir with a spone.	*poured [the liquid]*
	Then scho one slepe fell also sone,	
	Reght certeyne in hy.	
	Thus the lady there lyes	
	Thre nyghttis and thre dayes,	
2255	And the portere alwayes	
	Lay wakande hir by.	
	Thus the portare woke hir by —	*watched beside her*
	Ther whills hir luffed sekerly, —	*while [he]*
	Till at the laste the lady	
2260	Wakede, als I wene.	*awakened*
	Then scho was in hir awenn state	*(i.e., right mind)*
	And als wele in hir gate	*normal way*

Als scho hadde nowthir arely ne late   *formerly or recently*
    Never therowte bene.
2265 Thay sett tham down one thaire kne,
    Thanked Godde, alle three,
    That he wolde so appon tham see   *look*
      As it was there sene.
    Sythen aftir gan thay ta   *prepare*
2270 A riche bathe for to ma,   *make*
    And made the lady in to ga,
      In graye and in grene.

    Than Sir Percevell in hy
    Toke his modir hym by,
2275 I say yow than certenly,
      And home went hee.
    Grete lordes and the Qwene
    Welcomed hym al bydene;   *altogether*
    When thay hym on lyfe sene;
2280   Than blythe myghte thay bee.
    Sythen he went into the Holy Londe,   *Then*
    Wanne many cités full stronge,
    And there was he slayne, I undirstonde;
      Thusgatis endis hee.   *In this way*
2285 Now Jhesu Criste, hevens Kyng,
    Als He es Lorde of all thyng,
    Grante us all His blyssyng!
      Amen, for charyté!

    Quod Robert Thornton
    Explicit Sir Percevell de Gales
    Here endys the Romance of Sir Percevell of Gales, Cosyn to King Arthoure.

Notes

1   *Lef, lythes to me*. The opening formula links this poem to the minstrel tradition which often included a bid for attention, followed by the announcement of a subject. Minstrels favored tail-rhyme romances that could be more easily memorized and heard. The poet's contention that he will speak "two wordes or thre" sets a comic tone for a poem that continues for 2,288 lines.

7   This line is imitated by Chaucer in *The Tale of Sir Thopas* — "Hymself drank water of the well, / As dide the Knyght sire Percyvell" VII(B2), 915–16 — which appears to be, in part, a takeoff on the more creaky features of this poem. See Introduction and see also note at lines 2141–43.

23   The English poet is unique among romance writers in giving Arthur a sister named Acheflour. The name is perhaps a corruption of Blanchefleur, who in Chrétien's *Perceval*, is said to be Arthur's sister and the hero's mother.

26   Arthur provides dower for Acheflour. According to medieval law, the husband would control the "broad lands" and the wife would receive one-third of her husband's estate. The lands given by Arthur would revert to Acheflour upon her husband's death.

46   Jousts *à plaisance* (jousts of "pleasure"), peaceful skirmishes, were commonly held on occasions of celebration, such as a marriage, the birth of a son, or a coronation. Lances with slanted tips were used to reduce the chance of injury. The object was to unhorse one's opponent or to splinter his weapon, not to kill him.

78   *was he*. The line is a stress short. Holthausen emends it to *was that fre*.

95   *he*. MS: *it*. Holthausen's emendation.

152   *And stonayed that tyde*. "And stunned at that time" seems anticlimactic. Perhaps the sense is 1) "And, on that occasion, destroyed him" (as in

"smashed with a blow"); or 2) "And put an end to that lifetime"; or 3) "And dumbfounded the people celebrating his son's birthday."

160   Mills emends to *[v]aylede* and glsses the word as "helped."

179   This line might imply that Acheflour left her family and her king (*raye*). But *raye* was also a type of striped cloth popular among the nobility in the fourteenth century. Perhaps the point is that Lady Perceval abandoned both her kin and her finery when she left for the wild "wodde" (line 180).

200   French and Hale suggest that this "wande" is a kind of magic dart, which alone has power to bring down the Red Knight.

248   *day*. A hole in the MS obliterates the *a*.

261–63   Ewayne fytz Asoure (also spelled "Yvain") is a member of Arthur's court who stars in his own romance by Chrétien (see the Middle English translation/ adaptation in this volume), but also plays a minor role in *Perceval of Galles*. His father is usually said to be Uriens. Gawain is Arthur's nephew, being the son of Arthur's sister (or half-sister), Anna (as in Geoffrey of Monmouth), and, therefore, is Perceval's first cousin. He is often known for his bravery and courtesy. Kay, Arthur's seneschal, is a dark character, often, as here, a rude troublemaker and foil to noble knights of the court.

275   Perceval is traditionally portrayed as having exceptional physical prowess but being deficient in reason. Because his mother sheltered him as a child, he is also naive. As will become apparent, he has not learned courtly manners.

289   In Middle English *fole* did not necessarily carry the strongly negative connotations it does today, but, rather, simply comments on Perceval's naiveté.

302–05   Although *bukke* may mean body (i.e., Gawain's body), French and Hale delete *he* (line 302) to read: *Bot a grete bukke had bene*, thus implying that a buck stepped in between Perceval and Kay, thwarting Perceval's rude behavior. Stags frequently appear in fairy tales. Either way, the sense of the lines is obscure.

320   The top corner of the MS is frayed, obliterating most of the line. Reconstructed by Halliwell-Phillipps and others on the basis of the line following, which presumably repeats the key words according to tail-rhyme principles. All that remains of the line is *To . . . te his awenn.*

326   *stode.* A place where mares are kept for breeding. The word is derived from the German *die Stute* (mare).

339   Holthausen emends the line to read *Scho will telle [me] the name,* an emendation followed by French and Hale to maintain the meter.

356   The implication of *be moughte* ("must be") is that the mother knew her son would inevitably take the route of his father one day.

362   The reconstruction of *is* in "thiselfe" is Halliwell-Phillipps' suggestion. There is a hole here in the manuscript and an ink blot as well.

393   I.e., Christmas day. Coincidentally, as Arthur was popularly supposed to have held court on Easter, Ascension, Whitson, All Saints, and Christmas, the first day of the season would have been an opportune time for Perceval to set out in hopes of meeting him.

397   MS: *nuttoure.* French and Hale's emendation.

410   French and Hale gloss *payre* as "sets."

432   At this point the scribe interjects the words "Here is a ffyt of Percyvell of Galles." The next line begins with a large capital "0," extending over four lines.

434   The sudden appearance of a castle or hall to a travelling knight in a medieval romance often prepares the reader to expect some enchantment. Here Perceval will receive the magic ring that will figure heavily in his future actions.

493 ff.   A strange knight riding into the king's hall on horseback was a common episode in medieval romances. See *Sir Gawain and the Green Knight* and Chaucer's *Squire's Tale.*

606   The blood-red clothing worn by this character seems to indicate that he (like the green-clad figure in *Sir Gawain and the Green Knight*) is an enchanter against whom everyone is powerless except the one whose destiny it is to slay him.

611   French and Hale emend *inwith* to the more familiar "within."

617   Although the story of the cup is elliptically treated here, one may assume that this is no ordinary drinking vessel. Earlier critics suggested that it is somehow linked to the health of Arthur's kingdom, which will decline without it and, in this respect, is akin to a secularized grail trope. In line 1062, Arthur is said to have gone to "care-bedd," and even though this is supposedly on account of his concern for the safety of Perceval, it might earlier have been linked more directly to the stolen vessel.

633   *Fyve.* Holthausen emends to *fyftene*, imagining that the Red Knight has assailed Arthur every year since the death of Perceval senior.

642   *I.* Halliwell-Phillipps' emendation, which saves the meter and the sense and is followed by Holthausen and French and Hale.

657   MS: *wih*.

660   The unarmed "childe" (Perceval has only his dart) fighting and overcoming the armed and experienced foe smacks of the David and Goliath story that Chaucer also parodies in lines 807–27 of the Tale of Sir Thopas. Noting the short stanza, lines 557–60, Mills suggests that twelve lines have been omitted by the scribe. The text in the MS is continuous.

682   French and Hale note that in the Middle Ages, during the twelve days of the Christmas season, all fighting was forbidden. Casting one's foe in the marsh, however, seems to have been acceptable.

872   Mills suggests that Thornton's exemplar might have read: *To tham will I te* ("go"), which makes more immediate sense.

899   MS: *Thou hase the moste foo slayne*, which breaks the rhyme scheme, thus the emendation.

Notes

921   The brother who was slain fifteen years ago is the elder Perceval, and this man (unnamed) is thus young Perceval's uncle. Line 1050 alludes to this relationship.

977   *Sowdane.* A "Sultan," the chief ruler of a Muslim country, but the term is seldom used with much precision in medieval literature. Such a character was pagan, powerful, and, therefore, evil, and is commonly a foil to the hero.

1021   *The.* MS: *He.* The emendation is Halliwell-Phillipps'.

1043   *sprongen of a stane.* I.e., alone, as if he were just created. See Franklin's Tale line 1614: *cropen out of the ground.* The allusion is to the myth of Pyrrha and Deucalion and the repopulation of the world from stones thrown behind them.

1068   Arthur's concern for Perceval, which might seem excessive considering that he has never seen the boy before, can be explained in part by the king's affection for Perceval's father. But Arthur was also Perceval's *maternal* uncle. Thus he and the boy form that most special of medieval relationships, the avuncular — Arthur's blood most assuredly ran through Perceval's veins.

1165   French and Hale gloss *fade* as "determined." It could also mean "weak." But see line 616, where MED glosses the word as "eager for battle."

1173   Mills glosses this line as "Let anyone who can narrate [this story] in company [say that]. . . ."

1177   MED notes instances of *spede* used to imply "ease" or "alleviation," which seems to be the sense here. The point is that Perceval's spear is very busy.

1229–36 The sense of these lines is that Lady Lufamore, eager to find out who has slain the Saracens, asks that he come forth so that she might reward him. No one from inside the castle comes to claim the reward.

1294   Perceval's disposition to ignore the slaughter might be seen as a sign of his modesty, though more likely it signals his frustration at not having carried out his mission, namely, to slay the Sowdan, as he doggedly explains in lines 1298–1300.

73

1392   Although *kene* can mean "acrimonious," it also means "brave" or "bold," and it seems that the author intended one of the latter senses here, since Kay is not now playing his usual caustic role.

1540   The manuscript has been damaged so that only the beginnings of the last words recorded from lines 1537–39 remain at this point. The text continues with no space left for the sixteenth line. The omitted lines, the equivalent, perhaps, of the sixteenth line and the first four lines of the next stanza, tell of Lady Lufamore's greeting of King Arthur. They are missing apparently because of the scribe's oversight and not because of the damage to the manuscript.

1576–80   The beginnings of these lines were reconstructed by Holthausen. The lower left corner of the leaf is missing.

1589   *Then.* MS: *The.* Emendation by Halliwell-Phillipps.

1595   In the Middle Ages, a knight bent on peace did not wear shoes — only soft socks (see the Green Knight in *Sir Gawain and the Green Knight,* line 160); but a knight intent on battle wore both shoes and spurs. Arthur seems to be saying here that with the death of the Sultan, Perceval would have proven his battle skills to the fullest — i.e., he would be worthy of the shoes of a knight.

1615   The Sultan seems to be asking whether the slayer of his men (i.e., Perceval)
is   alive to fight with him.

1620   French and Hale note the break in rhyme to suggest the right reading is probably "with hym to fyghte."

1659   The sense of the line is uncertain. It perhaps refers to the distance the Sultan was hurled from his horse, since "land" was a unit of measure. See, for example, "plough*land*" (MED, OED), indicating the amount of land one could cultivate with one plough.

1693   The sense of this line seems to be that Perceval stood where he was and *thought,* an activity somewhat rare for him. The fact that the "mere" was actually a "steed" has come as a revelation.

1698   *Then.* MS *The.*

1755   French and Hale emend the line needlessly by adding *[wedded]* after *he had*.

1769–92 Although the interval might vary, a year was the usual length of time for a mortal to stay in fairyland before longing to return to the world.

1774   *with the gres*. The point seems to be that without Perceval to hunt for her, she now lives as a vegetarian, a detail that astonishes the narrator (lines 1778–80), but is nonetheless true — *without lesyng!*

1799   MS: *bot*.

1830   The noble lady is the same one with whom Perceval exchanged rings earlier in the poem, while she lay sleeping in the castle. Her magic ring protected him in battle, and it is thus much more valuable than the one he left with her.

1836   *in lande*. An expletive, used vaguely in ME poetry, comparable to *in towne*. Here, perhaps, it implies a situation or predicament. See *Sir Ferumbras*, line 2793, *Welawo to longe y lyve in londe*, where the sense is "on earth." Chaucer toys with the vacuous phrase in The Tale of Sir Thopas (CT VII 887), along with *in towne* (CT VII 793).

1839   *dighte*. The author's frequent use of this term pays rich dividends here. The lady is *hidden, adorned* (with the chains), *clothed* (in shame), *prepared* (for humiliation), *placed* (tied, etc.) — all meanings the poet has previously affiliated with *dighte*.

1963   Giants were popular creatures of medieval romance. See W. F. Bryan and Germaine Dempster, eds., *Sources and Analogues of Chaucer's "Canterbury Tales"* (New York: Humanities Press, 1958), pp. 530–54.

1985   *thay*. Holthausen and French and Hale read *thyn*, without acknowledging emendation, though the MS clearly reads *thay*.

1996   French and Hale gloss: "I gave it away." Mills emends the line to read: *[That] toke it fro me*. MED cites instances of *I* functioning as the pronoun *he*.

2027–28 *And one was behynde* apparently means that the iron clasp binding the head of the axe to the handle weighs another stone (c. 14 pounds), making the total axe weight 23 stone, or about 322 pounds in all.

2032   It is perhaps worth noting that *lome* is used in ME as a metaphor for the penis. Certainly, to this giant, his *playlome* (2013) or *cloblome* (2053) is a figure of his potency. Cf., MED *lome* (n.) 1.c.

2084   Perceval's is black comedy here; obviously a giant without a left foot cannot "leap," unless hopping is leaping.

2138   MS: *wonnade*. Holthausen's emendation.

2141–43 See Chaucer's Tale of Sir Thopas (VII, 748–50): *And so bifel upon a day, / For sothe, as I yow telle may, / Sire Thopas wolde out ride.*

2209–12 Critics such as Brown and Speirs contend that in earlier versions of this story, Perceval's mother was a water fairy, thus her repeated association with wells. Seen in this light, it is not surprising that she appears to her son just after he has taken a drink.

2251   The use of a magic portion to induce sleep and thus to restore one to the "proper" state of mind was commonplace in medieval romance.

2257–61 A v-shaped tear at the top center of fol. 176r deletes the end word of the first three long lines of the first column.

2257   *hir by*. French and Hale's reconstruction.

2258   *sekerly*. Halliwell-Phillipps' reconstruction, followed by Holthausen and French and Hale.

2261   *state*. Holthausen's reconstruction, followed by French and Hale. Halliwell-Phillipps supplies *wate*.

2272   Green is associated with vegetation, but it is also a restorative color, thus fitting for the reinstatement of the relationship between mother and son.

Ywain and Gawain

Introduction

Ywain and Gawain survives in a single copy preserved in the British Library as Cotton Galba E. ix. The parchment manuscript contains 114 folios, seventeen separate pieces. Most of these — *The Gospel of Nicodemus*, a treatise on the Seven Deadly Sins, *The Pricke of Conscience*, a "Book of Penance," a Rood poem, and a *Pater Noster*, for example — are didactic. But others, such as notes on the points of a horse, *The Prophecies of Merlin*, and the satirical poem, "Sir Penny," represent a diversity of secular tastes. The hands of six individual scribes can be discerned in the collection, four of these dating from the early fifteenth century. The first hand — that of *Ywain and Gawain* and *The Seven Sages of Rome* — is a clear *Anglicana Formata* and the text is in a Northern dialect. Because certain North-East Midland forms are often reflected in the rhyme, the language is assumed to be that of the original author, who probably composed the work some fifty to one hundred years before this particular version was written down. A lack of topical references in the text makes it impossible to date the composition of the poem precisely.

The manuscript is in generally good condition, although its upper edges show water damage, probably from the 1731 fire in the library of Robert Bruce Cotton, the book's only identifiable owner. The top portion is often marred by shrinkage, splitting, and staining; worm holes, tearing, and ink blots occur throughout. Few of these defects present difficulties for the reader, however. The text contains little decoration. It begins with a large, ornate blue capital, picked in red, and a long, downward flourish, extending through the title and four lines of the manuscript. A number of smaller initials, alternately red and blue, are scattered throughout the text, normally coinciding with our modern practice of paragraphing. Such initials contain non-representational foliage and sport tendrils both upward and downward into the margins. The text contains numerous paragraph markings, which are generally not consistent with modern usage. There is little punctuation, and capitalization is sporadically employed.

The poem itself, a translation and adaptation of Chrétien de Troyes' *Le Chevalier au Lion*, is the story of Ywain, son of Urien, and a knight of King Arthur's court, whom the English poet assumed to have been a king and who is historically believed to have fought against the Angles in the sixth century. Unlike most romances, this one is a tale of married love: Ywain weds his lady, only to lose her through the breaking of a vow, whereafter he must perform many feats of valor before winning her again. The story begins at Arthur's court when Sir Colgrevance tells of his adventure along a perilous path which led him to a monster herdsman, a magic storm-producing well, and an avenging knight who some time ago had defeated Colgrevance in battle. Immediately Ywain, fired by the prospect of such an encounter and hoping to be more successful than his kinsman, sets out on the path himself, followed at some distance by Arthur and his retinue. Ywain defeats the knight, who, mortally wounded, flees to his castle. Ywain pursues him, but upon reaching the castle, he is trapped by the portcullis which crashes down upon him, killing his horse. He is rescued by Lunette, the companion of the dead knight's wife, whom he has unknowingly befriended in the past, and she gives him a ring that makes him invisible. Thus he is able to escape capture within the castle walls. He falls in love with the grieving widow, Alundyne; subsequently, he marries her and becomes the protector of her property. When Arthur and his knights arrive, Ywain defeats Sir Kay and proudly entertains them all as host and lord.

His happiness is short-lived, however, for soon Gawain, who had accompanied Arthur to the castle, persuades Ywain to "follow arms" with him to prove his manliness alongside his friend in tournaments. Alundyne agrees to the venture — but only for the space of a year. When Ywain forgets to return on the appointed day, she publicly renounces him and subsequently withdraws *her* magic ring which had served to protect him from harm. Having lost his love, Ywain also loses his mind, roaming the forest like a wild "beste" until the kindness of a hermit and the magic of still another lady restore him. Brought, in effect, to his senses, he now fights for justice and truth. Seeing a dragon battling a lion, he saves the lion and the beast becomes his companion. He rescues hapless maidens, defeats an oppressing giant, and overcomes an evil steward. When at last he returns to Alundyne's castle, Lunette aids him in a reconciliation with his wife. Then all live happily, the poet assures us, "Until that death haves dreven tham down" (line 4026).

As with *Sir Perceval of Galles*, this poem has suffered by comparison with its French prototype, considered by many to have been Chrétien's consummate achievement. Unlike *Sir Perceval*, a work which the English poet took and made his own, *Ywain and Gawain* is more a translation and a streamlining of *Le Chevalier au Lion*, retaining the narrative, but reducing the earlier work by some twenty-eight hundred lines. That the reduction often comes at the expense of Chrétien's rich descriptive passages, eliminating not only the courtly elements, battle details, and character nuances, but also the subtle word play, irony, psychologizing, and suspense, has caused the English romance to be labeled as "flat," lacking in "wit and subtlety."

In addition, such streamlining has produced what some critics take to be lacunae in the text — gaps where the meaning is not clear. Such "gaps" may be the result of "faulty copying," or they may represent the English poet's conscious attempt at pandering to an audience who would eschew such subtleties in favor of a more fast-paced and action-filled plot. *Ywain and Gawain*, however, must not be judged solely by comparison to Chrétien, for it is a provocative, skillfully-wrought poem in its own right, reproducing the Ywain saga for an English audience that is rather different from the French courts for which Chrétien wrote, an audience seeking courtly sophistication rather than owning it.

Whatever the reason for the abridgements, the English poet does focus on action. Ywain's thoughts and feelings interest him less that the physical activities that effect character change. Ywain's adventures are not random, but progressive: his first act — his attack on the knight of the well — is motivated by family concerns. He is in pursuit of his own self-aggrandizement. Likewise, his year of "tournamenting" with Gawain is undertaken for personal glory. He becomes so self-absorbed that he forgets his vows to his wife. After he has lost and regained his sanity his adventures take on a different character. He now acts solely for justice and right as steps toward personal atonement. His deeds are performed not as the noted "Sir Ywain," but as the unknown "Knight of the Lion." In the final battle where he unknowingly fights against his best friend, Sir Gawain, he is willing to proclaim himself the loser — even though the battle was a draw — displaying a type of humility not known to him before. In humility Ywain's education is complete: He is *redeemed* and makes *ending . . . of al the sorows that he hade* (lines 4009–10). Only then can he be reconciled with his wife. Espousing chivalry in its ideal forms, *Ywain* contrasts with *Sir Perceval of Galles*. His courtly activities raise questions about the nature of *trowthe* and about the conflict between married love and personal honor, and thus the romance anticipates more fully developed treatments of such themes in later fourteenth-century works.

The poem is written in rhymed couplets; each line contains four stresses and is generally octosyllabic. Some degree of alliteration appears in approximately one third of the lines, sometimes in two or three syllables. The dialogue is often lively and colloquial, befitting a North-country poet writing for an audience more mercantile in its livelihood than Chrétien's courtly group.

Ywain and Gawain

Select Bibliography

Manuscript

British Library Cotton MS Galba E. ix, fols. 4–25.

Editions

French, Walter H., and Charles Brockway Hale, eds. *Ywain and Gawain* (lines 1–1448). In *Middle English Metrical Romances*. New York: Russell and Russell, 1964. Pp. 483–527.

Friedman, Albert B., and Norman T. Harrington, eds. *Ywain and Gawain*. EETS o.s. 254. London: Oxford University Press, 1964. Rpt. 1981. [The introduction, pp. ix–lxii, discusses the MS, the structure of the poem, and its relationship to Chrétien.]

Harrington, Norman Taylor, ed. *Ywain and Gawain: A Critical Edition*. Dissertation, Harvard University, 1960.

Mills, Maldwyn, ed. *Ywain and Gawain, Sir Percyvell of Gales, The Anturs of Arther*. London: J. M. Dent, 1992. [Everyman edition.]

Ritson, Joseph, ed. *Ancient Engleish Metrical Romanceës*. Vol. 1. London: W. Nicol, 1802. Pp. 1–169. Rpt. Edinburgh: Goldsmid, 1884.

Schleich, Gustav, ed. *Ywain and Gawain*. Oppeln/Leipzig: E. Franck, 1887.

Stevick, Robert D., ed. "Ywain and Gawain." In *Five Middle English Narratives*. New York: The Bobbs-Merrill Company, Inc., 1967. Pp. 140–283. [Normalized text.]

Taglicht, J., ed. *An Edition of the Middle English Romances [sic] Ywain and Gawain, with Introduction, Notes, Glossary*. Dissertation, Oxford University, 1963–64.

Introduction

Bibliographies

Hunt, Tony. "The Medieval Adaptations of Chrétien's *Yvain*: A Bibliographical Essay," In *An Arthurian Tapestry: Essays in Memory of Lewis Thorpe*. Ed. Kenneth Varty. Glasgow French Department, University of Glasgow, 1981. Pp. 203–13.

Roce, Joanne A. *Middle English Romance: An Annotated Bibliography, 1955–1985*. New York: Garland, 1987. Pp. 547–52.

Selected Critical Studies

de Caluwé-Dor, Juliette. "Yvain's Lion Again: A Comparative Analysis of Its Personality and Function in the Welsh, French, and English Versions." In *An Arthurian Tapestry: Essays in Memory of Lewis Thorpe*. Ed. Kenneth Varty. Glasgow French Department, University of Glasgow, 1981. Pp. 229–38. [Suggests that in the English version of the story, the lion does not have the personality of the vassal, as in Chrétien's, but rather that of a friendly dog, more faithful to Ywain than Ywain has been to the lady.]

Doob, Penelope B. R. *Nebuchadnezzar's Children: Conventions of Madness in Middle English Literature*. New Haven and London: Yale University Press, 1974. Pp. 134–53. [Views Ywain's lack of *trowthe* — his moral fault — as leading to his insanity (often a punishment for sin) and suggests that he can only be restored to reason by adhering to the virtues inherent in Alundyne's ring.]

Faris, David E. "The Art of Adventure in the Middle Englsh Romance: *Ywain and Gawain, Eger and Grime*." *Studia Neophilologica* 53 (1981), 91–100. [Argues for *Ywain* as an "imaginatively conceived" romance in which time and space exist to serve the hero's needs, not to limit them.]

Finlayson, John. "*Ywain and Gawain* and the Meaning of Adventure." *Anglia* 87 (1969), 312–37. [Claims that Ywain's adventures serve to characterize the hero who progresses from a self-serving knight to a king who seeks justice.]

Friedman, Albert B., and Norman T. Harrington. Introduction to *Ywain and Gawain*. EETS o.s. 254. London: Oxford University Press, 1964. Rpt. 1981. Pp. ix–lxii. [Discusses the manuscript of *Ywain*, the structure of the work, the relationship to Chrétien's *Yvain*.]

Hamilton, Gayle K. "The Breaking of the Troth in *Ywain and Gawain*." *Mediaevalia* 2 (1976), 111–35. [Argues that the poem is not only concerned with the keeping of one's vow in a feudal society, but also with that higher justice which is sometimes at odds with one's spoken vow.]

Hamilton, George L. "Storm-Making Springs: Rings of Invisibility and Protection — Studies on the Sources of the *Yvain* of Chrétien de Troyes." *The Romanic Review* 2 (1911), 355–75. [Traces the sources of the magic storm, concentrating on the Celtic folk-tale as a source for Chrétien.]

Harrington, Norman T. "The Problems of the Lacunae in *Ywain and Gawain*." *JEGP* 69 (1970), 659–65. [Sees the lacunae not as careless copying, but instead as deliberate attempts on the part of the English poet to avoid what his audience might consider as frivolous or unpalatable.]

Hunt, Tony. "Beginnings, Middles, and Ends: Some Interpretative Problems in Chrétien's *Yvain* and its Medieval Adaptations." In *The Craft of Fiction: Essays in Medieval Poetics*. Ed. Leigh A. Arrathoon. Rochester, Michigan: Solaris Press, 1984. Pp. 83–117. [Notes that *trowthe* is more important than the love element in *Ywain*, a poem which does not possess the ironies and complexities of the French original.]

Lacy, Norris J., *et al.* eds. *The New Arthurian Encyclopedia*. New York: Garland Publishing Inc., 1991. [See various characters, sites, works, s.v.]

Owens, Roger John. "'Ywain and Gawain': Style in the Middle English Romance." Dissertation, University of California, San Diego, 1977. [Argues for a certain set of English conventions that the *Ywain*-poet shared with his contemporaries and which he consciously manipulated in his work.]

Speirs, John. *Medieval English Poetry: The Non-Chaucerian Tradition*. London: Faber and Faber, 1957; rpt. 1971. Pp. 114–21. [Suggests that certain episodes in the poem (the monster herdsman, the storm-raising fountain, the keeper of the well) have their roots in pre-Christian rites which the English poet and Chrétien inherited even if they didn't fully understand.]

Taglicht, J. "Notes on *Ywain and Gawain*." *Neuphilologische Mitteilungen* 71 (1970), 641–47. [Corrects numerous errors, and supplements linguistic notes and glossary of Friedman and Harrington's edition.]

Introduction

Weston, Jessie L. "'Ywain and Gawain' and 'Le Chevalier au Lion.'" *MLQ* 1 (1898), 98–107 and 194–202. [Although conceding that the English poem is a "translation" of Chrétien's *Yvain*, Weston contends that the author also knew "The Lady of the Fountain" contained in the Welsh *Mabinogi*, which he used to supplement the French poem.]

Wilson, Anne. *The Magical Quest: The Use of Magic in Arthurian Romance*. Manchester and New York: Manchester University Press, 1988. Pp. 1–23 and 53–93. [Contends that *Ywain and Gawain* can best be understood by means of a four-step "magical plot" in which Ywain's ritualistic actions exorcise his theft of and treachery to Alundyne and allow him to achieve his goal.]

Ywain and Gawain

Here bigyns Ywain and Gawain

Almyghti God that made mankyn,	*mankind*
He schilde His servandes out of syn	*protects; from*
And mayntene tham with myght and mayne	
That herkens Ywayne and Gawayne;	*Who listens to*
5 Thai war knightes of the Tabyl Rownde,	
Tharfore listens a lytel stownde.	*little while*
Arthure, the Kyng of Yngland,	
That wan al Wales with his hand	*conquered*
And al Scotland, als sayes the buke,	*as*
10 And mani mo, if men wil luke,	*more*
Of al knightes he bare the pryse.	*was most worthy*
In werld was none so war ne wise.	*prudent*
Trew he was in alkyn thing.	*every*
Als it byfel to swilk a kyng,	*such*
15 He made a feste, the soth to say,	*feast; truth*
Opon the Witsononday	
At Kerdyf that es in Wales.	*Cardiff*
And efter mete thare in the hales	*after dinner; pavilions*
Ful grete and gay was the assemblé	
20 Of lordes and ladies of that cuntré,	
And als of kynghtes war and wyse	
And damisels of mykel pryse.	*great excellence*
Ilkane with other made grete gamin	*Each one; great pleasure*
And grete solace als thai war samin.	*as; were assembled*
25 Fast thai carped and curtaysly	*boasted*
Of dedes of armes and of veneri	*feats; hunting*
And of gude knightes that lyfed then,	*lived*
And how men might tham kyndeli ken	*truly know*
By doghtines of thaire gude dede	*valor*
30 On ilka syde, wharesum thai yede —	*every; wherever; went*

84

	For thai war stif in ilka stowre.	*strong; every fight*
	And tharfore gat thai grete honowre.	*got*
	Thai tald of more trewth tham bitwene	*accounted for; between*
	Than now omang men here es sene,	*among; is*
35	For trowth and luf es al bylaft;	*love; abandoned*
	Men uses now another craft.	
	With worde men makes it trew and stabil,	*words (i.e., writing)*
	Bot in thaire faith es noght bot fabil;	*nothing but lies*
	With the mowth men makes it hale,	*mouth; sweet*
40	Bot trew trowth es nane in the tale.	
	Tharfore hereof now wil I blyn,	*stop*
	Of the Kyng Arthure I wil bygin	
	And of his curtayse cumpany;	
	Thare was the flowre of chevallry.	
45	Swilk lose thai wan with speres-horde	*Such praise; spearpoint*
	Over al the werld went the worde.	
	After mete went the Kyng	
	Into chamber to slepeing,	
	And also went with him the Quene.	
50	That byheld thai al bydene,	*one and all*
	For thai saw tham never so	
	On high dayes to chamber go.	
	Bot sone, when thai war went to slepe,	
	Knyghtes sat the dor to kepe:	*guard*
55	Sir Dedyne and Sir Segramore,	
	Sir Gawayn and Sir Kay sat thore,	*there*
	And also sat thare Sir Ywaine	
	And Colgrevance of mekyl mayn.	*much strength*
	This knight that hight Colgrevance,	*was called*
60	Tald his felows of a chance	*situation*
	And of a stowre he had in bene,	*battle; been in*
	And al his tale herd the Quene.	
	The chamber dore sho has unshet,	*opened*
	And down omang tham scho hir set;	
65	Sodainli sho sat down right,	*Suddenly*
	Or ani of tham of hir had sight	*Before*
	Bot Colgrevance rase up in hy,	*rose; haste*
	And thareof had Syr Kay envy,	
	For he was of his tong a skalde,	*tongue a scold*

70	And forto boste was he ful balde.	*boast; bold*
	"Ow, Colgrevance," said Sir Kay,	*Oh*
	"Ful light of lepes has thou bene ay.	*quick to rise; ever been*
	Thou wenes now that the sal fall	*think; you shall be accounted*
	Forto be hendest of us all.	*To be most courteous*
75	And the Quene sal understand,	*shall*
	That here es none so unkunand	*ignorant*
	Al if thou rase and we sat styll.	*arose*
	We ne dyd it for none yll,	
	Ne for no manere of fayntise,	*sluggishness*
80	Ne us denyd noght forto rise,	*deigned (refused)*
	That we ne had resen had we hyr sene."	*arisen; seen*
	"Sir Kay, I wote wele," sayd the Quene,	*know*
	"And it war gude thou left swilk sawes	*quit such speech*
	And noght despise so thi felawes."	
85	"Madame," he said, "by Goddes dome,	*judgment*
	We ne wist no thing of thi come	*knew; coming*
	And if we did noght curtaysly,	*[behave] courteously*
	Takes to no velany.	*Account it no discourtesy*
	Bot pray ye now this gentil man	
90	To tel the tale that he bygan."	
	Colgrevance said to Sir Kay:	
	"Bi grete God that aw this day,	*made*
	Na mare manes me thi flyt	*bothers; reproach*
	Than it war a flies byt.	*bite*
95	Ful oft wele better men than I	
	Has thou desspised desspytusely.	*contemptuously*
	It es ful semeli, als me think,	*as it seems to me*
	A brok omang men forto stynk.	*badger*
	So it fars by the, Syr Kay:	*fares*
100	Of weked wordes has thou bene ay.	*evil words; ever been*
	And, sen thi wordes er wikked and fell,	*since; are; fierce*
	This time tharto na more I tell,	
	Bot of the thing that I bygan."	
	And sone Sir Kay him answerd than	
105	And said ful tite unto the Quene:	*quickly*
	"Madame, if ye had noght here bene,	
	We sold have herd a selly case;	*should; marvelous incident*
	Now let ye us of oure solace.	*you deprive us; entertainment*

86

	Tharfore, madame, we wald yow pray,	
110	That ye cumand him to say	*command; speak*
	And tel forth, als he had tyght."	*as; intended*
	Than answerd that hende knight:	*courteous*
	"Mi lady es so avyse,	*wise*
	That scho wil noght cumand me	
115	To tel that towches me to ill;	*what redounds to my discredit*
	Scho es noght of so weked will."	*wicked*
	Sir Kai said than ful smertli:	
	"Madame, al hale this cumpani	*whole*
	Praies yow hertly now omell,	*heartily; meanwhile*
120	That he his tale forth might tell.	
	If ye wil noght for oure praying,	
	For faith ye aw unto the kyng,	*owe*
	Cumandes him his tale to tell,	
	That we mai here how it byfell."	
125	Than said the Quene, "Sir Colgrevance,	
	I prai the tak to no grevance	
	This kene karping of Syr Kay;	*bitter nagging*
	Of weked wordes has he bene ay,	*always*
	So that none may him chastise.	
130	Tharfore I prai the, on al wise,	*wholeheartedly*
	That thou let noght for his sawes,	*cease*
	At tel to me and thi felawes	*But*
	Al thi tale, how it bytid.	*happened*
	For my luf I the pray and byd."	
135	"Sertes, madame, that es me lath	*reluctant*
	Bot for I wil noght mak yow wrath,	*angry*
	Yowre cumandment I sal fulfill,	
	If ye wil listen me untill,	*to*
	With hertes and eres understandes;	
140	And I sal tel yow swilk tithandes,	*such tidings*
	That ye herd never none slike	*like 'em*
	Reherced in no kynges ryke.	*Recounted; realm*
	Bot word fares als dose the wind,	
	Bot if men it in hert bynd;	
145	And, wordes wo so trewly tase,	*who; takes*
	By the eres into the hert it gase,	*goes*
	And in the hert thare es the horde	*treasury*

87

	And knawing of ilk mans worde.	*each*
	"Herkens, hende unto my spell.	*good sirs, gracious lady; story*
150	Trofels sal I yow nane tell,	*Trivial tales shall*
	Ne lesinges forto ger yow lagh,	*lies; make you laugh*
	Bot I sal say right als I sagh.	*saw*
	Now als this time sex yere	*six years ago*
	I rade allane, als ye sal here,	*rode; hear*
155	Obout forto seke aventurs,	*seek*
	Wele armid in gude armurs.	
	In a frith I fand a strete;	*wood; path*
	Ful thik and hard, I you bihete,	*assure*
	With thornes, breres, and moni a quyn.	*prickly branches; quince tree*
160	Nerehand al day I rade thareyn,	*Nearly*
	And thurgh I past with mekyl payn.	*great pain*
	Than come I sone into a playn,	*clearing*
	Whare I gan se a bretise brade,	*parapet broad*
	And thederward ful fast I rade.	
165	I saw the walles and the dyke,	*moat*
	And hertly wele it gan me lyke;	*heartily*
	And on the drawbrig saw I stand	
	A knight with fawkon on his hand.	*falcon*
	This ilk knight, that be ye balde,	*same; assured*
170	Was lord and keper of that halde.	*castle*
	I hailsed him kindly als I kowth;	*hailed; could*
	He answerd me mildeli with mowth.	*courteous speech*
	Mi sterap toke that hende knight	*stirrup*
	And kindly cumanded me to lyght;	*dismount*
175	His cumandment I did onane,	*straight away*
	And into hall sone war we tane.	*taken*
	He thanked God, that gude man,	
	Sevyn sithes or ever he blan,	*times before; ceased*
	And the way that me theder broght,	*thither*
180	And als the aventurs that I soght.	
	"Thus went we in, God do him mede,	*give him recompense*
	And in his hand he led my stede.	
	When we are in that fayre palays —	
	It was ful worthly wroght always —	
185	I saw no man of moder born.	
	Bot a burde hang us biforn,	*rectangular board*

	Was nowther of yren ne of tre,	*neither of iron nor wood*
	Ne I ne wist whareof it might be.	
	And by that bord hang a mall.	*hammer*
190	The knyght smate on tharwithal	
	Thrise, and by then might men se	*Thrice*
	Bifore him come a faire menye,	*group of followers*
	Curtayse men in worde and dede.	
	To stabil sone thai led mi stede.	
195	"A damisel come unto me,	
	The semeliest that ever I se,	
	Lufsumer lifed never in land.	*Lovelier lived*
	Hendly scho toke me by the hand,	*Courteously*
	And sone that gentyl creature	
200	Al unlaced myne armure.	
	Into a chamber sho me led,	
	And with a mantil scho me cled:	*clothed*
	It was of purpure faire and fine	*purple cloth*
	And the pane of riche ermyne.	*lining*
205	Al the folk war went us fra,	
	And thare was none than bot we twa.	
	Scho served me hendely to hend:	*courteously close by*
	Hir maners might no man amend.	
	Of tong sho was trew and renable	*tongue; eloquent*
210	And of hir semblant soft and stabile.	*demeanor*
	Ful fain I wald, if that I might,	*gladly*
	Have woned with that swete wight.	*lived; person*
	And, when we sold go to sopere,	*should*
	That lady with a lufsom chere	*gracious manner*
215	Led me down into the hall.	
	Thare war we served wele at all;	
	It nedes noght to tel the mese,	*food*
	For wonder wele war we at esse.	*ease*
	Byfor me sat the lady bright	
220	Curtaisly my mete to dyght;	*prepare*
	Us wanted nowther baken ne roste.	*lacked; meat pie; roast meat*
	And efter soper sayd myne oste	*host*
	That he cowth noght tel the day	*could not [more happily] recall*
	That ani knight are with him lay,	*previously*
225	Or that ani aventures soght.	

Tharfore he prayed me, if I moght,   *might*
On al wise, when I come ogayne,
That I sold cum to him sertayne.
I said, "Sir, gladly, yf I may."
230 It had bene shame have said him nay.
   "That night had I ful gude rest
And mi stede esed of the best.   *provided comfort*
Alsone als it was dayes lyght,
Forth to fare sone was I dyght.
235 Mi leve of mine ost toke I thare   *host*
And went mi way withowten mare,
Aventures forto layt in land.   *seek*
A faire forest sone I fand.   *came upon*
Me thoght mi hap thare fel ful hard,   *by chance*
240 For thare was mani a wilde lebard,   *leopard*
Lions, beres, bath bul and bare,   *boar*
That rewfully gan rope and rare.   *sorrowfully; cry out; roar*
Oway I drogh me, and with that   *drew*
I saw sone whare a man sat
245 On a lawnd, the fowlest wight   *clearing; ugliest creature*
That ever yit man saw in syght.
He was a lathly creature,   *loathsome*
For fowl he was out of mesure;   *ugly*
A wonder mace in hand he hade,   *wonderful club*
250 And sone mi way to him I made.
His hevyd, me thoght, was als grete   *head*
Als of a rowncy or a nete;   *saddle-horse; ox*
Unto his belt hang his hare,   *Down to; hair*
And efter that byheld I mare.   *more*
255 To his forhede byheld I than,
Was bradder than twa large span;   *two; handbreadths*
He had eres als ane olyfant   *like an elephant*
And was wele more than geant.   *bigger than a giant*
His face was ful brade and flat;   *broad*
260 His nese was cutted als a cat;   *snubbed*
His browes war like litel buskes;   *bushes*
And his tethe like bare tuskes.   *boar's tusks*
A ful grete bulge opon his bak —
Thare was noght made withowten lac.   *fault*

265	His chin was fast until his brest;	*firmly fixed*
	On his mace he gan him rest.	*club*
	Also it was a wonder wede,	*wondrous garment*
	That the cherle yn gede;	*was dressed in*
	Nowther of wol ne of line	*wool; linen*
270	Was the wede that he went yn.	*clothing*
	"When he me sagh, he stode upright.	
	I frayned him if he wolde fight,	*asked*
	For tharto was I in gude will,	
	Bot als a beste than stode he still.	
275	I hopid that he no wittes kowth,	*thought; had no ability to understand*
	No reson forto speke with mowth.	
	To him I spak ful hardily	
	And said, 'What ertow, belamy?'	*are you, fair friend*
	He said ogain, 'I am a man.'	
280	I said, 'Swilk saw I never nane.	*Such*
	What ertow?' alsone said he.	*instantly*
	I said, 'Swilk als thou here may se.'	
	I said, 'What does thou here allane?'	*alone*
	He said, 'I kepe thir bestes ilkane.'	*each one*
285	I said, 'That es mervaile, think me,	
	For I herd never of man bot the	
	In wildernes ne in forestes,	
	That kepeing had of wilde bestes,	
	Bot thai war bunden fast in halde.'	*bound; confinement*
290	He sayd, 'Of thire es none so balde	*fearless*
	Nowther by day ne bi night	
	Anes to pas out of mi sight.'	*Alone*
	I sayd, 'How so? Tel me thi scill.'	*skill*
	'Parfay,' he said, 'gladly I will.'	*By my faith*
295	He said, 'In al this faire foreste	
	Es thare none so wilde beste,	
	That remu dar, bot stil stand,	*dare to move*
	When I am to him cumand.	*coming*
	Any ay, when that I wil him fang	*seize*
300	With mi fingers that er strang,	
	I ger him cri on swilk manere,	*make; such*
	That al the bestes when thai him here,	*hear*
	Obout me than cum thai all,	

	And to mi fete fast thai fall,	
305	On thaire manere merci to cry.	
	Bot understand now redyli,	*readily*
	Olyve es thare lifand no ma	*Alive; more*
	Bot I that durst omang tham ga,	
	That he ne sold sone be al torent.	*should soon be torn to pieces*
310	Bot thai er at my comandment;	*Unless; are*
	To me thai cum when I tham call,	
	And I am maister of tham all.'	
	"Than he asked onone right,	*straight away*
	What man I was. I said, 'A knyght	
315	That soght aventurs in that land,	
	My body to asai and fande.	*test; try*
	And I the pray of thi kownsayle,	
	Thou teche me to sum mervayle.'	*direct*
	He sayd, 'I can no wonders tell,	
320	Bot here bisyde es a well.	
	Wend theder and do als I say;	*Go*
	Thou passes noght al quite oway.	*You won't get away so easily*
	Folow forth this ilk strete,	*same path*
	And sone sum mervayles sal thou mete.	
325	The well es under the fairest tre	
	That ever was in this cuntré;	
	By that well hinges a bacyne	*hangs; basin*
	That es of gold gude and fyne,	
	With a cheyne, trewly to tell,	
330	That wil reche into the well.	
	Thare es a chapel nere tharby,	
	That nobil es and ful lufely.	
	By the well standes a stane;	
	Tak the bacyn sone onane	*quickly*
335	And cast on water with thi hand,	
	And sone thou sal se new tithand.	*shall see; tidings*
	A storme sal rise and a tempest	
	Al obout, by est and west;	
	Thou sal here mani thonor-blast	*hear; thunderblasts*
340	Al obout the blawand fast.	*you blowing fiercely*
	And thare sal cum slik slete and rayne	*such sleet*
	That unnese sal thou stand ogayne;	*with difficulty*

	Of lightnes sal thou se a lowe,	*brightness; flame*
	Unnethes thou sal thi selven knowe.	*Hardly*
345	And if thou pas withowten grevance,	*harm*
	Than has thou the fairest chance,	
	That ever yit had any knyght,	
	That theder come to kyth his myght.'	*proclaim*
	"Than toke I leve and went my way	
350	And rade unto the midday.	*rode*
	By than I come whare I sold be,	*By [the time] when; should*
	I saw the chapel and the tre.	
	Thare I fand the fayrest thorne	
	That ever groued sen God was born.	*grew since*
355	So thik it was with leves grene,	
	Might no rayn cum tharbytwene;	
	And that grenes lastes ay,	*always*
	For no winter dere yt may.	*may harm it*
	I fand the bacyn als he talde,	*basin*
360	And the wel with water kalde.	*cold*
	An amerawd was the stane —	*emerald; stone*
	Richer saw I never nane —	
	On fowre rubyes on heght standand.	*standing aloft*
	Thaire light lasted over al the land,	*shone*
365	And when I saw that semely syght,	*pleasing*
	It made me bath joyful and lyght.	*both; light-hearted*
	I toke the bacyn sone onane	*at once*
	And helt water opon the stane.	*poured*
	The weder wex than wonder-blak,	
370	And the thoner fast gan crak.	*thunder*
	Thare come slike stormes of hayl and rayn,	*such*
	Unnethes I might stand thare ogayn;	*With difficulty*
	The store windes blew ful lowd,	*violent*
	So kene come never are of clowd.	*bitter; before from*
375	I was drevyn with snaw and slete,	*driven*
	Unnethes I might stand on my fete.	*Scarcely*
	In my face the levening smate,	*lightning smote*
	I wend have brent, so was it hate,	*expected to have [been] burned; hot*
	That weder made me so will of rede,	*at a loss*
380	I hopid sone to have my dede;	*death*
	And sertes, if it lang had last,	

93

	I hope I had never thethin past.	*I expect I'd never have left that place*
	Bot thorgh His might that tholed wownd,	*suffered wounds (i.e., Christ)*
	The storme sesed within a stownde.	*moment*
385	Than wex the weder fayre ogayne,	
	And thareof was I wonder-fayne;	*wondrously joyous*
	For best comforth of al thing	*comfort*
	Es solace efter myslikeing.	*unhappiness*
	"Than saw I sone a mery syght:	
390	Of al the fowles that er in flyght,	
	Lighted so thik opon that tre,	
	That bogh ne lefe none might I se.	*bough; leaf*
	So merily than gon thai sing,	
	That al the wode bigan to ring;	
395	Ful mery was the melody	
	Of thaire sang and of thaire cry.	
	Thare herd never man none swilk,	*heard; such*
	Bot if ani had herd that ilk.	*Unless; same [song]*
	And when that mery dyn was done,	
400	Another noyse than herd I sone,	
	Als it war of horsmen	*As if*
	Mo than owther nyen or ten.	*More; either*
	"Sone than saw I cum a knyght;	
	In riche armurs was he dight,	*dressed*
405	And sone, when I gan on him loke,	
	Mi shelde and spere to me I toke.	
	That knight to me hied ful fast,	*hastened*
	And kene wordes out gan he cast.	*bold*
	He bad that I sold tel him tite,	*commanded; immediately*
410	Whi I did him swilk despite,	*such injury*
	With weders wakened him of rest	*storms; from*
	And done him wrang in his forest.	*wrong*
	'Tharfore,' he said, 'thou sal aby!'	*shall pay for it*
	And with that come he egerly	
415	And said I had ogayn resowne	*against reason*
	Done him grete destrucciowne,	
	And might it never more amend.	
	Tharfore he bad I sold me fend.	*defend myself*
	And sone I smate him on the shelde,	*as soon as*
420	Mi schaft brac out in the felde,	*broke*

	And than he bare me sone bi strenkith	*strength*
	Out of my sadel my speres lenkith.	*the length of my spear*
	I wate that he was largely	*knew; larger*
	By the shuldres mare than I;	
425	And bi the ded that I sal thole,	*death; suffer*
	Mi stede by his was bot a fole.	*foal*
	For mate I lay down on the grownde,	*Defeated (check-mated)*
	So was I stonayd in that stownde.	*stunned; time*
	A worde to me wald he noght say,	
430	Bot toke my stede and went his way.	*horse*
	Ful sarily than thare I sat,	*then*
	For wa I wist noght what was what.	*woe; knew not*
	With my stede he went in hy	*quickly*
	The same way that he come by.	
435	And I durst folow him no ferr	*farther*
	For dout me solde bitide werr.	*fear I should suffer worse*
	And also yit, by Goddes dome,	*heaven*
	I ne wist whare he bycome.	*didn't know; went*
	"Than I thoght how I had hight	*promised*
440	Unto myne ost, the hende knyght,	*host; gracious*
	And also til his lady bryght,	*to*
	To com ogayn if that I myght.	
	Mine armurs left I thare ilkane,	*armor; also*
	For els myght I noght have gane.	
445	Unto myne in I come by day.	*lodging*
	The hende knight and the fayre may	*maiden*
	Of my come war thai ful glade,	*coming were; glad*
	And nobil semblant thai me made.	*reception*
	In al thinges thai have tham born	
450	Als thai did the night biforn.	
	Sone thai wist whare I had bene,	*learned*
	And said that thai had never sene	
	Knyght that ever theder come,	
	Take the way ogayn home.	
455	On this wise that tyme I wroght;	*In this manner*
	I fand the folies that I soght."	*found*
	"Now sekerly," said Sir Ywayne,	
	"Thou ert my cosyn jermayne;	*close kinsman*
	Trew luf suld be us bytwene,	

460	Als sold bytwyx brether bene.	*brother*
	Thou ert a fole at thou ne had are	*not to have [told me] earlier*
	Tald me of this ferly fare,	*weird event*
	For sertes I sold onone ryght	*at once*
	Have venged the of that ilk knyght.	*avenged you; same*
465	So sal I yit, if that I may."	
	And than als smertly sayed Syr Kay —	*sharply*
	He karpet to tham wordes grete:	*spoke; insolent*
	"It es sene, now es efter mete,	*is*
	Mare boste es in a pot of wyne	
470	Than in a karcas of Saynt Martyne.	*(see note)*
	Arme the smertly, Syr Ywayne,	
	And sone that thou war cumen ogayne;	*again*
	Luke thou fil wele thi panele,	*saddlepad*
	And in thi sadel set the wele.	*place yourself well*
475	And when thou wendes, I the pray,	*goes*
	Thi baner wele that thou desplay;	
	And, rede I, or thou wende,	*ere you go*
	Thou tak thi leve at ilka frende.	*of every friend*
	And if it so bytide this nyght,	
480	That the in slepe dreche ani wight	*vex*
	Or any dremis mak the rad,	*you frightened*
	Turn ogayn and say I bad."	*predicted [it]*
	The quene answerd with milde mode	*mood*
	And said, "Sir Kay, ertow wode?	*are you crazy*
485	What the devyl es the withyn,	
	At thi tong may never blyn	*That; tongue; cease*
	Thi felows so fowly to shende?	*shame*
	Sertes, Sir Kay, thou ert unhende.	*discourteous*
	By Him that for us sufferd pine,	*(i.e., Christ); torment*
490	Syr, and thi tong war myne	*if*
	I sold bical it tyte of treson,	*should accuse it quickly*
	And so might thou do, by gude reson.	
	Thi tong dose the grete dishonowre,	
	And tharefore es it thi traytowre."	
495	And than alsone Syr Ywayne	*instantly*
	Ful hendly answerd ogayne,	*courteously*
	Al if men sayd hym velany,	*Always*
	He karped ay ful curtaysly:	*spoke*

96

"Madame," he said unto the quene,
500 "Thare sold na stryf be us bytwene.
Unkowth men wele may he shende   *Stupid; shamed*
That to his felows es so unhende.   *discourteous*
And als, madame, men says sertayne   *also*
That, wo so flites or turnes ogayne,   *whosoever reproaches; against*
505 He bygins al the melle: *fight*
So wil I noght it far by me.
Lates him say haley his thoght;   *Let; wholly*
His wordes greves me right noght."   *not at all*
     Als thai war in this spekeing
510 Out of the chamber come the kyng.
The barons that war thare, sertayn,
Smertly rase thai him ogayne.   *rose themselves for him*
He bad tham sit down al bydene,   *one and all*
And down he set him by the quene.   *himself*
515 The quene talde him fayre and wele,
Als sho kowth, everilka dele   *understood every bit*
Ful apertly al the chance   *plainly; occurrence*
Als it bifel Syr Colgrevance.
When sho had talde him how it ferd,   *happened*
520 And the king hyr tale had herd,
He sware by his owyn crowne
And his fader sowl Uter Pendragowne,   *father's soul*
That he sold se that ilk syght   *same*
By that day thethin a fowretenight,   *from thence; fortnight*
525 On Saint Johns evyn, the Baptist,
That best barn was under Crist.   *man; next to*
"Swith," he sayd, "wendes with me,   *Quickly; go*
Who so wil that wonder se."
     The kynges word might noght be hid,
530 Over al the cowrt sone was it kyd;   *made known*
And thare was none so litel page
That he ne was fayn of that vayage;   *eager for; journey*
And knyghtes and swiers war ful fayne;   *squires*
Mysliked none bot Syr Ywayne.   *None was displeased*
535 To himself he made grete mane,
For he wald have went allane.
In hert he had grete myslykyng   *displeasure*

	For the wending of the kyng,	*going*
	Al for he hopid, withowten fayle,	
540	That Sir Kay sold ask the batayle,	*should*
	Or els Sir Gawayn, knyght vailant;	
	And owther wald the king grant.	
	Who so it wald first crave	
	Of tham two, sone might it have.	
545	The kynges wil wald he noght bide,	*would he (i.e., Ywain) not await*
	Worth of him, what may bityde;	*Become; happen*
	Bi him allane he thoght to wend	*By himself alone*
	And tak the grace that God wald send.	
	He thoght to be wele on hys way,	
550	Or it war passed the thryd day,	*Ere*
	And to asay if he myght mete	
	With that ilk narow strete	*path*
	With thornes and with breres set,	*briars*
	That mens way might lightli let,	*hinder*
555	And also forto fynd the halde,	*fortress*
	That Sir Colgrevance of talde.	*told*
	The knyght and the mayden meke,	
	The forest fast than wald he seke,	
	And als the karl of Kaymes kyn	*also; churl of Cain's*
560	And the wilde bestes with him,	
	The tre with briddes thare opon,	
	The chapel, the bacyn, and the stone.	
	His thoght wald he tel to no frende,	
	Until he wyst how it wald ende.	
565	Than went Ywaine to his yn;	*household*
	His men he fand redy thareyn.	*found*
	Unto a swier gan he say,	*squire*
	"Go swith and sadel my palfray,	*quickly*
	And so thou do my strang stede,	*also; powerful*
570	And tak with the my best wede.	*armor*
	At yone gate I wil outryde;	
	Withowten town I sal the bide.	*Outside; await you*
	And hy the smertly unto me,	*hasten quickly*
	For I most make a jorné.	*journey*
575	Ogain sal thou bring my palfra,	
	And forbede the oght to say.	

If thou wil any more me se,
Lat none wit of my preveté;   *know; secrecy*
And if ani man the oght frayn,   *should ask you*
580   Luke now lely that thou layn."   *loyally; lie*
"Sir," he said, "with ful gude will,
Als ye byd, I sal fulfyll.
At yowre awyn wil may ye ride,   *own*
For me ye sal noght be ascryed."   *because of; informed upon*
585   Forth than went Sir Ywayne;
He thinkes, or he cum ogayne,
To wreke his kosyn at his myght.   *avenge his cousin with all*
The squier has his hernays dyght;   *armor prepared*
He did right als his mayster red;   *advised*
590   His stede, his armurs he him led.   *equipment; [to] him*
When Ywayn was withowten town,   *outside*
Of his palfray lighted he down   *Off*
And dight him right wele in his wede   *dressed; armor*
And lepe up on his gude stede.
595   Furth he rade onone right,   *straight away*
Until it neghed nere the nyght.
He passed many high mowntayne
In wildernes and mony a playne,
Til he come to that lethir sty,   *treacherous crossing*
600   That him byhoved pass by.   *of necessity [had to]*
Than was he seker for to se   *sure*
The wel and the fayre tre.
The chapel saw he at the last,
And theder hyed he ful fast.   *hastened*
605   More curtaysi and more honowre
Fand he with tham in that toure,
And mare conforth by monyfalde,   *many times over*
Than Colgrevance had him of talde.
That night was he herberd thare: *lodged*
610   So wele was he never are.   *before*
    At morn he went forth by the strete,
And with the cherel sone gan he mete   *churl*
That sold tel to him the way.   *should*
He sayned him, the soth to say,   *crossed himself*
615   Twenty sith or ever he blan;   *times; ceased*

99

Swilk mervayle had he of that man;
For he had wonder that nature
Myght mak so fowl a creature.
Than to the well he rade gude pase,   *at a good pace (i.e., rapidly)*
620 And doun he lighted in that place;
And sone the bacyn has he tane
And kest water opon the stane;
And sone thare wex withowten fayle,   *soon; blew up*
Wind and thonor and rayn and haile.   *thunder*
625 When it was sesed, than saw he
The fowles light opon the tre;   *birds*
Thai sang ful fayre opon that thorn,
Right als thai had done byforn.
 And sone he saw cumand a knight
630 Als fast so the fowl in flyght   *as*
With rude sembland and sterne chere,   *rough appearance; fierce manner*
And hastily he neghed nere.   *approached*
To speke of lufe na time was thare,
For aither hated uther ful sare.   *either; sorely*
635 Togeder smertly gan thai drive,
Thaire sheldes sone bigan to ryve,   *split*
Thaire shaftes cheverd to thaire hand,   *splintered in*
Bot thai war bath ful wele syttand.   *[in the saddle]*
Out thai drogh thaire swerdes kene
640 And delt strakes tham bytwene;
Al to peces thai hewed thaire sheldes,
The culpons flegh out in the feldes.   *pieces flew*
On helmes strake thay so with yre,   *ire*
At ilka strake outbrast the fyre.
645 Aither of tham gude buffettes bede,   *Either; blows offered*
And nowther wald styr of the stede.   *budge from*
Ful kenely thai kyd thaire myght   *bravely; made known*
And feyned tham noght forto fight.
On thaire hauberkes that men myght ken,   *coats of mail; see*
650 The blode out of thaire bodyes ren;
Aither on other laid so fast,
The batayl might noght lang last.
Hauberkes er broken and helmes reven,   *Coats of mail are; split*
Stif strakes war thare gyfen;

100

655	Thai faght on hors stifly always;	*stoutly*
	The batel was wele more to prays.	
	Bot at the last Syr Ywayne	
	On his felow kyd his mayne:	*made known; strength*
	So egerly he smate him than,	*then*
660	He clefe the helme and the hernpan.	*skull*
	The knyght wist he was nere ded;	*knew*
	To fle than was his best rede,	*plan*
	And fast he fled with al hys mayne,	*strength*
	And fast folowd Syr Ywayne.	
665	Bot he ne might him overtake,	*(Ywain); (the knight)*
	Tharfore grete murning gan he make.	
	He folowd him ful stowtlyk	*resolutely*
	And wald have tane him ded or quik.	*dead or alive*
	He folowd him to the ceté;	*city*
670	Na man lyfand met he.	*living*
	When thai come to the kastel gate,	
	In he folowd fast thareate.	
	At aither entré was, iwys,	*truly*
	Straytly wroght a portculis	*Finely*
675	Shod wele with yren and stele	*steel*
	And also grunden wonder wele.	*sharpened*
	Under that than was a swyke,	*treacherous snare*
	That made Syr Ywain to myslike.	
	His hors fote toched thareon	
680	Than fel the portculis onone	*iron gate instantly*
	Bytwyx him and his hinder arsown.	*cantle (rear part of saddle)*
	Thorgh sadel and stede it smate al down,	
	His spores of his heles it schare;	*spurs off; heels; cut*
	Than had Ywaine murnyng mare.	*mourning more*
685	Bot so he wend have passed quite,	*as he thought to; free*
	Than fel the tother bifore als tyte.	*quickly*
	A faire grace yit fel him swa,	*so*
	Al if it smate his hors in twa	
	And his spors of aither hele,	*from*
690	That himself passed so wele.	
	Bytwene tha gates now es he tane;	
	Tharfore he mase ful mukel mane,	*makes; much moan*
	And mikel murnyng gan he ma,	*great; make*

101

	For the knyght was went him fra.	*from*
695	Als he was stoken in that stall,	*trapped (stoked)*
	He herd byhind him in a wall	
	A dore opend faire and wele,	
	And thareout come a damysel.	
	Efter hir the dore sho stak,	*shut*
700	Ful hinde wordes to him sho spak.	*courteous; she*
	"Syr," sho said, "by Saint Myghell,	*Michael*
	Here thou has a febil ostell.	*poor hostelry*
	Thou mon be ded, es noght at laine,	*shall; certainly*
	For my lord that thou has slayne.	
705	Seker it es that thou him slogh;	*Certain; killed*
	My lady makes sorow ynogh	
	And al his menye everilkane.	*attendants everyone*
	Here has thou famen many ane	*foes*
	To be thi bane er thai ful balde.	*cause your death are; eager*
710	Thou brekes noght out of this halde.	
	And, for thai wate thai may noght fayl,	*since they know*
	Thai wil the sla in playn batayl."	
	He sayd, "Thai ne sal, so God me rede.	*shall not; counsel*
	For al thaire might do me to dede,	*slay me*
715	Ne no handes opon me lay."	
	Sho said, "Na, sertes, if that I may!	
	Al if thou be here straytly stad,	*sore beset*
	Me think thou ert noght ful adrad.	
	And sir," sho said, "on al wise	
720	I aw the honore and servyse.	*owe you*
	I was in message at the king	*on a mission to*
	Bifore this time, whils I was ying;	*young*
	I was noght than savese,	*[as] discreet*
	Als a damysel aght to be.	
725	Fro the tyme that I was lyght	*alighted*
	In cowrt was none so hend knyght,	*courteous*
	That unto me than walde take hede,	
	Bot thou allane, God do the mede.	*alone; reward you*
	Grete honore thou did to me,	
730	And that sal I now quite the.	*repay*
	I wate, if thou be seldom sene,	*know even though you*
	Thou ert the Kyng son Uriene,	*are the son of King Uriene*

And thi name es Sir Ywayne.
Of me may thou be sertayne.
735 If thou wil my kownsail leve,   *counsel believe*
Thou sal find na man the to greve;
I sal lene the here mi ring,   *lend you*
Bot yelde it me at myne askyng.
When thou ert broght of al thi payn,
740 Yelde it than to me ogayne.
Als the bark hilles the tre,   *protects*
Right so sal my ring do the;
When thou in hand has the stane,
Dere sal thai do the nane;   *Harm*
745 For the stane es of swilk myght,   *such*
Of the sal men have na syght."
    Wit ye wele that Sir Ywayne   *Know*
Of thir wordes was ful fayne.   *these; joyful*
In at the dore sho him led
750 And did him sit opon hir bed.
A quylt ful nobil lay thareon,   *quilt*
Richer saw he never none.
Sho said if he wald any thing,   *wanted*
He sold be served at his liking.   *pleasure*
755 He said that ete wald he fayn.   *eat; gladly*
Sho went and come ful sone ogain;
A capon rosted broght sho sone,
A clene klath and brede tharone   *cloth; bread*
And a pot with riche wine
760 And a pece to fil it yne.   *cup; in*
He ete and drank with ful gude chere,
For tharof had he grete mystere.   *need*
When he had eten and dronken wele,
Grete noyse he herd in the kastele.
765 Thai soght overal him to have slayn,   *everywhere*
To venge thaire lorde war thai ful bayn   *eager*
Or that the cors in erth was layd.   *Ere; corpse*
The damysel sone to him sayd,
"Now seke thai the fast forto sla,
770 Bot whosoever com or ga,
Be thou never the more adred,   *afraid*

	Ne styr thou noght out of this stede;	*Nor move; place*
	In this here seke thai wyll,	*[place]*
	Bot on this bed luke thou be styll,	
775	Of tham al mak thou na force.	
	Bot when that thai sal bere the cors	*body*
	Unto the kyrk for to bery,	*church; bury*
	Than sal thou here a sary cry;	*hear; grievous*
	So sal thai mak a doleful dyn.	
780	Than wil thay seke the eft herein;	*seek you afterwards*
	Bot loke thou be of hert lyght,	
	For of the sal thai have no syght.	
	Here sal thou be, mawgré thaire berd,	*despite their best efforts*
	And tharfore be thou noght aferd.	
785	Thi famen sal be als the blynd,	*foes*
	Both byfor the and byhind,	
	On ilka side sal thou be soght.	*every*
	Now most I ga, bot drede the noght,	*go*
	For I sal do that the es lefe,	*what is agreeable [to] you*
790	If al it turn me to mischefe."	*Even if*
	When sho come unto the gate,	
	Ful many men fand sho tharate	
	Wele armed, and wald ful fayn	
	Have taken and slane Sir Ywaine.	
795	Half his stede thare fand thai	*horse*
	That within the gates lay;	
	Bot the knight thare fand thai noght:	
	Than was thare mekil sorow unsoght.	*unrelieved*
	Dore ne window was thare nane,	
800	Whare he myght oway gane.	
	Thai said he sold thare be laft,	
	Or els he cowth of wechecraft,	*knew*
	Or he cowth of nygromancy,	*knew*
	Or he had wenges forto fly.	
805	Hastily than went thai all	
	And soght him in the maydens hall,	
	In chambers high (es noght at hide),	*to*
	And in solers on ilka side.	*upper rooms; each*
	Sir Ywaine saw ful wele al that,	
810	And still opon the bed he sat.	

	Thare was nane that anes mynt	*who once made a movement*
	Unto the bed at smyte a dynt;	*Toward; to*
	Al obout thai smate so fast,	
	That mani of thaire wapins brast.	*broke*
815	Mekyl sorow thai made ilkane,	*each one*
	For thai ne myght wreke thaire lord bane.	*avenge; lord's death*
	Thai went oway with dreri chere,	
	And sone thare efter come the bere.	*bier*
	A lady folowd white so mylk,	*as*
820	In al that land was none swilk;	*such*
	Sho wrang hir fingers, outbrast the blode.	*out burst*
	For mekyl wa sho was nere wode.	*gone mad*
	Hir fayre hare scho al todrogh,	*hair; pulled out*
	And ful oft fel sho down in swogh;	*in a swoon*
825	Sho wepe with a ful dreri voice.	
	The hali water and the Croyce	*Cross*
	Was born bifore the procession;	*Were*
	Thare folowd mani a moder son;	
	Bifore the cors rade a knyght	*corpse rode*
830	On his stede that was ful wight,	*(the dead knight's) steed; strong*
	In his armurs wele arayd,	*(the dead knight's) armor*
	With spere and target gudely grayd.	*shield; equipped*
	Than Sir Ywayn herd the cry	
	And the dole of that fayre lady;	*sorrow*
835	For more sorow myght nane have,	
	Than sho had when he went to grave.	
	Prestes and monkes on thaire wyse	*in every way*
	Ful solempnly did the servyse.	
	Als Lunet thare stode in the thrang,	*Also*
840	Until Sir Ywaine thoght hir lang.	*long away*
	Out of the thrang the wai sho tase,	*takes*
	Unto Sir Ywaine fast sho gase.	*goes*
	Sho said, "Sir, how ertow stad?	*how are you doing?*
	I hope ful wele thou has bene rad."	*expect; frightened*
845	"Sertes," he said, "thou sais wele thare;	
	So abayst was I never are."	*upset; before*
	He said, "Leman, I pray the,	*Sweetheart*
	If it any wise may be,	
	That I might luke a litel throw	*look; while*

850	Out at sum hole or sum window,	
	For wonder fayn," he sayd, "wald I	*would*
	Have a sight of the lady."	
	The maiden than ful sone unshet	*then; opened up*
	In a place a prevé weket.	*secret window*
855	Thare of the lady he had a syght.	
	Lowd sho cried to God almyght,	
	"Of his sins do hym pardowne,	
	For sertanly in no regyowne	*region*
	Was never knight of his bewté,	
860	Ne efter him sal never nane be;	
	In al the werld fro end to ende	
	Es none so curtayse ne so hende.	*gracious*
	God grant the grace thou mai won	*dwell*
	In hevyn with His owyn son;	
865	For so large lifs none in lede	*generous; on earth*
	Ne none so doghty of gude dede."	*worthy*
	When sho had thus made hir spell,	*speech*
	In swownyng ful oft sithes sho fell.	*times*
	Now lat we the lady be,	
870	And of Sir Ywaine speke we.	
	Luf, that es so mekil of mayne,	*mighty of power*
	Sare had wownded Sir Ywayne,	*Sore*
	That whareso he sal ride or ga,	
	His hert sho has that es his fa.[1]	*foe*
875	His hert he has set al bydene,	*altogether*
	Whare himself dar noght be sene.	*dare*
	Bot thus in langing bides he	*longing*
	And hopes that it sal better be.	
	Al that war at the enterement,	*burial*
880	Toke thaire leve at the lady gent,	*of; gracious*
	And hame now er thai halely gane;	*wholly*
	And the lady left allane	
	Dweland with hir chamberere	*lady-in-waiting*
	And other mo that war hir dere.	*were close to her*
885	Than bigan hir noyes al new,	*weeping*

---

[1]*She who is his foe possesses his heart*

	For sorow failed hir hide and hew.	*permeated; skin*
	Unto his sawl was sho ful hulde;	*loyal*
	Opon a sawter al of gulde	*psalter; gold*
	To say the salmes fast sho bigan	*psalms*
890	And toke no tent unto no man.	*heed of any*
	Than had Sir Ywain mekyl drede,	
	For he hoped noght to spede;	*(i.e., he did not expect success)*
	He said, "I am mekil to blame,	
	That I luf tham that wald me shame.	
895	Bot yit I wite hir al with wogh,	*blame; wrongfully*
	Sen that I hir lord slogh.	*Since*
	I can noght se by nakyn gyn,	*any scheme*
	How that I hir luf sold wyn.	
	That lady es ful gent and small,	*gracious*
900	Hir yghen clere als es cristall;	*eyes*
	Sertes thare es no man olive,	*alive*
	That kowth hir bewtese wele descrive."	*could; beauty*
	Thus was Syr Ywayne sted that sesowne;	*situated; time*
	He wroght ful mekyl ogayns resowne	
905	To set his luf in swilk a stede,	*place*
	Whare thai hated him to the dede.	*death*
	He sayd he sold have hir to wive,	
	Or els he sold lose his lyve.	
	Thus als he in stody sat,	*reverie*
910	The mayden come to him with that.	
	Sho sayd, "How hasto farn this day,	*have you fared*
	Sen that I went fro the oway?"	
	Sone sho saw him pale and wan,	
	Sho wist wele what him ayled than.	*ailed him then*
915	Sho said, "I wote thi hert es set,	
	And sertes I ne sal noght it let;	*allow*
	Bot I sal help the fra presowne	*from prison*
	And bring the to thi warisowne."	*reward*
	He said, "Sertes, damysele,	
920	Out of this place wil I noght stele;	
	Bot I wil wende by dayes lyght,	
	That men may of me have sight	
	Opinly on ilka syde.	
	Worth of me what so bityde,	*Become*

925	Manly wil I hethin wende."	*Nobly; hence depart*
	Than answerd tha mayden hende,	
	"Sir, thow sal wend with honowre,	
	For thou sal have ful gude socowre.	*assistance*
	Bot, sir, thou sal be here sertayne	
930	A while unto I cum ogayne."	
	Sho kend al trewly his entent,	*knew*
	And tharfore es sho wightly went	*busily gone*
	Unto the lady faire and bright,	
	For unto hir right wele sho myght	
935	Say whatsom hyr willes es.	*whatsoever*
	For sho was al hir maystres,	*(Lunette); (Alundyne's) governess*
	Her keper, and hir cownsaylere.	*manager of her affairs*
	To hir sho said, als ye sal here,	
	Bytwix tham twa in gude cownsayl,	
940	"Madame," sho sayd, "I have mervayl	
	That ye sorow thus ever on ane.	*so persistently (all the time)*
	For Goddes luf, lat be yowre mane.	*grief*
	Ye sold think over alkyn thyng	*every*
	Of the Kinges Arthurgh cumyng.	*King Arthur's*
945	Menes yow noght of the message	*Don't you recall*
	Of the Damysel Savage,	
	That in hir lettre to yow send?	
	Allas, who sal yow now defend	
	Yowre land and al that es thareyn,	
950	Sen ye wil never of wepeing blyn?	*stop*
	A, madame, takes tent to me.	*pay attention*
	Ye ne have na knyght in this cuntré,	
	That durst right now his body bede	*offer*
	Forto do a doghty dede,	
955	Ne forto bide the mekil boste	
	Of King Arthurgh and of his oste;	
	And if he find none hym ogayn,	
	Yowre landes er lorn, this es sertayn."	*lost*
	The lady understode ful wele,	
960	How sho hyr cownsaild ilka dele;	*every part*
	Sho bad hyr go hir way smertly,	
	And that sho war na more hardy	*bold*
	Swilk wordes to hyr at speke;	*to*

For wa hir hert wold al tobreke. — *woe; break into pieces*
965 Sho bad, "Go wightly hethin oway." — *swiftly hence*
Than the maiden thus gan say,
"Madame, it es oft wemens will
Tham forto blame that sais tham scill." — *reasons with them*
Sho went oway, als sho noght roght, — *as if she didn't care*
970 And than the lady hyr bythoght,
That the maiden said no wrang, — *wrong*
And so sho sat in stody lang.
In stody thus allane sho sat;
The mayden come ogayn with that.
975 "Madame," sho said, "ye er a barn; — *child*
Thus may ye sone yowre self forfarn." — *destroy*
Sho sayd, "Chastise thi hert, madame; — *(Lunete)*
To swilk a lady it es grete shame
Thus to wepe and make slike cry; — *such*
980 Think opon thi grete gentri. — *gentility*
Trowes thou the flowre of chevalry — *Believe*
Sold al with thi lord dy
And with him be put in molde? — *earth*
God forbede that it so solde! — *should be*
985 Als gude als he and better bene."
"Thou lyes," sho sayd, "by hevyn-quene!
Lat se if thoue me tel kan,
Whar es any so doghty man,
Als he was that wedded me."
990 "Yis, and ye kun me na mawgré, — *if you will bear me no spite*
And that ye mak me sekernes, — *give me reassurance*
That ye sal luf me never the les."
Sho said, "Thou may be ful sertayn,
That for na thing that thou mai sayn,
995 Wil I me wreth on nane manere." — *grow angry*
"Madame," sho said, "than sal ye here;
I sal yow tel a preveté, — *secret*
And na ma sal it wit bot we. — *more; know except the two of us*
Yf twa knyghtes be in the felde — *two*
1000 On twa stedes with spere and shelde
And the tane the tother may sla, — *one; other; slay*
Whether es the better of tha?" — *those*

109

Sho said, "He that has the bataile."   *won*
"Ya," said the mayden, "sawnfayle,   *without fail*
1005 The knyght that lifes es mare of maine   *powerful*
Than yowre lord that was slayne.
Yowre lord fled out of the place,
And the tother gan hym chace   *the other*
Heder into his awyn halde;   *Hither; own fortress*
1010 Thare may ye wit, he was ful balde."   *know; brave*
The lady said, "This es grete scorne,
That thou nevyns him me biforne;   *speaks of; before me*
Thou sais nowther soth ne right.   *truth*
Swith, out of myne eghen syght!"   *Instantly get out; eye*
1015 The mayden said, "So mot I the,   *As I hope to prosper*
Thus ne hight ye noght me,   *promised*
That ye sold so me myssay,"   *abuse*
With that sho turned hir oway,
And hastily sho went ogayn   *(Lunette)*
1020 Unto the chameber to Sir Ywayne.
    The lady thoght than al the nyght,   *(Alundyne)*
How that sho had na knyght
Forto seke hir land thorghout   *defend*
To kepe Arthurgh and hys rowt.   *defend against; army*
1025 Than bigan hir forto shame
And hirself fast forto blame.
Unto hirself fast gan sho flyte   *reproach*
And said, "With wrang now I hir wite.   *(Lunette) blame*
Now hopes sho I wil never mare   *thinks*
1030 Luf hir als I have done are.   *Love*
I wil hir luf with main and mode;   *strength of mind and will*
For that sho said was for my gode."
    On the morn the mayden rase,   *arose*
And unto chamber sone sho gase.
1035 Thare sho fyndes the faire lady
Hingand hir hevyd ful drerily   *Hanging; head*
In the place whare sho hir left;
And ilka dele sho talde hir eft,   *Every bit; then*
Als sho had said to hir bifore.
1040 Than said the lady, "Me rewes sore,   *I sorely regret*
That I missayd the yisterday.   *spoke gruffly to you*

110

	I wil amend, if that I may.	
	Of that knyght now wald I here,	*would; hear*
	What he war and whethen he were.	*whence*
1045	I wate that I have sayd omys;	*know; amiss*
	Now wil I do als thou me wys.	*direct*
	Tel me baldely, or thou blin,	*fearlessly; cease*
	If he be cumen of gentil kyn."	
	"Madame," sho said, "I dar warand,	*dare guarantee*
1050	A genteler lord es none lifand;	*living*
	The hendest man ye sal him fynde,	*most gracious*
	That ever come of Adams kynde."	
	"How hat he? Sai me for sertayne."	*What is his name*
	"Madame," sho said, "Sir Ywayne;	
1055	So gentil knight have ye noght sene;	
	He es the King son Uryene."	
	Sho held hir paid of that tithyng,	*pleased; news*
	For that his fader was a kyng;	
	"Do me have him here in my sight	*Bring him here*
1060	Bitwene this and the thrid night	
	And are, if that it are myght be.	*sooner; sooner*
	Me langes sare him forto se;	*longs sorely*
	Bring him, if thou mai, this night."	
	"Madame," sho sayd, "that I ne might,	
1065	For his wonyng es hethin oway	*dwelling; hence*
	More than the jorné of a day.	
	Bot I have a wele rinand page,	*fast-running*
	Wil stirt thider right in a stage	*pretty quick*
	And bring him by to-morn at nyght."	*tomorrow*
1070	The lady saide, "Loke yf he myght	
	To-morn by evyn be here ogayn."	
	Sho said, "Madame, with al his mayn."	
	"Bid him hy on alkyn wyse.	*hasten in every way*
	He sal be quit wele his servyse;	*repaid*
1075	Avancement sal be hys bone,	*reward*
	If he wil do this erand sone."	
	"Madame," sho said, "I dar yow hight	*promise*
	To have him here or the thrid nyght.	*before*
	Towhils, efter yowre kownsayl send	*Meanwhile*
1080	And ask tham wha sal yow defend	

Yowre well, yowre land, kastel, and towre
Ogayns the nobil King Arthure.
For thare es nane of tham ilkane,   *each one*
That dar the batel undertane.   *undertake*
1085   Than sal ye say, "Nedes bus me take   *It is necessary that*
A lorde to do that ye forsake."
Nedes bus yow have sum nobil knyght,   *It is necessary that*
That wil and may defend yowre right;
And sais also, to suffer ded   *say; death*
1090   Ye wil noght do out of thaire rede.   *counsel*
Of that worde sal thai be blyth
And thank yow ful many sithe."   *times*
The lady said, "By God of myght,
I sal areson tham this night.   *question*
1095   Me think thou dwelles ful lang here;
Send forth swith the messangere."   *at once*
      Than was the lady blith and glad.
Sho did al als hir mayden bad.
Efter hir cownsail sho sent onane.
1100   And bad thai sold cum sone ilkane.
The maiden redies hyr ful rath.   *quickly*
Bilive sho gert Syr Ywaine bath   *Quickly she drew; bath*
And cled him sethin in gude scarlet   *clothed; afterwards*
Forord wele and with gold fret,   *Trimmed with fur; fastened*
1105   A girdel ful riche for the nanes   *occasion*
Of perry and of preciows stanes.   *jewelry; [other]*
Sho talde him al how he sold do,
When that he come the lady to.
And thus when he was al redy,
1110   Sho went and talde to hyr lady,
That cumen was hir messagere.
Sho said smertly, "Do lat me here,
Cumes he sone, als have thou wyn?"   *as you hope to have joy*
"Medame," sho said, "I sal noght blin,   *cease*
1115   Or that he be byfor yow here."
Than said the lady with light chere,
"Go bring him heder prevely,   *hither secretly*
That none wit bot thou and I."   *knows*
Than the maiden went ogayn

112

1120	Hastily to Sir Ywayn.	
	"Sir," sho sayd, "als have I wyn,	*joy*
	My lady wate thou ert hereyn.	*knows*
	To cum bifore hir luke thou be balde,	*fearless*
	And tak gode tent what I have talde."	*pay close attention*
1125	By the hand sho toke the knyght	
	And led him unto chamber right	
	Byfor hir lady (es noght at layne),	*(it can't be hidden)*
	And of that come was sho ful fayne.	*arrival; joyful*
	Bot yit Sir Ywayne had grete drede,	
1130	When he unto chamber yede.	*went*
	The chamber flore and als the bed	
	With klothes of gold was al overspred.	
	Hir thoght he was withowten lac,	*It seemed to her he was without fault*
	Bot no word to him sho spak.	
1135	And he for dred oway he drogh.	*drew*
	Than the mayden stode and logh.	*laughed*
	Sho sayd, "Mawgré have that knyght	*Ill luck befall*
	That haves of swilk a lady syght	*such*
	And can noght shew to hir his nede.	
1140	Cum furth, sir; the thar noght drede,	*you need not*
	That mi lady wil the smyte;	
	Sho loves the wele withouten lite.	*fault*
	Pray to hir of hir mercy,	
	And for thi sake right so sal I,	
1145	That sho forgif the in this stede	*situation*
	Of Salados the Rouse ded,	*Salados the Rouse's death*
	That was hir lord, that thou has slayne."	
	On knese him set than Syr Ywaine.	
	"Madame, I yelde me yow untill	
1150	Ever to be at yowre wyll;	
	Yf that I might, I ne wald noght fle."	
	Sho said, "Nay, whi sold so be?	
	To ded yf I gert do the now,	*death; caused to*
	To me it war ful litel prow.	*advantage*
1155	Bot for I find the so bowsum,	*gracious*
	That thou wald thus to me cum,	
	And for thou dose the in my grace,	*since you place yourself*
	I forgif the thi trispase.	

Syt down," sho said, "and lat me here,
1160 Why thou ert thus debonere."   *meek*
"Madame," he said, "anis with a luke,   *once; look*
Al my hert with the thou toke.
Sen I first of the had syght,
Have I the lufed with al my might.
1165 To mo than the, mi lady hende,   *more; gracious*
Sal never more my luf wende.
For thi luf ever I am redy
Lely forto lif or dy."   *Loyally*
Sho said, "Dar thou wele undertake
1170 In my land pese forto make
And forto maintene al mi rightes
Ogayns King Arthure and his knyghtes?"
He said, "That dar I undertane
Ogaynes ilka lyfand man."
1175 Swilk kownsail byfore had sho tane.   *Such; taken*
Sho said, "Sir, than er we at ane."   *are*
Hir barons hir ful rathly red   *quickly advised*
To tak a lord hir forto wed.
    Than hastily sho went to hall;
1180 Thare abade hir barons all
Forto hald thaire parlement
And mari hir by thaire asent.   *marry*
Sho sayd, "Sirs, with an acorde,
Sen me bus nedely have a lord   *Since I needs must*
1185 My landes forto lede and yeme,   *oversee*
Sais me sone howe ye wil deme."   *Tell; judge*
"Madame," thai said, "how so ye will,
Al we sal assent thartyll."   *thereto*
    Than the lady went ogayne
1190 Unto chameber to Sir Ywaine.
"Sir," sho said, "so God me save,
Other lorde wil I nane have.
If I the left, I did noght right,
A king son and a noble knyght."
1195 Now has the maiden done hir thoght: *accomplished her intention*
Sir Ywayne out of anger broght.
The lady led him unto hall;

114

Ogains him rase the barons all.   *Before him arose*
And al thai said ful sekerly:
1200 "This knight sal wed the lady."
And ilkane said thamself bitwene   *each one*
(So faire a man had thai noght sene),
"For his bewté in hal and bowre
Him semes to be an emperowre.
1205 We wald that thai war trowth-plight   *wish; engaged*
And weded sone this ilk nyght."   *wedded immediately; very*
The lady set hir on the dese
And cumand al to hald thaire pese,   *all came to her*
And bad hir steward sumwhat say,
1210 Or men went fra cowrt oway.   *Before; court*
The steward said, "Sirs, understandes,
Were es waxen in thir landes: *Danger increases*
The king Arthure es redy dight   *is already prepared*
To be here byn this fowretenyght.   *within; fortnight*
1215 He and his menye ha thoght   *followers have*
To win this land if thai moght.   *are able*
Thai wate ful wele that he es ded,   *know*
That was lord here in this stede.
None es so wight wapins to welde   *courageous*
1220 Ne that so boldly mai us belde.   *protect*
And wemen may maintene no stowre —   *women; withstand no battle*
Thai most nedes have a governowre.
Tharfor mi lady most nede
Be weded hastily for drede;
1225 And to na lord wil sho tak tent,   *take heed*
Bot if it be by yowre assent."
  Than the lordes al on raw   *in turn*
Held tham wele payd of this saw;   *contented; speech*
Al assented hyr untill   *to*
1230 To tak a lord at hyr owyn wyll.
Than said the lady onone right,
"How hald ye yow paid of this knight?   *(i.e., Are you contented with)*
He profers hym on al wyse
To myne honore and my servyse.
1235 And sertes, sirs, the soth to say,
I saw him never or this day;   *before*

115

Bot talde unto me has it bene,
He es the kyng son Uriene.
He es cumen of hegh parage   *high lineage*
1240 And wonder doghty of vasselage.   *bold in knightly deeds*
War and wise and ful curtayse,
He yernes me to wife alwayse.
And nere the lese, I wate, he might   *know*
Have wele better, and so war right."
1245 With a voice halely thai sayd,   *sweetly*
"Madame, ful wele we hald us payd.   *contented*
Bot hastes fast, al that ye may,
That ye war wedded this ilk day."
And grete prayer gan thai make
1250 On al wise, that sho suld hym take.
      Sone unto the kirk thai went
And war wedded in thaire present.   *presence*
Thare wedded Ywaine in plevyne   *pledge*
The riche lady Alundyne,
1255 The dukes doghter of Landuit;
Els had hyr lande bene destruyt.
Thus thai made the maryage
Omang al the riche barnage.   *nobility*
Thai made ful mekyl mirth that day,
1260 Ful grete festes on gude aray.
Grete mirthes made thai in that stede,
And al forgetyn es now the ded   *death*
Of him that was thaire lord fre.   *gracious*
Thai say that this es worth swilk thre,   *this [lord] (i.e., Ywain)*
1265 And that thai lufed him mekil more
Than him that lord was thare byfore.
      The bridal sat, for soth to tell,   *wedding festivities lasted*
Til Kyng Arthure come to the well
With al his knyghtes everilkane;   *everyone*
1270 Byhind leved thare noght ane.
Than sayd Sir Kay, "Now, whare es he
That made slike bost here forto be   *such*
Forto venge his cosyn germayne?   *kinsman*
I wist his wordes war al in vayne.
1275 He made grete boste bifor the quene,

116

And here now dar he noght be sene.

His prowd wordes er now al purst,   *shut up*

For, in fayth, ful ill he durst

Anes luke opon that knyght   *Once look*

1280 That he made bost with to fyght."

Than sayd Gawayn hastily:

"Syr, for Goddes luf, mercy!

For I dar hete the for sertayne,   *promise*

That we sal here of Sir Ywayne   *hear*

1285 This ilk day, that be thou balde,   *same; assured*

Bot he be ded or done in halde;   *Unless; put in confinement*

And never in no cumpany

Herd I him speke the velany."   *of you*

Than sayd Sir Kay, "Lo, at thi will

1290 Fra this time forth I sal be still."

    The king kest water on the stane;

The storme rase ful sone onane   *at once*

With wikked weders, kene and calde,

Als it was byforehand talde.

1295 The king and his men ilkane

Wend tharwith to have bene slane,   *Thought*

So blew it store with slete and rayn;   *violently*

And hastily than Syr Ywayne

Dight him graythly in his gere   *Prepared himself readily*

1300 With nobil shelde and strong spere.

When he was dight in seker wede,   *safe armor*

Than he umstrade a nobil stede.   *mounted*

Him thoght that he was als lyght

Als a fowl es to the flyght.

1305 Unto the well fast wendes he,

And sone, when thai myght him se,

Syr Kay (for he wald noght fayle)

Smertly askes the batayl.   *Arrogantly requests*

And alsone than said the kyng,   *instantly*

1310 "Sir Kay, I grante the thine askyng."

Than Sir Ywayn neghed tham nere   *approached*

Thaire cowntenance to se and here.

Sir Kay than on his stede gan spring;

"Bere the wele now," sayd the kyng.

117

1315	Ful glad and blith was Syr Ywayne,	
	When Sir Kay come him ogayn.	
	Bot Kay wist noght wha it was;	*who*
	He findes his fere now or he pas.	*companion; goes forth*
	Syr Ywaine thinkes now to be wroken	*avenged*
1320	On the grete wordes that Kay has spoken.	
	Thai rade togeder with speres kene;	
	Thare was no reverence tham bitwene.	
	Sir Ywayn gan Sir Kay bere	
	Out of his sadel lenkith of his spere;	*the length*
1325	His helm unto the erth smate;	
	A fote depe tharein yt bate.	*stuck*
	He wald do him na more despite,	*injury*
	Bot down he lighted als tyte.	*quickly*
	Syr Kay stede he toke in hy	*Kay's horse; haste*
1330	And presand the king ful curtaysly.	*presented [it to]*
	Wonder glad than war thai all	
	That Kay so fowl a shame gan fall;	
	And ilkone sayd til other then,	*to the*
	"This es he that scornes al men";	
1335	Of his wa war thai wele paid.	*woe; pleased*
	Syr Ywain than to the kyng said,	
	"Sir Kyng, I gif to the this stede,	
	For he may help the in thi nede;	
	And to me war it grete trispas	
1340	Forto withhald that yowres was."	*what rightly belongs to you*
	"What man ertow?" quod the kyng;	
	"Of the have I ne knawyng,	
	Bot if thou unarmed were	
	Or els thi name that I might here."	
1345	"Lord," he sayd, "I am Ywayne."	
	Than was the king ferly fayne;	*wondrous joyful*
	A sari man than was Sir Kay,	
	That said that he was stollen oway;	
	Al descumfite he lay on grownde,	
1350	To him that was a sary stownde.	*grevious moment*
	The king and his men war ful glad,	
	That they so Sir Ywayne had,	
	And ful glad was Sir Gawayne	

Of the welefare of Sir Ywayne.
1355 For nane was to him half so dere
Of al that in the court were.
The king Sir Ywayn sone bisoght
To tel him al how he had wroght;   *what he had done*
And sone Sir Ywaine gan him tell
1360 Of al his fare how it byfell:
With the knight how that he sped,
And how he had the lady wed,
And how the mayden hym helped wele.
Thus tald he to him ilka dele.   *all the details*
1365   "Sir King," he sayd, "I yow byseke
And al yowre menye milde and meke,   *company*
That ye wald grante to me that grace
At wend with me to my purchace,   *To dwell; newly acquired property*
And se my kastel and my towre;
1370 Than myght ye do me grete honowre."
The kyng granted him ful right   *(i.e., Ywain)*
To dwel with him a fowretenyght.
Sir Ywayne thanked him oft sith;   *many times*
The knyghtes war al glad and blyth
1375 With Sir Ywaine forto wend.
And sone a squier has he send;
Unto the kastel the way he nome   *went*
And warned the lady of thaire come,   *arrival*
And that his lord come with the kyng.
1380 And when the lady herd this thing,
It es no lifand man with mowth,   *There's not a living soul; mouth*
That half hir cumforth tel kowth.   *delight could tell*
Hastily that lady hende   *gracious*
Cumand al hir men to wende   *Ordered; attend*
1385 And dight tham in thaire best aray   *dressed*
To kepe the king that ilk day.   *receive*
Thai keped him in riche wede   *received; decor*
Rydeand on many a nobil stede;
Thai hailsed him ful curtaysly
1390 And also al his cumpany.
Thai said he was worthy to dowt,   *of fear (reverence)*
That so fele folk led obowt.   *many*

Thare was grete joy, I yow bihete,

With clothes spred in ilka strete *banners; every*

1395 And damysels danceand ful wele *dancing*

With trompes, pipes, and with fristele. *flute*

The castel and the ceté rang

With mynstralsi and nobil sang.

Thai ordand tham ilkane infere *all together*

1400 To kepe the king on faire manere.

The lady went withowten towne

And with hir many bald barowne *brave*

Cled in purpure and ermyne *purple clothing*

With girdels al of gold ful fyne,

1405 The lady made ful meri chere; *decked out with precious lovetokens*

Sho was al dight with drewries dere.

Abowt hir was ful mekyl thrang;

The puple cried and sayd omang, *people; among [themselves]*

"Welkum ertou, Kyng Arthoure —

1410 Of al this werld thou beres the flowre.

Lord Kyng of all kynges,

And blissed be he that the brynges."

When the lady the kyng saw,

Unto him fast gan sho draw

1415 To hald his sterap whils he lyght. *dismounted*

Bot sone, when he of hir had syght,

With mekyl myrth thai samen met. *together*

With hende wordes sho him gret,

"A thowsand sithes welkum," sho says,

1420 "And so es Sir Gawayne the curtayse."

The king said, "Lady white so flowre,

God gif the joy and mekil honowre,

For thou ert fayre with body gent."

With that he hir in armes hent, *embraced*

1425 And ful faire he gan hir falde. *enfold*

Thare was many to bihalde. *bihold*

It es no man with tong may tell

The mirth that was tham omell. *among*

Of maidens was thare so gude wane, *a number*

1430 That ilka knight myght tak ane. *have one*

Ful mekil joy Syr Ywayn made

	That he the king til his hows hade;	
	The lady omang tham al samen	*together*
	Made ful mekyl joy and gamen.	
1435	In the kastel thus thai dwell,	
	Ful mekyl myrth wase tham omell;	*among*
	The king was thare with his knyghtes	
	Aght dayes and aght nyghtes;	*Eight; eight*
	And Ywayn tham ful mery made	
1440	With alkyn gamyn tham forto glade.	*every pleasure; move*
	He prayed the kyng to thank the may,	*maiden*
	That hym had helpid in his jornay;	
	And ilk day had thai solace sere	*diverse*
	Of huntyng and als of revere;	*hawking*
1445	For thare was a ful fayre cuntré	
	With wodes and parkes grete plenté,	
	And castels wroght with lyme and stane,	
	That Ywayne with his wife had tane.	*taken*
	Now wil the king no langer lende,	*dwell*
1450	Bot til his cuntré wil he wende.	*to; go*
	Aywhils thai war thare, for sertayne,	*As long as*
	Syr Gawayn did al his mayne	
	To pray Sir Ywaine on al manere	
	Forto wende with tham infere.	*together*
1455	He said, "Sir, if thou ly at hame,	
	Wonderly men wil the blame.	*Greatly*
	That knight es no thing to set by	
	That leves al his chevalry	
	And ligges bekeand in his bed,	*lies warming himself*
1460	When he haves a lady wed.	
	For when that he has grete endose,	*support*
	Than war tyme to win his lose;	*renown*
	For when a knyght es chevalrouse,	
	His lady es the more jelows.	
1465	Also sho lufes him wele the bet.	
	Tharfore, sir, thou sal noght let	*delay*
	To haunt armes in ilk cuntré;	*follow; every*
	Than wil men wele more prayse the.	
	Thou hase inogh to thi despens;	*use*
1470	Now may thow wele hante turnamentes.	*frequent*

	Thou and I sal wende infere,	*travel together*
	And I will be at thi banere.	
	I dar noght say, so God me glad,	
	If I so fayre a leman had,	
1475	That I ne most leve al chevalry	
	At hame ydel with hir to ly.	
	Bot yit a fole that litel kan,	
	May wele cownsail another man."	
	So lang Sir Gawayn prayed so,	
1480	Syr Ywayne grantes him forto go	
	Unto the lady and tak his leve;	
	Loth him was hir forto greve.	
	Til hyr onane the way he nome,	*took*
	Bot sho ne wist noght whi he come.	
1485	In his arms he gan hir mete,	*embrace*
	And thus he said, "My leman swete,	*beloved*
	My life, my hele, and al my hert,	
	My joy, my comforth, and my quert,	*health*
	A thing prai I the unto	
1490	For thine honore and myne also."	
	The lady said, "Sir, verrayment,	*truly*
	I wil do al yowre cumandment."	
	"Dame," he said, "I wil the pray,	
	That I might the king cumvay	*accompany*
1495	And also with my feres founde	*companions seek*
	Armes forto haunte a stownde.	*To follow arms for a while*
	For in bourding men wald me blame,	*(i.e., men would think me a joke)*
	If I sold now dwel at hame."	
	The lady was loth him to greve.	
1500	"Sir," sho said, "I gif yow leve	
	Until a terme that I sal sayn,	
	Bot that ye cum than ogayn!	*Only if*
	Al this yere hale I yow grante	*entire*
	Dedes of armes forto hante;	*follow*
1505	Bot, syr, als ye luf me dere,	
	On al wise that ye be here	
	This day twelmoth how som it be,	
	For the luf ye aw to me.	*owe*
	And if ye com noght by that day,	

1510	My luf sal ye lose for ay.	
	Avise yow wele now or ye gone.	*before you leave*
	This day es the evyn of Saint Jon;	
	That warn I yow now or ye wende,	
	Luke ye cum by the twelmoth ende."	
1515	"Dame," he sayd, "I sal noght let	*fail*
	To hald the day that thou has set;	
	And if I might be at my wyll,	
	Ful oft are sold I cum the till.	*to*
	Bot, madame, this understandes:	
1520	A man that passes divers landes,	
	May sum tyme cum in grete destres,	
	In preson or els in sekenes;	
	Tharfore I pray yow, or I ga,	
	That ye wil out-tak thir twa."	*exclude these two [possibilities]*
1525	The lady sayd, "This grant I wele,	
	Als ye ask, everilka dele;	*every bit*
	And I sal lene to yow my ring,	
	That es to me a ful dere thing.	*precious*
	In nane anger sal ye be,	*trouble*
1530	Whils ye it have and thinkes on me.	
	I sal tel to yow onane	
	The vertu that es in the stane:	
	It es na preson thow sal halde,	*hold*
	Al if yowre fase be manyfalde;	*foes; manifold*
1535	With sekenes sal ye noght be tane,	*taken*
	Ne of yowre blode ye sal lese nane;	
	In batel tane sal ye noght be,	*taken*
	Whils ye it have and thinkes on me;	
	And ay, whils ye er trew of love,	
1540	Over al sal ye be obove.	
	I wald never for nakyn wight	*any kind of circumstance*
	Lene it are unto na knyght.	*Give; ever*
	For grete luf I it yow take;	*give it to you*
	Yemes it wele now for my sake."	*Care for*
1545	Sir Ywayne said, "Dame, gramercy!"	
	Than he gert ordain in hy	*made ready in haste*
	Armurs and al other gere,	
	Stalworth stedes, both sheld and spere,	

123

	And also squyere, knave, and swayne.	
1550	Ful glad and blith was Sir Gawayne.	
	No lenger wald Syr Ywayne byde,	
	On his stede sone gan he stride	
	And thus he has his leve tane.	
	For him murned many ane.	
1555	The lady took leve of the kyng	
	And of his menye, ald and ying;	*followers; young*
	Hir lord, Sir Ywayne, sho bisekes	
	With teris trikland on hir chekes,	
	On al wise that he noght let	*fail*
1560	To halde the day that he had set.	*hold*
	The knightes thus thaire ways er went	
	To justing and to turnament.	
	Ful dughtily did Sir Ywayne,	*worthily performed*
	And also did Sir Gawayne;	
1565	Thai war ful doghty both infere,	*together*
	Thai wan the prise both fer and nere.	
	The kyng that time at Cester lay;	*Chester*
	The knightes went tham forto play.	
	Ful really thai rade obout	
1570	Al that twelmoth out and out	
	To justing and to turnament;	
	Thai wan grete wirships, als thai went;	
	Sir Ywayne oft had al the lose,	*praise*
	Of him the word ful wide gose;	*goes*
1575	Of thaire dedes was grete renown	
	To and fra in towre and towne.	
	On this wise in this life they last,	
	Unto Saint Johns day was past.	
	Then hastily they hied home	*hurried*
1580	And sone unto the kyng thai come;	
	And thare thai held grete mangeri,	*feasts*
	The kyng with al his cumpany.	
	Sir Ywaine umbithoght him than,	*remembered*
	He had forgeten his leman.	*beloved*
1585	"Broken I have hir cumandment.	
	Sertes," he said, "now be I shent;	*ruined*
	The terme es past that sho me set.	

124

	How ever sal this bale be bet?	*grief be remedied*
	Unnethes he might him hald fra wepe.	*Barely; from weeping*
1590	And right in this than toke he kepe,	*just as he was remembering all this*
	Into court come a damysele	
	On a palfray ambland wele;	
	And egerly down gan sho lyght	
	Withouten help of knave or knyght.	
1595	And sone sho lete hyr mantel fall	
	And hasted hir fast into hall.	
	"Syr Kyng," sho sayde, "God mot the se,	*"May God favor you"*
	My lady gretes the wele by me,	
	And also Sir gude Gawayne	
1600	And al thi knyghtes bot Sir Ywayne.	*except*
	He es ateyned for trayture,	*condemned*
	A fals and lither losenjoure;	*wicked rascal*
	He has bytrayed my lady,	
	But sho es war with his gilry.	*aware of; deceit*
1605	Sho hopid noght, the soth to say,	*expected*
	That he wald so have stollen oway.	
	He made to hir ful mekyl boste	
	And said, of al he lufed hir moste.	
	Al was treson and trechery,	
1610	And that he sal ful dere haby.	*dearly pay for*
	It es ful mekyl ogains the right	
	To cal so fals a man a knight.	
	My lady wend he had hir hert	
	Ay forto kepe and hald in quert,	*health*
1615	Bot now with grefe he has hir gret	*harmed*
	And broken the term that sho him set,	
	That was the evyn of Saynt John;	
	Now es that tyme for ever gone.	
	So lang gaf sho him respite,	
1620	And thus he haves hir led with lite.	*treated her viciously*
	Sertainly, so fals a fode	*creature*
	Was never cumen of kynges blode,	
	That so sone forgat his wyfe,	
	That lofed him better than hyr life."	*loved*
1625	Til Ywayne sais sho thus, "Thou es	
	Traytur untrew and trowthles	

	And also an unkind cumlyng.	*upstart*
	Deliver me my lady ring!	
	Sho stirt to him with sterne loke,	
1630	The ring fro his finger sho toke;	
	And alsone als sho had the ring,	*as soon as*
	Hir leve toke sho of the king	
	And stirted up on hir palfray.	*lept*
	Withowten more sho went hir way;	
1635	With hir was nowther knave ne grome,	
	Ne no man wist where sho bycome.	*went*
	Sir Ywayn, when he this gan here,	
	Murned and made simpil chere;	*dismal countenance*
	In sorrow than so was he stad,	
1640	That nere for murning wex he mad.	*became*
	It was no mirth that him myght mend;	
	At worth to noght ful wele he wend,	
	For wa he es ful wil of wane.	*totally confused*
	"Allas, I am myne owin bane;	*destroyer (evil, poison)*
1645	Allas," he sayd, "that I was born,	
	Have I my leman thus forlorn,	*lost utterly*
	And al es for myne owen foly.	
	Allas, this dole wil mak me dy."	
	An evyl toke him als he stode;	*evil spirit possessed him*
1650	For wa he wex al wilde and wode.	*woe; crazy*
	Unto the wod the way he nome;	*forest; took*
	No man wist whore he bycome.	*knew where he went*
	Obout he welk in the forest,	*lurked*
	Als it wore a wilde beste;	*As if he were*
1655	His men on ilka syde has soght	
	Fer and nere and findes him noght.	
	On a day als Ywayne ran	
	In the wod, he met a man;	
	Arowes brade and bow had he,	
1660	And when Sir Ywayne gan him se,	
	To him he stirt with bir ful grim,	*assault*
	His bow and arwes reft he him.	*robbed*
	Ilka day than at the leste	*Every*
	Shot he him a wilde beste;	
1665	Fless he wan him ful gude wane,	*Flesh; abundance*

126

And of his arows lost he nane.
Thare he lifed a grete sesowne;   *lived*
With rotes amd raw venysowne;   *roots*
He drank of the warm blode,
1670 And that did him mekil gode.
    Als he went in that boskage,   *woods*
He fand a litil ermytage.   *hermitage*
The ermyte saw and sone was war,   *hermit; cognizant of*
A naked man a bow bare.
1675 He hoped he was wode that tide;   *thought; gone mad; time*
Tharfore no lenger durst he bide.
He sperd his gate and in he ran   *fastened*
Forfered of that wode man;   *Terrified by; crazy*
And for him thoght it charité,
1680 Out at his window set he
Brede and water for the wode man;
And tharto ful sone he ran.
Swilk als he had, swilk he him gaf,   *such; such*
Barly-brede with al the chaf;
1685 Tharof ete he ful gude wane,   *in abundance*
And are swilk ete he never nane.   *previously such ate*
Of the water he drank tharwith;
Than ran he forth into the frith,   *forest*
For if a man be never so wode,
1690 He wil kum whare man dose him gode,
And, sertanly, so did Ywayne.
Everilka day he come ogayne,
And with him broght he redy boun   *prepared*
Ilka day new venisowne;
1695 He laid it at the ermite gate
And ete and drank and went his gate.   *way*
Ever alsone als he was gane,
The ermyt toke the flesh onane;
He flogh it and seth it fayre and wele;   *flayed; boiled*
1700 Than had Ywayne at ilka mele   *every*
Brede and sothen venysowne.   *boiled*
Than went the ermyte to the towne
And salde the skinnes that he broght,
And better brede tharwith he boght;

1705	Than fand Sir Ywayne in that stede	*place*
	Venyson and better brede.	
	This life led he ful fele yere,	*for several years*
	And sethen he wroght als ye sal here.	*afterwards; toiled*
	Als Ywaine sleped under a tre,	
1710	By him come thare rideand thre:	
	A lady, twa bourewemen alswa.	*ladies-in-waiting*
	Than spak ane of the maidens twa,	
	"A naked man me think I se;	
	Wit I wil what it may be."	*know*
1715	Sho lighted doun and to him yede,	*went*
	And unto him sho toke gude hede;	*heed*
	Hir thoght wele sho had him sene	
	In many stedes whare sho had bene.	*places*
	Sho was astonyd in that stownde,	*moment*
1720	For in hys face sho saw a wonde,	*wound*
	Bot it was heled and hale of hew;	
	Tharby, hir thoght, that sho him knew.	
	Sho sayd, "By God that me has made,	
	Swilk a wound Sir Ywayne hade.	
1725	Sertaynly, this ilk es he.	*person*
	Allas," sho sayd, "how may this be?	
	Allas, that him es thus bityd,	*come to pass*
	So nobil a knyght als he was kyd.	*known to be*
	It es grete sorow that he sold be	
1730	So ugly now opon to se."	*to look upon*
	So tenderly for him sho gret,	*wept*
	That hir teres al hir chekes wet.	
	"Madame," sho said, "for sertayn,	
	Here have we funden Sir Ywayne,	
1735	The best knyght that on grund mai ga.	
	Allas, him es bytid so wa;	*on him some woe has happened*
	In sum sorow was he stad,	*With; afflicted*
	And tharfore es he waxen mad.	
	Sorow wil meng a mans blode	*stir up*
1740	And make him forto wax wode.	*go crazy*
	Madame, and he war now in quert	*if; good health*
	And al hale of will and hert,	
	Ogayns yowre fa he wald yow were,	*foe; protect*

128

	That has yow done so mekyl dere.	*great harm*
1745	And he ware hale, so God me mend,	*If*
	Yowre sorow war sone broght to end."	
	The lady said, "And this ilk be he	
	And than he wil noght hethin fle,	*hence*
	Thorgh Goddes help than, hope I yit	
1750	We sal him win ynto his wyt.	
	Swith at hame I wald we were,	
	For thare I have an unement dere;	*ointment*
	Morgan the Wise gaf it to me	
	And said als I sal tel to the.	
1755	He sayd, "This unement es so gode,	*ointment*
	That if a man be braynwode	*gone mad*
	And he war anes anoynt with yt,	
	Smertly sold he have his wit."	
	Fro hame thai wer bot half a myle;	
1760	Theder come thai in a whyle.	
	The lady sone the boyst has soght,	*box*
	And the unement has sho broght.	*ointment*
	"Have," sho said, "this unement here,	
	Unto me it es ful dere;	
1765	And smertly that thou wend ogayne.	
	Bot luke thou spend it noght in vaine;	
	And fra the knight anoynted be,	
	That thou leves, bring it to me."	
	Hastily that maiden meke	
1770	Tok hose and shose and serk and breke.	*shirt; undergarment*
	A riche robe als gan sho ta	*take*
	And a saint of silk alswa	*girdle*
	And also a gude palfray,	
	And smertly come sho whare he lay.	
1775	On slepe fast yit sho him fande.	
	Hir hors until a tre sho band,	*bound*
	And hastily to him sho yede,	*went*
	And that was ful hardy dede.	
	Sho enoynt hys heved wele	
1780	And his body ilka dele.	*everywhere*
	Sho despended al the unement	
	Over hir ladies cumandment.	*Against*

129

	For hir lady wald sho noght let;	*fail*
	Hir thoght that it was ful wele set.	
1785	Al his atyre sho left hym by	
	At his rising to be redy	
	That he might him cleth and dyght,	*clothe; prepare*
	Or he sold of hyr have syght.	
	Than he wakend of his slepe;	*from*
1790	The maiden to him toke gude kepe;	
	He luked up ful sarily	*wretchedly*
	And said, "Lady Saynt Mary,	
	What hard grace to me es maked,	
	That I am here now thus naked?	
1795	Allas, wher any have here bene?	
	I trow, sum has my sorow sene."	
	Lang he sat so in a thoght,	*Long*
	How that gere was theder broght.	
	Than had he noght so mekyl myght	
1800	On his fote to stand upright;	
	Him failed might of fote and hand,	
	That he myght nowther ga ne stand.	*walk*
	Bot yit his clathes on he wan;	*put*
	Tharfore ful wery was he than.	
1805	Than had he mister forto mete	*desire*
	Sum man that myght his bales bete.	*grief abate*
	Than lepe the maiden on hir palfray	
	And nere byside him made hir way.	
	Sho lete als sho him noght had sene	*let [on] as*
1810	Ne wetyn that he thare had bene.	*knew*
	Sone when he of hir had syght,	
	He cried unto hyr on hight.	*he cried to her by name*
	Than wald sho no ferrer ride,	
	Bot fast sho luked on ilka syde	
1815	And waited obout fer and nere.	
	He cried and sayd, "I am here."	
	Than sone sho rade him till	
	And sayd, "Sir, what es thi will?"	
	"Lady, thi help war me ful lefe,	*would be to me most desirable*
1820	For I am here in grete meschefe.	
	I ne wate never by what chance	*don't know by what circumstance*

That I have al this grevance.
Thar charité I walde the pray
Forto lene me that palfray,
1825   That in thi hand es redy bowne   *prepared*
And wis me sone unto som towne.   *guide*
I wate noght how I had this wa,   *don't know; woe*
Ne how that I sal hethin ga."   *go hence*
Sho answered him with wordes hende,   *gracious*
1830   "Syr, if thou wil with me wende,
Ful gladly wil I ese the,   *attend you*
Until that thou amended be."
    Sho helped him up on his hors ryg,   *horse's back*
And sone thai come until a bryg;   *bridge*
1835   Into the water the boist sho cast,   *box*
And sethin hame sho hied fast.   *afterwards; hastened*
When thai come to the castel gate,
Thai lighted and went in tharate.
The maiden to the chameber went;
1840   The lady asked the unement.   *inquired about; ointment*
"Madame," sho said, "the boyst es lorn,   *box; lost*
And so was I nerehand tharforn."   *nearly as a result*
"How so," sho said, "for Goddes Tre?"   *by the Cross*
"Madame," she said, "I sal tel the
1845   Al the soth how that it was.   *Exactly (All the truth)*
Als I over the brig sold pas,   *bridge should pass*
Evyn in myddes, the soth to say,   *middle*
Thare stombild my palfray;
On the brig he fell al flat,   *sprawling*
1850   And the boyst right with that   *box*
Fel fra me in the water down;
And had I noght bene titter boun   *quickly prepared*
To tak my palfray by the mane,
The water sone had bene my bane."   *doom*
1855   The lady said, "Now am I shent,   *ruined*
That I have lorn my gude unement;
It was to me, so God me glade,   *make glad*
The best tresure that ever I hade.
To me it es ful mekil skath,   *injury*
1860   Bot better es lose it than yow bath.

	"Wend," sho said, "unto the knight	*Betake thyself*
	And luke thou ese him at thi myght."	
	"Lady," sho said, "els war me lathe."	*loathsome*
	Than sho gert him washe and bathe	*caused him to be*
1865	And gaf him mete and drink of main,	*for strengthening*
	Til he had geten his might ogayn.	
	Thai ordand armurs ful wele dight,	*requisitioned; wrought*
	And so thai did stedes ful wight.	*powerful*
	So it fell sone on a day,	
1870	Whils he in the castel lay,	
	The ryche eryl, Syr Alers,	*powerful*
	With knightes, serjantes and swiers,	*squires*
	And with swith grete vetale	*an abundance of provisions*
	Come that kastel to asayle.	
1875	Sir Ywain than his armurs tase	*dons*
	With other socure that he hase.	
	The erel he kepes in the felde,	*encounters*
	And sone he hit ane on the shelde,	*landed such a blow*
	That the knyght and als the stede	*also*
1880	Stark ded to the erth thai yede.	*went*
	Sone another, the thrid, the ferth	
	Feld he doun ded on the erth;	
	He stird him so omang tham than,	
	At ilka dint he slogh a man.	*each blow; slew*
1885	Sum he losed of hys men,	
	Bot the eril lost swilk ten.	*ten times as many*
	Al thai fled fast fra that syde,	
	Whare thai saw Sir Ywayn ride.	
	He herted so his cumpany,	*inspired*
1890	The moste coward was ful hardy	*greatest*
	To fel al that thai fand in felde.	
	The lady lay ever and bihelde;	
	Sho sais, "Yon es a nobil knyght,	
	Ful eger and of ful grete myght;	
1895	He es wele worthy forto prayse,	
	That es so doghty and curtayse."	
	The mayden said, "Withowten let,	*Doubtless*
	Yowre oynement may ye think wele set;	*ointment; well applied*
	Sese, madame, how he prikes,	*See; spurs*

132

1900	And sese also how fele he stikes	*see; many*
	Lo, how he fars omang his fase;	*foes*
	Al that he hittes sone he slase.	*slays*
	War thare swilk other twa als he,	
	Than, hope I, sone thaire fase sold fle.	*foes*
1905	Sertes, than sold we se ful tyte,	*quickly*
	The eril sold be descumfite.	
	Madame, God gif, his wil were	*may God grant*
	To wed yow and be loverd here."	*lord*
	The erils folk went fast to ded;	*death*
1910	To fle than was his best rede.	*plan*
	The eril sone bigan to fle,	
	And than might men bourd se,	*entertainment*
	How Sir Ywayne and his feres	*companions*
	Folowd tham on fel maners;	*fierce*
1915	And fast thai slogh the erils men,	
	Olive thai left noght over ten.	*Alive*
	The eril fled ful fast for drede,	
	And than Sir Ywaine strake his stede	
	And overtoke him in that tide	*time*
1920	At a kastel thar bysyde.	
	Sir Ywayne sone withset the gate,	*blocked*
	That the eril myght noght in tharate.	
	The eril saw al might noght gain;	
	He yalde him sone to Sir Ywayn.	*yielded himself*
1925	And sone he has his trowth plyght	*(the earl); pledged*
	To wend with him that ilk night	
	Unto the lady of grete renowne	
	And profer him to hir presowne,	*himself; prison*
	And to do him in hir grace	*put himself*
1930	And also to mend his trispase.	
	The eril than unarmed his hevid,	*head*
	And none armure on him he levid.	*left*
	Helm, shelde, and als his brand,	
	That he bare naked in his hand,	
1935	Al he gaf to Sir Ywayne,	
	And hame with him he went ogaine.	
	In the kastel made thai joy ilkane,	
	When thai wist the eril was tane.	*taken*

And, when thai saw tham cumand nere,
1940 Ogayns him went thai al infere;
And when the lady gan tham mete,
Sir Ywaine gudely gan hir grete.
He said, "Madame, have thi presoun   *prisoner*
And hald him here in thi baundoun."   *power*
1945 Bot he gert hir grante him grace   *made*
To mak amendes yn that space.
On a buke the erl sware
Forto restore bath les and mare,
And big ogayn bath toure and toune,   *build; both tower; fortress*
1950 That by him war casten doune,
And evermare to be hir frende.
Umage made he to that hende;   *Homage; gracious woman*
To this forward he borows fand,   *promise; inscribed pledges*
The best lordes of al that land.
1955   Sir Ywaine wald no lenger lend,   *stay*
Bot redies him fast forto wend.
At the lady his leve he takes,
Grete murnyng tharfore sho makes.
Sho said, "Sir, if it be yowre will,
1960 I pray yow forto dwel here still;
And I wil yelde into yowre handes
Myne awyn body and al my landes."
Hereof fast sho hym bysoght,   *earnestly*
Bot al hir speche avayles noght.
1965 He said, "I wil no thing to mede   *will [take]; as reward*
Bot myne armurs and my stede."
Sho said, "Bath stede and other thing
Es yowres at yowre owyn likyng;
And if ye walde here with us dwell,
1970 Mekyl mirth war us omell."   *with all of us*
It was na bote to bid him bide,   *use; stay*
He toke his stede and on gan stride;
The lady and hyr maydens gent   *gracious*
Wepid sare when that he went.
1975   Now rides Ywayn als ye sal here,
With hevy herte and dreri chere
Thurgh a forest by a sty;   *narrow pathway*

134

And thare he herd a hydose cry.   *hideous*

The gaynest way ful sone he tase,   *straightest; takes*

1980   Til he come whare the noys was.

Than was he war of a dragoun,

Had asayled a wilde lyown;   *attacked; lion*

With his tayl he drogh him fast,   *(the dragon)*

And fire ever on him he cast.

1985   The lyoun had over litel myght   *lion*

Ogaynes the dragon forto fyght.

Than Sir Ywayn made him bown   *ready*

Forto sucore the lyown;   *help the lion*

His shelde bifore his face he fest   *held*

1990   For the fyre that the dragon kest;

He strake the dragon in at the chavyl,   *jowl*

That it come out at the navyl.

Sunder strake he the throte-boll,   *Asunder; larynx*

That fra the body went the choll.   *jowl*

1995   By the lioun tail the hevid hang yit,   *head still hung*

For tharby had he tane his bit;   *bites*

The tail Sir Ywayne strake in twa,

The dragon hevid than fel tharfra.

He thoght, "If the lyoun me asayle,

2000   Redy sal he have batayle."   *Ready*

Bot the lyoun wald noght fyght.

Grete fawnyng made he to the knyght.

Down on the grund he set him oft,   *placed himself*

His fortherfete he held oloft,   *forefeet*

2005   And thanked the knyght als he kowth,   *could*

Al if he myght noght speke with mowth;   *Even though*

So wele the lyon of him lete,   *paid homage*

Ful law he lay and likked his fete.   *low; licked*

When Syr Ywayne that sight gan se,

2010   Of the beste him thoght peté,   *beast; pity*

And on his wai forth gan he ride;

The lyown folowd by hys syde.

In the forest al that day

The lyoun mekely foloud ay,   *followed always*

2015   And never for wele ne for wa

Wald he part Sir Ywayn fra.

	Thus in the forest als thai ware,	
	The lyoun hungerd swith sare.	*very sorely*
	Of a beste savore he hade;	*smell*
2020	Until hys lord sembland he made,	*Unto; signs*
	That he wald go to get his pray;	
	His kind it wald, the soth to say.	*nature demanded it*
	For his lorde sold him noght greve,	
	He wald noght go withowten leve.	*permission*
2025	Fra his lord the way he laght	*took*
	The mountance of ane arow-draght;	*distance; arrow's flight*
	Sone he met a barayn da,	*barren doe*
	And ful sone he gan hir sla;	
	Hir throte in twa ful sone he bate	*bit*
2030	And drank the blode whils it was hate.	*hot*
	That da he kest than in his nek,	*doe; cast; across*
	Als it war a mele sek.	*sack of meal*
	Unto his lorde than he it bare;	
	And Sir Ywayn parsayved thare,	*observed*
2035	That it was so nere the nyght,	
	That no ferrer ride he might.	
	A loge of bowes sone he made,	*lodging; boughs*
	And flynt and fire-yren bath he hade,	
	And fire ful sone thare he slogh	*struck*
2040	Of dry mos and many a bogh.	*bough*
	The lion has the da undone;	*doe*
	Sire Ywayne made a spit ful sone,	
	And rosted sum to thaire sopere.	*for*
	The lyon lay als ye sal here:	
2045	Unto na mete he him drogh	*drew near*
	Until his maister had eten ynogh.	*enough*
	Him failed thare bath salt and brede,	*lacked*
	And so him did whyte wine and rede;	*also he lacked*
	Bot of swilk thing als thai had,	
2050	He and his lyon made tham glad.	
	The lyon hungerd for the nanes,	*you can be certain*
	Ful fast he ete raw fless and banes.	
	Sir Ywayn in that ilk telde	*same lodging place*
	Laid his hevid opon his shelde;	
2055	Al nyght the lyon about gede	*paced*

136

To kepe his mayster and his stede.   *protect*
Thus the lyon and the knyght
Lended thare a fouretenyght.   *Stayed*
   On a day so it byfell,
2060 Syr Ywayne come unto the well.
He saw the chapel and the thorne
And said allas that he was born;
And when he loked on the stane,
He fel in swowing sone onane.   *swooning once again*
2065 Als he fel his swerde outshoke;
The pomel into the erth toke,   *stuck*
The poynt toke until his throte —   *stuck*
Wel nere he made a sari note!   *Very nearly; sorry piece of work*
Thorgh his armurs sone it smate,   *pierced*
2070 A litel intil hys hals it bate;   *neck; bit*
And wen the lyon saw his blude,   *when*
He brayded als he had bene wode.   *roared; gone insane*
Than kest he up so lathly rerde,   *hideous a roar*
Ful mani fok myght he have ferde.   *frightened*
2075 He wend wele, so God me rede,   *thought; advise*
That his mayster had bene ded.
It was ful grete peté to here
What sorow he made on his manere.
He stirt ful hertly, I yow hete,   *leaped up; promise*
2080 And toke the swerde bytwix his fete;
Up he set it by a stane,
And thare he wald himself have slane;
And so he had sone, for sertayne,
Bot right in that rase Syr Ywayne;   *that [instant] arose*
2085 And alsone als he saw hym stand,   *[the lion] saw [Ywain]*
For fayn he liked fote and hand.   *Eagerly he licked*
Sir Ywayn said oft sithes, "Allas,   *repeatedly*
Of alkins men hard es my grace.
Mi leman set me sertayn day,
2090 And I it brak, so wayloway.
Allas, for dole how may I dwell   *grief*
To se this chapel and this well,
Hir faire thorn, hir riche stane?
My gude dayes er now al gane,

137

2095	My joy es done now al bidene,	*entirely*
	I am noght worthi to be sene.	
	I saw this wild beste was ful bayn	*eager*
	For my luf himself have slayne.	
	Than sold I, sertes, by more right	
2100	Sla my self for swilk a wyght	*person*
	That I have for my foly lorn.	*lost*
	Allas the while that I was born!"	
	Als Sir Ywayn made his mane	*lament*
	In the chapel ay was ane	*even so was one*
2105	And herd his murnyng haly all	*all his mourning*
	Thorgh a crevice of the wall,	
	And sone it said with simepel chere,	*manner*
	"What ertou, that murnes here?"	
	"A man," he sayd, "sum tyme I was.	
2110	What ertow? Tel me or I pas."	*go forth*
	"I am," it sayd, "the sariest wight,	*sorriest*
	That ever lifed by day or nyght."	
	"Nay," he said, "by Saynt Martyne,	
	Thare es na sorow mete to myne,	*equal*
2115	Ne no wight so wil of wane.	*homeless*
	I was a man, now am I nane;	
	Whilom I was a nobil knyght	
	And a man of mekyl myght;	
	I had knyghtes of my menye	
2120	And of reches grete plenté;	*wealth*
	I had a ful fayre seignory,	*domain*
	And al I lost for my foly.	
	Mi maste sorow als sal thou here:	
	I lost a lady that was me dere."	
2125	The tother sayd, "Allas, allas,	
	Myne es a wele sarier case:	
	To-morn I mun bere my jewyse,	*must; judgment (doom)*
	Als my famen wil devise."	*foes*
	"Allas," he said, "what es the skill?"	*reason*
2130	"That sal thou here, sir, if thou will.	
	I was a mayden mekil of pride	
	With a lady here nere biside;	
	Men me bikalles of tresown	*accuse*

138

And has me put here in presown.
2135 I have no man to defend me,
Tharfore to-morn brent mun I be."   *burned*
He sayd, "What if thou get a knyght,
That for the with thi fase wil fight?"   *enemies*
"Sir," sho sayd, "als mot I ga,
2140 In this land er bot knyghtes twa,   *are*
That me wald help to cover of care: *recover from*
The tane es went, I wate noght whare;   *one is gone; know*
The tother es dweland with the king   *other; dwelling*
And wate noght of my myslykyng.   *misfortune*
2145 The tane of tham hat Syr Gawayn.   *is called*
And the tother hat Syr Ywayn.
For hym sal I be done to dede   *Because of him; put to death*
To-morn right in this same stede;
He es the Kinges son Uriene."
2150 "Parfay," he sayd, "I have hym sene;
I am he, and for my gilt
Sal thou never more be spilt.   *killed*
Thou ert Lunet, if I can rede,   *discern*
That helpyd me yn mekyl drede;
2155 I had bene ded had thou noght bene.
Tharfore tel me us bytwene,
How bical thai the of treson   *accuse*
Thus forto sla and for what reson?"
"Sir, thai say that my lady
2160 Lufed me moste specially,
And wroght al efter my rede;   *counsel*
Tharefore thai hate me to the ded.   *sentenced; death*
The steward says that done have I
Grete tresone unto my lady.
2165 His twa brether sayd it als,
And I wist that thai said fals;
And sone I answerd als a sot —   *foolishly*
For fole bolt es sone shot —   *fool's*
I said that I sold find a knyght,
2170 That sold me mayntene in my right
And feght with tham al thre;
Thus the batayl wajed we.   *waged*

139

Than thai granted me als tyte   *immediately*
Fourty dayes unto respite;
2175 And at the kynges court I was;
I fand na cumfort ne na solase
Nowther of knyght, knave, ne swayn."
Than said he, "Whare was Syr Gawayn?
He has bene ever trew and lele,   *fair*
2180 He fayled never no damysele."
Scho said, "In court he was noght sene,
For a knyght led oway the quene.
The king tharfore es swith grym;   *very angry*
Syr Gawayn folowd efter him,
2185 He coms noght hame, for sertayne,
Until he bryng the quene ogayne.
Now has thou herd, so God me rede,
Why I sal be done to ded."
He said, "Als I am trew knyght,
2190 I sal be redy forto fyght
To-morn with tham al thre,
Leman, for the luf of the.
At my might I sal noght fayl.
Bot how so bese of the batayle,   *it shall be*
2195 If ani man my name the frayne,   *ask*
On al manere luke thou yt layne;   *conceal*
Unto na man my name thou say."
"Syr," sho sayd, "for soth, nay.
I prai to grete God alweldand,   *almighty*
2200 That thai have noght the hegher hand;   *victory*
Sen that ye wil my murnyng mend,
I tak the grace that God wil send."
Syr Ywayn sayd, "I sal the hyght   *promise*
To mend thi murnyng at my myght:
2205 Thorgh grace of God in Trenyté
I sal the wreke of tham al thre."   *avenge you against*
    Than rade he forth into frith,   *woods*
And hys lyoun went hym with.
Had he redyn bot a stownde,   *ridden; while*
2210 A ful fayre castell he fownde;
And Syr Ywaine, the soth to say,

Unto the castel toke the way.
When he come at the castel gate,
Foure porters he fand tharate.
2215 The drawbryg sone lete thai doun,
Bot al thai fled for the lyown.   *because of*
Thai said, "Syr, withowten dowt,
That beste byhoves the leve tharout."   *you're obliged to leave outside*
He sayd, "Sirs, so have I wyn,   *bliss*
2220 Mi lyoun and I sal noght twyn;   *part*
I luf him als wele, I yow hete,   *assure*
Als my self at ane mete;   *equally*
Owther sal we samyn lende,   *together remain*
Or els wil we hethin wende.   *go away*
2225 Bot right with that the lord he met,
And ful gladly he him gret,
With knyghtes and swiers grete plenté
And faire ladies and maydens fre;
Ful mekyl joy of him thai made,
2230 Bot sorow in thaire hertes thai hade.
Unto a chameber was he led
And unharmed and sethin cled   *unarmed; afterwards dressed*
In clothes that war gay and dere.   *costly*
Bot ofttymes changed thaire chere;   *manner*
2235 Sum tyme, he saw, thai weped all
Als ai wald to water fall;   *ever would; turn*
Thai made slike murnyng and slik mane   *such*
That gretter saw he never nane;
Thai feynyd tham oft for hys sake
2240 Fayre semblant forto make.
Ful grete wonder Sir Ywayn hade
For thai swilk joy and sorow made.
"Sir," he said, "if yowre wil ware,   *if it be your will*
I wald wyt why ye make slike kare."   *mourning*
2245 "This joy," he said, "that we mak now,
Sir, es al for we have yow;   *is all because you're here*
And, sir, also we mak this sorow
For dedys that sal be done to-morow.
A geant wons here nere bysyde,   *dwells*
2250 That es a devil of mekil pryde;

141

His name hat Harpyns of Mowntain.
For him we lyf in mekil payn;
My landes haves he robbed and reft,   *pillaged; stolen*
Noght bot this kastel es me left.
2255   And, by God that in hevyn wons,   *dwells*
Syr, I had sex knyghtis to sons;
I saw my self the twa slogh he,
To-morn the foure als slane mun be —   *must*
He has al in hys presowne.
2260   And, sir, for nane other enchesowne,   *reason*
Bot for I warned hym to wyve   *refused his marrying*
My doghter, fayrest fode olyve.   *creature alive*
Tharfore es he wonder wrath,
And depely has he sworn hys ath,   *oath*
2265   With maystry that he sal hir wyn,
And that the laddes of his kychyn
And also that his werst fote-knave
His wil of that woman sal have,
Bot I to-morn might find a knight,   *Unless*
2270   That durst with hym selven fyght;
And I have none to him at ga.
What wonder es if me be wa?"
Syr Ywayn lystend hym ful wele,
And when he had talde ilka dele,   *every bit*
2275   "Syr," he sayd, "me think mervayl
That ye soght never no kounsayl
At the kynges hous here bysyde;
For, sertes, in al this werld so wyde
Es no man of so mekil myght,
2280   Geant, champioun, ne knight,   *Giant*
That he ne has knyghtes of his menye   *company*
That ful glad and blyth wald be
Forto mete with swilk a man
That thai myght kyth thaire myghtes on."   *make known; prowess*
2285   He said, "Syr, so God me mend,
Unto the kynges kourt I send
To seke my mayster Syr Gawayn;   *assist*
For he wald socore me ful fain.
He wald noght leve for luf ne drede,

142

2290	Had he wist now of my nede;	*known*
	For his sister es my wyfe,	
	And he lufes hyr als his lyfe.	
	Bot a knyght this other day,	
	Thai talde, has led the quene oway.	
2295	Forto seke hyr went Sir Gawayn,	
	And yit ne come he noght ogayn."	
	Than Syr Ywayne sighed sare	
	And said unto the knyght right thare;	
	"Syr," he sayd, "for Gawayn sake	
2300	This batayl wil I undertake	
	Forto fyght with the geant;	
	And that opon swilk a covenant,	
	Yif he cum at swilk a time,	
	So that we may fight by prime.	*If*
2305	No langer may I tent tharto,	*attend*
	For other thing I have to do;	
	I have a dede that most be done	
	To-morn nedes byfor the none."	*noon*
	The knyght sare sighand sayd him till,	
2310	"Sir, God yelde the thi gode wyll."	
	And al that ware thare in the hall,	
	On knese byfor hym gan thai fall.	
	Forth thare come a byrd ful bryght,	*lady*
	The fairest man might se in sight;	
2315	Hir moder come with hir infere,	*together*
	And both thai morned and made yll chere.	
	The knight said, "Lo, verraiment,	*truly*
	God has us gude socure sent,	
	This knight that of his grace wil grant	
2320	Forto fyght with the geant."	
	On knese thai fel doun to his fete	
	And thanked him with wordes swete.	
	"A, God forbede," said Sir Ywain,	
	"That the sister of Sir Gawayn	
2325	Or any other of his blode born	
	Sold on this wise knel me byforn."	
	He toke tham up tyte both infere	
	And prayd tham to amend thaire chere.	

143

"And praies fast to God alswa,

2330 That I may venge yow on yowre fa,

And that he cum swilk tyme of day,

That I by tyme may wend my way

Forto do another dede;

For, sertes, theder most I nede.

2335 Sertes, I wald noght tham byswike   *betray*

Forto win this kinges rike."   *realm*

His thoght was on that damysel,

That he left in the chapel.

Thai said, "He es of grete renowne,

2340 For with hym dwels the lyoun."

Ful wele confort war thai all

Bath in boure and als in hall.

Ful glad war thai of thaire gest,   *guest*

And when tyme was at go to rest,

2345 The lady broght him to his bed;

And for the lyoun sho was adred.

Na man durst negh his chamber nere,   *approach*

Fro thai war broght thareyn infere.

Sone at morn, when it was day,

2350 The lady and the fayre may

Til Ywayn chamber went thai sone,

And the dore thai have undone.

    Sir Ywayn to the kyrk gede   *went*

Or he did any other dede;   *Before; deed*

2355 He herd the servise of the day

And sethin to the knyght gan say,

"Sir," he said, "now most I wend,

Lenger here dar I noght lende;

Til other place byhoves me fare."   *I'm obliged to go*

2360 Than had the knyght ful mekel care;

He said, "Syr, dwells a litel thraw   *while longer*

For luf of Gawayn that ye knaw;

Socore us now or ye wende.   *Help*

I sal yow gif withowten ende

2365 Half my land with toun and toure,

And ye wil help us in this stoure."   *If; battle*

Sir Ywayn said, "Nai, God forbede

	That I sold tak any mede."	*reward*
	Than was grete dole, so God me glade,	*grief; make me glad*
2370	To se the sorow that thai made.	
	Of tham Sir Ywayn had grete peté;	
	Him thoght his hert myght breke in thre,	
	For in grete drede ay gan he dwell	
	For the mayden in the chapell.	
2375	For, sertes, if sho war done to ded,	
	Of him war than none other rede	*plan*
	Bot oither he sold hymselven sla	*either; slay*
	Or wode ogain to the wod ga.	*become insane again in the wilderness*
	Ryght with that thare come a grome	*At that instant; lad*
2380	And said tham that geant come:	*told them*
	"Yowre sons bringes he him byforn,	
	Wel nere naked als thai war born."	
	With wreched ragges war thai kled	*dressed*
	And fast bunden; thus er thai led.	*securely*
2385	The geant was bath large and lang	
	And bare a levore of yren ful strang;	*bar; iron*
	Tharwith he bet tham bitterly.	*beat*
	Grete rewth it was to here tham cry;	*pity*
	Thai had no thing tham forto hyde.	*to hide themselves with*
2390	A dwergh gode on the tother syde,	*dwarf went*
	He bare a scowrge with cordes ten;	
	Tharewith he bet tha gentil men	*beat those*
	Ever on ane als he war wode.	*as if he were mad*
	Efter ilka band brast out the blode;	*After each stroke burst*
2395	And when thai at the walles were,	
	He cried loud that men myght here,	
	"If thou wil have thi sons in hele,	*health*
	Deliver me that damysele.	
	I sal hir gif to warisowne	*give as a prize*
2400	Ane of the foulest quisteroun,	*scullions*
	That ever yit ete any brede.	*ate*
	He sal have hir maydenhede.	
	Thar sal none other lig hir by	*lie down*
	Bot naked herlotes and lowsy."	*contemptible persons*
2405	When the lord thir wordes herd,	
	Als he war wode for wa he ferd.	*As if; woe; became (fared)*

Sir Ywayn than that was curtays,   *then who*
Unto the knyght ful sone he sais:
"This geant es ful fers and fell   *ferocious; bold*
2410 And of his wordes ful kruell;
I sal deliver hir of his aw   *power*
Or els be ded within a thraw.   *short while*
For, sertes, it war a misaventure
That so gentil a creature
2415 Sold ever so foul hap byfall
To be defouled with a thrall."   *slave*
Sone was he armed, Sir Ywayn;
Tharfore the ladies war ful fayn.   *joyous*
Thai helpid to lace him in his wede,   *armor*
2420 And sone he lepe up on his stede.
Thai prai to God that grace him grant
Forto sla that foul geant.
The drawbrigges war laten doun,
And forth he rides with his lioun.
2425 Ful mani sari murnand man
Left he in the kastel than,
That on thaire knese to God of might *knees*
Praied ful hertly for the knyght.
  Syr Ywayn rade into the playne,
2430 And the geant come hym ogayne.
His levore was ful grete and lang   *steel pole*
And himself ful mekyl and strang;
He said, "What devil made the so balde
Forto cum heder out of thi halde?
2435 Whosoever the heder send,   *sent you here*
Lufed the litel, so God me mend.
Of the he wald be wroken fayn."   *avenged gladly*
"Do forth thi best," said Sir Ywayn.
Al the armure he was yn,   *(i.e., the giant)*
2440 Was noght bot of a bul-skyn.
Sir Ywayn was to him ful prest,   *at him quickly*
He strake to him in middes the brest. *the middle of*
The spere was both stif and gode —
Whare it toke bit, outbrast the blode. *pierced*
2445 So fast Sir Ywayn on yt soght,

	The bul-scyn availed noght.	
	The geant stombild with the dynt,	*blow*
	And unto Sir Ywayn he mynt,	*aimed a blow*
	And on the shelde he hit ful fast,	
2450	It was mervayl that it myght last.	
	The levore bended tharwithall,	*pole*
	With grete force he lete it fall,	
	The geant was so strong and wight,	
	That never for no dint of knyght	
2455	Ne for batayl that he sold make,	*should*
	Wald he none other wapyn take.	
	Sir Ywain left his spere of hand	
	And strake obout him with his brand,	*sword*
	And the geant mekil of mayn	*giant great of strength*
2460	Strake ful fast to him ogayn,	
	Til at the last within a throw	*for a while*
	He rest him on his sadelbow;	*(i.e., rested himself)*
	And that parcayved his lioun,	
	That his hevid so hanged doun,	
2465	He hopid that hys lord was hyrt,	*thought*
	And to the geant sone he styrt.	
	The scyn and fless bath rafe he down	*skin; flesh; tore*
	Fro his hals to hys cropoun;	*neck; buttocks*
	His ribbes myght men se onane,	
2470	For al was bare unto bane.	*bone*
	At the lyown oft he mynt,	*aimed a blow*
	Bot ever he lepis fro his dynt,	*(i.e., the lion dodges his blows)*
	So that no strake on him lyght.	
	By than was Ywain cumen to myght,	
2475	Than wil he wreke him if he may.	
	The geant gaf he ful gude pay;	*It cost the giant dearly*
	He smate oway al his left cheke,	
	His sholder als of gan he kleke,	*off did he snatch*
	That both his levore and his hand	
2480	Fel doun law opon the land.	*low*
	Sethin with a stoke to him he stert	*thrust*
	And smate the geant unto the hert:	
	Than was nane other tale to tell,	
	Bot fast unto the erth he fell,	

2485	Als it had bene a hevy tre.	
	Than myght men in the kastel se	
	Ful mekil mirth on ilka side.	
	The gates kest thai opyn wyde;	
	The lord unto Syr Ywaine ran,	
2490	Him foloud many a joyful man;	
	Also the lady ran ful fast,	
	And hir doghter was noght the last.	
	I may noght tel the joy thai had;	
	And the foure brether war ful glad,	
2495	For thai war out of bales broght.	evil fate
	The lord wist it helpid noght	
	At pray Sir Ywayn for to dwell,	To; stay
	For tales that he byfore gan tell.	
	Bot hertly with his myght and mayn	
2500	He praied him forto cum ogayn	
	And dwel with him a litel stage,	time
	When he had done hys vassage.	knightly obligations
	He said, "Sir, that may I noght do;	(Ywain)
	Bileves wele, for me bus go."	I must go
2505	Tham was ful wo — he wald noght dwell —	
	Bot fain thai war that it so fell.	joyous; came about
	The neghest way than gan he wele,	closest; take
	Until he come to the chapele.	
	Thare he fand a mekil fire	
2510	And the mayden with lely lire	flesh white as a lily
	In hyr smok was bunden fast	smock
	Into the fire forto be kast.	
	Unto himself he sayd in hy	in haste
	And prayed to God almyghty,	
2515	That he sold for his mekil myght	
	Save fro shame that swete wight.	
	"Yf thai be many and mekil of pryse,	great in excellence
	I sal let for no kouwardise;	desist; cowardice
	For with me es bath God and right,	
2520	And thai sal help me forto fight.	
	And my lyon sal help me —	
	Than er we foure ogayns tham thre."	
	Sir Ywayn rides and cries then,	

148

"Habides, I bid yow, fals men!   *Stay*

2525   It semes wele that ye er wode,

That wil spill this sakles blode.   *innocent person's blood*

Ye sal noght so, yf that I may."

His lyown made hym redy way.

Naked he saw the mayden stand

2530   Bihind hir bunden aither hand:

Than sighed Ywain wonder-oft,

Unnethes might he syt oloft.   *barely; set up on [his horse]*

Thare was no sembland tham bitwene,   *semblance*

That ever owther had other sene.

2535   Al obout hyr myght men se

Ful mykel sorow and grete peté

Of other ladies that thare were,

Wepeand with ful sory chere.

"Lord," thai sayd, "what es oure gylt?

2540   Oure joy, oure confort sal be spilt.

Who sal now oure erandes say?   *messages*

Allas, who sal now for us pray?"

Whils thai thus karped, was Lunet   *spoke*

On knese byfore the prest set,   *priest*

2545   Of hir syns hir forto schrive.   *confess*

And unto hir he went bylive,   *(Ywain) went quickly*

Hir hand he toke, and up sho rase;

"Leman," he sayd, "whore er thi fase?"   *where are*

"Sir, lo tham yonder in yone stede

2550   Bideand until I be ded;   *Waiting*

Thai have demed me with wrang.   *judged me falsely*

Wel nere had ye dwelt over lang!   *Nearly*

I pray to God He do yow mede   *grant you reward*

That ye wald help me in this nede."

2555   Thir wordes herd than the steward;   *These*

He hies him unto hir ful hard.   *hastens; cruelly*

He said, "Thou lies, fals woman!

For thi treson ertow tane.

Sho has bitraied hir lady,

2560   And, sir, so wil sho the in hy.   *haste*

And tharfore, syr, by Goddes dome,   *heaven*

I rede thou wend right als thou com;   *advise*

Thou takes a ful febil rede, *counsel*
If thou for hir will suffer ded."
2565 Unto the steward than said he,
"Who so es ferd, I rede he fle; *Whoever's afraid I suggest*
And, sertes, I have bene this day,
Whare I had ful large pay; *satisfaction*
And yit," he sayd, "I sal noght fail."
2570 To tham he waged the batayl.
"Do oway thi lioun," said the steward,
"For that es noght oure forward. *agreement*
Allane sal thou fight with us thre."
And unto him thus answerd he,
2575 "Of my lioun no help I crave;
I ne have none other fote-knave;
If he wil do yow any dere, *harm*
I rede wele that ye yow were." *advise; you protect yourself*
The steward said, "On alkins wise *every way*
2580 Thi lyoun, sir, thou most chastise, *restrain*
That he do here no harm this day,
Or els wend forth on thi way;
For hir warand mai thou noght be, *guarantee*
Bot thou allane fight with us thre.
2585 Al thir men wote, and so wote I, *these; know; know*
That sho bitrayed hir lady.
Als traytures sal sho have hyre, *reward*
Sho be brent here in this fire."
Sir Ywayn sad, "Nai, God forbede!"
2590 (He wist wele how the soth gede.) *stood*
"I trow to wreke hir with the best.' *plan to avenge her*
He bad his lyoun go to rest;
And he laid him sone onane
Doun byfore tham everilkane;
2595 Bitwene his legges he layd his tail
And so biheld to the batayl.
    Al thre thai ride to Sir Ywayn,
And smertly rides he tham ogayn;
In that time nothing tint he, *wasted*
2600 For his an strake was worth thaires thre. *one*
He strake the steward on the shelde,

That he fel doun flat in the felde;

Bot up he rase yit at the last   *yet*

And to Sir Ywayn strake ful fast.

2605   Tharat the lyoun greved sare;

No lenger wald he than lig thare.   *lie there*

To help his mayster he went onane;

And the ladies everilkane,

That war thare forto se that sight,

2610   Praied ful fast ay for the knight.

     The lyoun hasted him ful hard,

And sone he come to the steward.

A ful fel mynt to him he made: *fierce blow*

He bigan at the shulder-blade,

2615   And with his pawm al rafe he downe   *paws; tore*

Bath hauberk and his actoune   *mail; jerkin (leather vest)*

And al the fless doun til his kne,   *flesh*

So that men myght his guttes se;

To ground he fell so al torent   *torn to pieces*

2620   Was thare no man that him ment.   *mourned*

The lioun gan hym sla.

Than war thai bot twa and twa,

And, sertanly, thare Sir Ywayn

Als with wordes did his main   *best*

2625   Forto chastis hys lyowne;

Bot he ne wald na more lig doun.

The liown thoght, how so he sayd,

That with his help he was wele payd.   *satisfied*

Thai smate the lyoun on ilka syde   *(The remaining two assailants)*

2630   And gaf him many woundes wide.

When that he saw hys lyoun blede,   *(i.e., Ywain)*

He ferd for wa als he wald wede,   *would go mad*

And fast he strake than in that stoure,   *battle*

Might thare none his dintes doure.   *endure*

2635   So grevosly than he bygan

That doun he bare bath hors and man.

Thai yald tham sone to Sir Ywayn,   *yielded*

And tharof war the folk ful fayne;

And sone quit to tham thaire hire,   *paid; reward*

2640   For both he kest tham in the fire

And said, "Wha juges men with wrang,
The same jugement sal thai fang."   *receive*
Thus he helpid the maiden ying,   *young*
And sethin he made the saghtelyng   *afterwards; peace*
2645   Bitwene hyr and the riche lady.
    Than al the folk ful hastily
Proferd tham to his servise
To wirship him ever on al wise.
Nane of tham al wist bot Lunet
2650   That thai with thaire lord war met.
The lady prayed him als the hend   *courteously*
That he hame with tham wald wende
Forto sojorn thare a stownd,   *awhile*
Til he wer warist of his wound.   *healed*
2655   By his sare set he noght a stra,   *wound; straw*
Bot for his lioun was him wa.
"Madame," he said, "sertes, nay,
I mai noght dwel, the soth to say."
Sho said, "Sir, sen thou wyl wend,
2660   Sai us thi name, so God the mend."   *Tell*
"Madame," he said, "bi Saint Symoun,
I hat the Knight with the Lyoun."   *am called*
Sho said, "We saw yow never or now,   *before*
Ne never herd we speke of yow."
2665   "Tharby," he sayd, "ye understand,
I am noght knawen wide in land."
Sho said, "I prai the forto dwell,
If that thou may, here us omell."   *among*
If sho had wist wele wha it was,
2670   She wald wele lever have laten him pas;   *rather*
And tharfore wald he noght be knawen
Both for hir ese and for his awyn.   *ease*
He said, "No lenger dwel I ne may;
Beleves wele and haves goday.   *remain*
2675   I prai to Crist, hevyn kyng,
Lady, len yow gude lifing,   *grant*
And len grace, that al yowre anoy
May turn yow unto mykel joy."
Sho said, "God grant that it so be."

2680   Unto himself than thus said he,

"Thou ert the lok and kay also   *lock; key*

Of al my wele and al my wo."

    Now wendes he forth and morning mase,   *makes [his] lament*

And nane of tham wist what he was,

2685   Bot Lunet that he bad sold layn,   *bade; conceal*

And so sho did with al hir mayne.

Sho cunvayd him forth on his way;

He said, "Gude leman, I the pray,

That thou tel to no moder son,

2690   Who has bene thi champion;

And als I pray the, swete wight,

Late and arly thou do thi might

With speche unto my lady fre

Forto make hir frende with me.

2695   Sen ye er now togeder glade,   *happily*

Help thou that we war frendes made."   *Help us to become friends*

"Sertes, sir," sho sayd, "ful fayn

Thareobout wil I be bayn;   *eager*

And that ye have done me this day,

2700   God do yow mede, als he wele may."

    Of Lunet thus his leve he tase,   *takes*

Bot in hert grete sorow he hase;

His lioun feled so mekill wa,

That he ne myght no ferrer ga.   *farther go*

2705   Sir Ywayn puld gres in the felde

And made a kouche opon his shelde;

Thareon his lyoun laid he thare,

And forth he rides and sighes sare;

On his shelde so he him led.   *(i.e., the lion)*

2710   Than was he ful evyl sted.   *unhappily situated*

Forth he rides by frith and fell,   *forest; hill*

Til he come to a fayre castell.

Thare he cald and swith sone   *immediately*

The porter has the gates undone,

2715   And to him made he ful gude chere.

He said, "Sir, ye er welcum here."

Syr Ywain said, "God do the mede,   *reward thee*

For tharof have I mekil nede."

	Yn he rade right at the gate;	
2720	Faire folk kepid hym tharate.	
	Thai toke his shelde and his lyoun,	
	And ful softly thai laid it doun;	
	Sum to stabil led his stede,	
	And sum also unlaced his wede.	*armor*
2725	Thai talde the lord than of that knyght;	
	And sone he and his lady bryght	
	And thaire sons and doghters all	
	Come ful faire him forto kall;	
	Thai war ful fayn he thore was sted.	*there; situated*
2730	To chaumber sone thai have him led;	
	His bed was ordand richely,	*prepared*
	And his lioun thai laid him by.	
	Him was no mister forto crave,	*did not need anything*
	Redy he had what he wald have.	
2735	Twa maydens with him thai laft	
	That wele war lered of lechecraft;	*learned in medicine*
	The lordes doghters both thai wore	*were*
	That war left to kepe hym thore.	
	Thai heled hym everilka wound,	
2740	And hys lyoun sone made thai sownd.	*healthy*
	I can noght tel how lang he lay;	
	When he was helyd he went his way.	*healthy*
	Bot whils he sojorned in that place,	
	In that land byfel this case.	
2745	A litil thethin in a stede	*distance away*
	A grete lord of the land was ded.	
	Lifand he had none other ayre	*heir*
	Bot two doghters that war ful fayre.	
	Als sone als he was laid in molde,	*buried in the earth*
2750	The elder sister sayd sho wolde	
	Wend to court sone als sho myght	
	Forto get hir som doghty knyght	
	Forto win hir al the land	
	And hald it haley in hir hand.	*wholly*
2755	The yonger sister saw sho ne myght	
	Have that fell until hir right,	
	Bot if that it war by batail;	

154

To court sho wil at ask cownsayl.
The elder sister sone was gare,   *prepared*
2760 Unto the court fast gan sho fare.
To Sir Gawayn sho made hir mane,
And he has granted hyr onane,
"Bot yt bus be so prevely,   *must; secretly*
That nane wit bot thou and I.
2765 If thou of me makes any yelp,   *boast*
Lorn has thou al my help."   *Lost*
Than efter on the tother day
Unto kourt come the tother may,
And to Sir Gawayn sone sho went
2770 And talde unto him hir entent;
Of his help sho him bysoght.
"Sertes," he sayd, "that may I noght."
Than sho wepe and wrang hir handes;
And right with that come new tithandes,   *tidings*
2775 How a knyght with a lyoun
Had slane a geant ful feloun.   *fierce*
The same knight thare talde this tale
That Syr Ywayn broght fra bale   *grief*
That had wedded Gawayn sister dere.
2780 Sho and hir sons war thare infere;
Thai broght the dwergh, that be ye balde,   *dwarf; assured*
And to Sir Gawayn have thai talde
How the knyght with the lyowne
Delivred tham out of presowne,
2785 And how he for Syr Gawayn sake
Gan that batayl undertake,
And als how nobilly that he wroght.
Sir Gawayn said, "I knaw him noght."
The yonger mayden than alsone   *instantly*
2790 Of the king askes this bone   *boon*
To have respite of fourti dais,
Als it fel to landes lays.   *laws*
Sho wist thare was no man of main   *strength*
That wald fyght with Sir Gawayn;
2795 Sho thoght to seke by frith and fell   *woodland; hill*
The knyght that sho herd tham of tell.

Respite was granted of this thing;
The mayden toke leve at the king
And sethen at al the baronage,
2800　And forth sho went on hir vayage.　　　　*journey*
　　Day ne nyght wald sho noght spare;
Thurgh al the land fast gan sho fare,
Thurgh castel and thurgh ilka toun
To seke the knight with the lyown:
2805　He helpes al in word and dede,
That unto him has any nede.
Sho soght hym thurgh al that land,
Bot of hym herd sho na tythand.　　　　*tidings*
Na man kouth tel hir whare he was.
2810　Ful grete sorow in hert sho has.
So mikel murning gan sho make
That a grete sekenes gan sho take.　　　　*sickness*
Bot in hir way right wele sho sped.
At that kastell was sho sted　　　　*did she find herself*
2815　Whare Sir Ywayn are had bene　　　　*earlier*
Helid of his sekenes clene.　　　　*completely*
Thare sho was ful wele knawen
And als welcum als til hyr awyn;　　　　*own (people)*
With alkyn gamyn thai gan hir glade,　　　　*every kind of pleasure*
2820　And mikel joy of hir thai made.
Unto the lord sho tald hyr case,
And helping hastily sho hase.　　　　*hath*
　　Stil in lecheing thare sho lay;　　　　*undergoing medical treatment*
A maiden for hir toke the way
2825　For to seke yf that sho myght
In any land here of that knyght;
And that same kastel come sho by,
Whare Ywayn wedded the lavedy;　　　　*lady*
And fast sho spird in ylk sesown　　　　*inquired*
2830　Efter the knight with the lioun.
Thai tald hir how he went tham fra,
And also how thay saw him sla
Thre nobil knyghtes for the nanes　　　　*occasion*
That faght with him al at anes.　　　　*all at once*
2835　Sho said, "Par charité, I yow pray,

156

If that ye wate, wil ye me say,
Whederward that he es went?"
Thai said, for soth, thai toke na tent; *paid no attention*
"Ne here es nane that the can tell,
2840 Bot if it be a damysell,
For whas sake he heder come,
And for hir the batayl he name. *undertook*
We trow wele that sho can the wis; *believe; direct you*
Yonder in yone kyrk sho ys;
2845 Tharfore we rede to hyr thou ga."
And hastily than did sho swa. *so*
Aither other ful gudeli gret, *Either; greeted*
And sone she frayned at Lunet *quickly she inquired of*
If sho kouth ani sertan sayne. *knew any definite news*
2850 And hendly answerd sho ogayne,
"I sal sadel my palfray
And wend with the forth on thi way
And wis the als wele als I can." *guide you as well as*
Ful oft sithes thanked sho hir than.
2855 Lunet was ful smertly gare, *ready*
And with the mayden forth gan sho fare.
Als thai went, al sho hyr talde,
How sho was taken and done in halde,
How wikkedly that sho was wreghed, *accused*
2860 And how that trayturs on hir leghed, *against her alleged*
And how that sho sold have bene brent,
Had noght God hir socore sent
Of that knight with the lyoun:
"He lesed me out of presoun." *released*
2865 Sho broght hir sone into a playn, *(Lunette)*
Whare sho parted fra Sir Ywayn;
Sho said, "Na mare can I tel the,
Bot here parted he fra me.
How that he went wate I no mare;
2870 Bot wounded was he wonder-sare.
God that for us sufferd wounde.
Len us to se him hale and sownde. *Grant*
No lenger with the may I dwell;
Bot cumly Crist that heried hell, *holy; harried*

157

2875	Len the grace that thou may spede	
	Of thine erand als thou has nede."	
	Lunet hastily hies hir home,	
	And the mayden sone to the kastel come	
	Whare he was helid byforehand.	*(i.e., Ywain)*
2880	The lord sone at the gate sho fand	
	With knyghtes and ladies grete cumpani;	
	Sho haylsed tham al ful hendely,	
	And ful fayre praied sho to tham then	
	If thai couth thai sold hyr ken	*knew; make known*
2885	Whare sho myght fynd in toure or toun	
	A kumly knyght with a lyoun.	*noble*
	Than said the lord, "By swete Jhesus,	
	Right now parted he fra us;	
	Lo here the steppes of his stede,	
2890	Evyn unto him thai wil the lede."	
	Than toke sho leve and went hir way,	
	With sporrs sho sparid noght hir palfray;	
	Fast sho hyed with al hyr myght,	
	Until sho of him had a syght	
2895	And of hys lyoun that by him ran.	
	Wonder joyful was sho than,	
	And with hir force sho hasted so fast	*strength*
	That sho overtoke him at the last.	
	Sho hailsed him with hert ful fayn,	*greeted*
2900	And he hir hailsed fayre ogayn.	
	Sho said, "Sir, wide have I yow soght,	
	And for my self ne es it noght,	
	Bot for a damysel of pryse	
	That halden es both war and wise.	*is held to be*
2905	Men dose to hir ful grete outrage,	
	Thai wald hir reve hyr heritage;	*rob her of*
	And in this land now lifes none	*lives*
	That sho traystes hyr opone	*trusts; upon*
	Bot anly opon God and the,	*only*
2910	For thou ert of so grete bounté;	
	Thorgh help of the sho hopes wele	
	To win hyr right everilka dele.	*every bit*
	Scho sais no knyght that lifes now	

Mai help hir half so wele als thou;

2915 Gret word sal gang of thi vassage,   *prowess*
If that thou win hir heritage.
For thoght sho toke slike sekenes sare,   *such*
So that sho might travail no mare,
I have yow soght on sydes sere.   *various*

2920 Tharfore yowre answer wald I here,
Whether ye wil with me wend,
Or elswhare yow likes to lend."   *remain*
He said, "That knyght that idil lies
Oft sithes winnes ful litel pries.   *prize*

2925 Forthi mi rede sal sone be tane:
Gladly with the wil I gane,   *go*
Wheder so thou wil me lede,
And hertly help the in thi nede.
Sen thou haves me so wide soght,

2930 Sertes, fail the sal I noght."
    Thus thaire wai forth gan thai hald
Until a kastel that was cald
The Castel of the Hevy Sorow.
Thare wald he bide until the morow;

2935 Thare to habide him thoght it best,
For the son drogh fast to rest.   *sun drew*
Bot al the men that thai with met,
Grete wonder sone on tham thai set
And said, "Thou wreche, unsely man,   *unhappy*

2940 Whi wil thou here thi herber tane?   *lodging taken*
Thou passes noght without despite."   *injury*
Sir Ywain answerd tham als tyte   *quickly*
And said, "For soth, ye er unhende   *ungracious*
An unkouth man so forto shende;   *unknown; scorn*

2945 Ye sold noght say hym velany,
Bot if ye wist encheson why."   *reason*
Thai answerd than and said ful sone,
"Thou sal wit or to-morn at none."
Syr Ywaine said, "For al yowre saw   *talk*

2950 Unto yon castel wil I draw."
He and his lyoun and the may   *maiden*
Unto the castel toke the way.

When the porter of tham had sight,
Sone he said unto the knight,
2955 "Cumes forth," he said, "ye al togeder!
Ful ille hail er ye cumen heder."   *With much misfortune*
Thus war thai welkumd at the gate,
And yit thai went al in tharate;
Unto the porter no word thai said.
2960 A hal thai fand ful gudeli graid,   *prepared*
And als Sir Ywaine made entré,
Fast bisyde him than saw he
A proper place and faire, iwis,
Enclosed obout with a palis.   *palisade*
2965 He loked in bitwix the trese,
And many maidens thare he sese
Wirkand silk and gold-wire;
Bot thai war al in pover atire.
Thaire clothes war reven on evil arai;   *torn*
2970 Ful tenderly al weped thai.
Thaire face war lene and als unclene,
And blak smokkes had thai on bidene;   *smocks; one and all*
Thai had mischefs ful manifalde   *troubles*
Of hunger, of threst, and of calde;   *thirst*
2975 And ever onane thai weped all,
Als thai wald to water fall.   *As if they would turn to water*
When Ywaine al this understode,
Ogayn unto the gates he gode;   *went*
Bot thai war sperred ferli fast   *fastened*
2980 With lokkes that ful wele wald last.   *locks*
The porter kepid tham with his main   *defended; strength*
And said, "Sir, thou most wend ogain;
I wate thou wald out at the gate,
Bot thou mai noght by na gate.   *any path*
2985 Thi herber es tane til to-morow,   *lodging*
And tharfore getes thou mekill sorow.
Omang thi fase here sted ertow."   *foes; you are placed*
He said, "So have I bene or now
And past ful wele; so sal I here.
2990 Bot, leve frend, wiltou me lere   *dear; will you explain to me*
Of thise maidens what thai are,

160

	That wirkes al this riche ware?"	*goods*
	He said, "If thou wil wit trewly,	*know*
	Forthermare thou most aspy."	*find out*
2995	"Tharfore," he said, "I sal noght lett."	*delay*
	He soght and fand a dern weket,	*concealed gate*
	He opind it and in he gede.	*went*
	"Maidens," he said, "God mot yow spede,	
	And als He sufferd woundes sare,	
3000	He send yow covering of yowre care,	
	So that ye might mak merier chere."	
	"Sir," thai said, "God gif so were."	*God grant it!*
	"Yowre sorow," he said, "unto me say,	
	And I sal mend it, yf I may."	
3005	Ane of tham answerd ogayne	
	And said, "The soth we sal noght layne;	*hide*
	We sal yow tel or ye ga ferr,	*further*
	Why we er here and what we err.	
	Sir, ye sal understand	
3010	That we er al of Maydenland.	
	Oure kyng opon his jolité	*pleasure*
	Passed thurgh many cuntré	
	Aventures to spir and spy	*seek out*
	Forto asay his owen body.	*test*
3015	His herber here anes gan he ta;	*once*
	That was biginyng of oure wa.	
	For heryn er twa champions;	*herein*
	Men sais thai er the devil sons,	
	Geten of a woman with a ram;	
3020	Ful many man have thai done gram.	*harm*
	What knight so herbers here a nyght,	
	With both at ones bihoves him fight.	
	So bus the do, by bel and boke;	*must*
	Allas, that thou thine thus here toke.	
3025	Oure king was wight himself to welde	*capable of looking after himself*
	And of fourtene yeres of elde,	
	When he was tane with tham to fyght;	
	Bot unto tham had he no myght,	
	And when he saw him bud be ded,	*that he would be killed*
3030	Than he kouth no better rede,	*plan*

	Bot did him haly in thaire grace	*put himself entirely*
	And made tham sureté in that place,	
	Forto yeld tham ilka yere,	*each year*
	So that he sold be hale and fere,	*sound*
3035	Threty maidens to trowage,	*tribute*
	And al sold be of hegh parage	*rank*
	And the fairest of his land;	
	Herto held he up his hand.	
	This ilk rent byhoves hym gyf,	*revenue*
3040	Als lang als the fendes lyf,	*fiends*
	Or til thai be in batayl tane,	
	Or els unto thai be al slane.	
	Than sal we pas al hethin quite,	*hence free*
	That here suffers al this despite.	
3045	Bot herof es noght for speke;	
	Es none in werld that us mai wreke.	*avenge*
	We wirk here silver, silk, and golde,	
	Es none richer on this molde,	
	And never the better er we kled,	*are we clothed*
3050	And in grete hunger er we sted;	*are we always*
	For al that we wirk in this stede,	
	We have noght half oure fil of brede;	
	For the best that sewes here any styk,	*stitch*
	Takes bot foure penys in a wik,	*week*
3055	And that es litel wha som tase hede,	*to whoever takes heed*
	Any of us to kleth and fede.	*clothe; feed*
	Ilkone of us withouten lesyng	*Each one; lying*
	Might win ilk wike fourty shilling;	*each week*
	And yit, bot if we travail mare,	*unless*
3060	Oft thai bete us wonder sare.	
	It helpes noght to tel this tale,	
	For thare bese never bote of oure bale.	*relief; suffering*
	Oure maste sorow, sen we bigan,	*greatest*
	That es that we se mani a man,	
3065	Doghty dukes, yrels, and barouns,	
	Oft sithes slane with thir champiowns;	*slain by*
	With tham to-morn bihoves the fight."	*you're obliged to fight*
	Sir Ywayn said, "God, maste of myght,	
	Sal strenkith me in ilka dede	*strengthen*

3070	Ogains tha devils and al thaire drede;	
	That lord deliver yow of yowre fase."	*foes*
	Thus takes he leve and forth he gase.	
	He passed forth into the hall,	
	Thare fand he no man him to call;	
3075	No bewtese wald thai to him bede,	*kindness; offer*
	Bot hastily thai toke his stede	
	And also the maydens palfray,	
	War served wele with corn and hay.	
	For wele thai hoped that Sir Ywayn	*thought*
3080	Sold never have had his stede ogayn.	
	Thurgh the hal Sir Ywain gase	
	Intil ane orcherd playn pase;	*walking quickly*
	His maiden with him ledes he.	*leads*
	He fand a knyght under a tre;	
3085	Opon a clath of gold he lay.	
	Byfor him sat a ful fayre may;	*maiden*
	A lady sat with tham infere.	*in company*
	The mayden red at thai myght here,	*read so that; hear*
	A real romance in that place,	*courtly (royal) romance*
3090	Bot I ne wote of wham it was.	*don't know about whom*
	Sho was bot fiftene yeres alde;	
	The knyght was lord of al that halde,	
	And that mayden was his ayre;	*heir*
	Sho was both gracious, gode, and fare.	
3095	Sone, when thai saw Sir Ywaine,	
	Smertly rase thai hym ogayne,	*they rose to meet him*
	And by the hand the lord him tase,	
	And unto him grete myrth he mase.	*makes*
	He said, "Sir, by swete Jhesus,	
3100	Thou ert ful welcum until us."	
	The mayden was bowsom and bayne	*gracious; willing*
	Forto unarme Syr Ywayne;	
	Serk and breke bath sho hym broght,	*Shirt; undergarment*
	That ful craftily war wroght	
3105	Of riche cloth soft als the sylk	
	And tharto white als any mylk.	
	Sho broght hym ful riche wedes to were,	
	Hose and shose and alkins gere.	*shoes; all sorts of other clothing*

	Sho payned hir with al hir myght	*tried conscientiously*
3110	To serve him and his mayden bright.	
	Sone thai went unto sopere,	
	Ful really served thai were	*royally*
	With metes and drinkes of the best,	
	And sethin war thai broght to rest.	*then*
3115	In his chaumber by hym lay	
	His owin lyoun and his may.	
	At morn, when it was dayes lyght,	
	Up thai rase and sone tham dyght.	*dressed*
	Sir Ywayn and hys damysele	
3120	Went ful sone til a chapele,	
	And thare thai herd a mes in haste	*mass*
	That was sayd of the Haly Gaste.	
	Efter Mes ordand he has	*Mass*
	Forth on his way fast forto pas;	
3125	At the lord hys leve he tase,	
	And grete thanking to him he mase.	*makes*
	The lord said, "Tak it to na greve,	*grievance*
	To gang hethin yit getes thou na leve.	*go hence yet you have no permission*
	Herein es ane unsely law,	*unhappy*
3130	That has bene used of ald daw	*since olden days*
	And bus be done for frend or fa.	*must be adhered to by*
	I sal do com byfor the twa	*shall make [you] come before*
	Grete serjantes of mekil myght;	
	And, whether it be wrang or right,	
3135	Thou most tak the shelde and spere	
	Ogaynes tham the forto were.	*fight*
	If thou overcum tham in this stoure,	*struggle*
	Than sal thou have al this honoure	
	And my doghter in mariage,	
3140	And also al myne heritage."	
	Than said Sir Ywayn, "Als mot I the,	*prosper*
	Thi doghter sal thou have for me;	*on behalf of*
	For a king or ane emparoure	
	May hir wed with grete honoure."	
3145	The lord said, "Here sal cum na knyght,	
	That he ne sal with twa champions fight;	
	So sal thou do on al wise,	*on this occasion*

164

For it es knawen custum assise."   *established*
Sir Ywaine said, "Sen I sal so,   *Since*
3150   Than es the best that I may do
       To put me baldly in thaire hend   *hands*
       And tak the grace that God wil send."
       The champions sone war forth broght.
       Sir Ywain sais, "By Him me boght,   *[who] redeemed me*
3155   Ye seme wele the devils sons,
       For I saw never swilk champions."
       Aither broght unto the place   *Each*
       A mikel rownd talvace   *great; shield*
       And a klub ful grete and lang,
3160   Thik fret with mani a thwang;   *fastened; thong*
       On bodies armyd wele thai ware,
       Bot thare hedes bath war bare.
       The lioun bremly on tham blist;   *fiercely; stared*
       When he tham saw ful wele he wist
3165   That thai sold with his mayster fight.
       He thoght to help him at his myght;
       With his tayl the erth he dang,   *struck*
       For to fyght him thoght ful lang.
       Of him a party had thai drede;   *somewhat [the fiends] were afraid*
3170   Thai said, "Syr knight, thou most nede
       Do thi lioun out of this place   *Remove*
       For to us makes he grete manace,
       Or yelde the til us als creant."   *defeated*
       He said, "That war noght mine avenant."   *honorable for me*
3175   Thai said, "Than do thi beste oway,   *Then put your beast away*
       And als sone sal we samyn play."   *together*
       He said, "Sirs, if ye be agast,   *frightened*
       Takes the beste and bindes him fast."
       Thai said, "He sal be bun or slane,   *bound*
3180   For help of him sal thou have nane.
       Thi self allane sal with us fight,
       For that es custume and the right."
       Than said Sir Ywain to tham sone:
       "Whare wil ye that the best be done?"   *put*
3185   "In a chamber he sal be loken   *locked*
       With gude lokkes ful stifly stoken."   *firmly closed*

165

Sir Ywain led than his lioun
Intil a chamber to presoun;
Than war bath tha devils ful balde,   *fearless*
3190   When the lioun was in halde.
Sir Ywayn toke his nobil wede   *armor*
And dight him yn, for he had nede;
And on his nobil stede he strade,
And baldely to tham bath he rade.
3195   His mayden was ful sare adred,
That he was so straitly sted,   *sore beset*
And unto God fast gan sho pray
Forto wyn him wele oway.
Than strake thai on him wonder sare
3200   With thaire clubbes that ful strang ware;
Opon his shelde so fast thai feld
That never a pece with other held;
Wonder it es that any man
Might bere the strakes that he toke than.
3205   Mister haved he of socoure,   *Greatly was he in need*
For he come never in swilk a stoure;
Bot manly evyr with al his mayn
And graithly hit he tham ogayn;   *readily*
And als it telles in the boke,
3210   He gaf the dubbil of that he toke.   *double*
    Ful grete sorow the lioun has
In the chameber whare he was;
And ever he thoght opon that dede,
How he was helpid in his nede,
3215   And he might now do na socowre   *assistance*
To him that helpid him in that stoure;
Might he out of the chamber breke,
Sone he walde his maister wreke.   *avenge*
He herd thaire strakes that war ful sterin,   *injurious (fierce)*
3220   And yern he waytes in ilka heryn,   *eagerly searches in every corner*
And al was made ful fast to hald.
At the last he come to the thriswald;   *threshold*
The erth thare kest he up ful sone,
Als fast als foure men sold have done
3225   If thai had broght bath bill and spade;   *pickaxe*

166

	A mekil hole ful sone he made.	*large*
	Yn al this was Sir Ywayn	
	Ful straitly parred with mekil payn,	*hemmed in*
	And drede he had, als him wele aght,	*ought*
3230	For nowther of tham na woundes laght.	*took*
	Kepe tham cowth thai wonder wele	*Protect themselves*
	That dintes derid tham never a dele;	*blows harmed; bit*
	It was na wapen that man might welde,	
	Might get a shever out of thaire shelde.	
3235	Tharof cowth Ywayn no rede,	
	Sare he douted to be ded;	*feared; dead*
	And also his damysel	
	Ful mekil murnyng made omell,	
	And wele sho wend he sold be slane,	
3240	And, sertes, than war hir socore gane.	
	Bot fast he stighteld in that stowre,	*fought; battle*
	And hastily him come socowre.	*help*
	Now es the lioun outbroken,	
	His maister sal ful sone be wroken.	*avenged*
3245	He rynnes fast with ful fell rese,	*runs; fierce rush*
	Than helpid it noght to prai for pese!	
	He stirt unto that a glotowne,	*jumped; vile fellow (glutton)*
	And to the erth he brayd him downe.	*pushed*
	Than was thare nane obout that place,	
3250	That thai ne war fayn of that faire chace.	*chase (pursuit)*
	The maiden had grete joy in hert;	
	Thai said, "He sal never rise in quert."	*good health (alive)*
	His felow fraisted with al his mayn	*tried*
	To raise him smertly up ogayn;	
3255	And right so als he stowped doun,	
	Sir Ywain with his brand was boun,	*sword; ready*
	And strake his nek-bane right insonder,	*asunder*
	Thareof the folk had mekil wonder.	
	His hevid trindeld on the sand:	*rolled*
3260	Thus had Ywain the hegher hand.	*upper*
	When he had feld that fowl feloun,	
	Of his stede he lighted down.	
	His lioun on that other lay:	
	Now wil he help him, if he may.	

3265	The lioun saw his maister cum,	
	And to hys part he wald have som.	*(i.e., eat)*
	The right sholder oway he rase,	*tore*
	Both arm and klob with him he tase,	*club*
	And so his maister gan he wreke.	*avenge*
3270	And, als he might, yit gan he speke	
	And said, "Sir knight, for thi gentry,	
	I pray the have of me mercy;	
	And by scill sal he mercy have,	*reason*
	What man so mekely wil it crave;	
3275	And tharfore grantes mercy to me."	
	Sir Ywain said, "I grant it the,	
	If that thou wil thi selven say,	
	That thou ert overcumen this day."	
	He said, "I grant, withowten fail,	
3280	I am overcumen in this batail	
	For pure ataynt and recreant."	*To the utmost extent; admitting defeat*
	Sir Ywayn said, "Now I the grant	
	Forto do the na mare dere,	*injury*
	And fro my liown I sal the were;	*protect*
3285	I grant the pese at my powere."	
	Than come the folk ful faire infere;	
	The lord and the lady als	
	Thai toke him faire obout the hals;	*neck*
	Thai saide, "Sir, now saltou be	
3290	Lord and syre in this cuntré,	
	And wed oure doghter, for sertayn."	
	Sir Ywain answerd than ogayn;	
	He said, "Sen ye gif me hir now,	
	I gif hir evyn ogayn to yow;	
3295	Of me forever I grant hir quite.	
	Bot, sir, takes it til no despite;	
	For, sertes, whif may I none wed,	*wife*
	Until my nedes be better sped.	
	Bot this thing, sir, I ask of the,	
3300	That al thir prisons may pas fre.	*these prisoners (the women in the sweatshops)*
	God has granted me this chance,	
	I have made thaire delyverance."	
	The lord answerd than ful tyte	

168

And said, "I grant the tham al quite.   *released*
3305 My doghter als, I rede, thou take;
Sho es noght worthi to forsake."
Unto the knyght Sir Ywain sais,
"Sir, I sal noght hir mysprays;   *disparage*
For sho es so curtays and hende,   *lovely*
3310 That fra hethin to the werldes ende   *hence*
Es no king ne emparoure
Ne no man of so grete honowre,
That he ne might wed that bird bright;   *noble lady*
And so wald I, if that I myght.
3315 I wald hir wed with ful gude chere,
Bot, lo, I have a mayden here;
To folow hir now most I nede,
Wheder so sho wil me lede.
Tharfore at this time haves goday."   *good day*
3320 He said, "Thou passes noght so oway,
Sen thou wil noght do als I tell,
In my prison sal thou dwell."
He said, "If I lay thare al my live,
I sal hir never wed to wive;
3325 For with this maiden most I wend
Until we cum whare sho wil lend."   *dwell*
The lord saw it was no bote   *avail*
Obout that mater more to mote.   *argue*
He gaf him leve oway to fare,
3330 Bot he had lever he had bene thare.   *rather; stayed*
  Sir Ywayn takes than forth infere
Al the prisons that thare were;   *prisoners*
Bifore hym sone thai come ilkane,
Nerehand naked and wo-bigane;   *Nearly*
3335 Stil he hoved at the gate,   *lingered*
Til thai war went al forth thareate.
Twa and twa ay went thai samyn   *together*
And made omang tham mikel gamyn.   *pleasure*
If God had cumen fra hevyn on hight
3340 And on this mold omang tham light,   *earth; dwelt*
Thai had noght made mare joy, sertain,
Than thai made to Syr Ywayne.

169

Folk of the toun com him biforn
And blissed the time that he was born;
3345 Of his prowes war thai wele payd: *pleased*
"In this werld es none slike," thai said.
Thai cunvayd him out of the toun
With ful faire processiowne.
The maidens than thaire leve has tane,
3350 Ful mekil myrth thai made ilkane;   *each one*
At thaire departing prayed thai thus:
"Oure lord God, mighty Jhesus,
He help yow, sir, to have yowre will
And shilde yow ever fra alkyns ill.'
3355 "Maidens," he said, "God mot yow se
And bring yow wele whare ye wald be."   *prosperity*
Thus thaire way forth er thai went: *onwards*
Na more unto tham wil we tent.   *attend*
    Sir Ywayn and his faire may
3360 Al the sevenight traveld thai.
The maiden knew the way ful wele
Hame until that ilk castele
Whare sho left the seke may;   *sick maiden*
And theder hastily come thai.
3365 When thai come to the castel gate,
Sho led Sir Ywain yn thareate.
The mayden was yit seke lyand;   *sick lying*
Bot, when thai talde hir this tithand,   *news*
That cumen was hir messagere
3370 And the knyght with hyr infere,
Swilk joy thareof sho had in hert,
Hir thoght that sho was al in quert.   *good health*
Sho said, "I wate my sister will
Gif me now that falles me till."
3375 In hir hert sho was ful light;
Ful hendly hailsed sho the knight: *greeted*
"A, sir," sho said, "God do the mede,
That thou wald cum in swilk a nede."
And al that in that kastel were
3380 Welkumd him with meri chere.
I can noght say, so God me glade,

170

Half the myrth that thai him made.
That night he had ful nobil rest
With alkins esment of the best.

3385 Als sone als the day was sent,
Thai ordaind tham and forth thai went. *prepared themselves*
  Until that town fast gan thai ride *To*
Whare the kyng sojorned that tide; *at that time*
And thare the elder sister lay,

3390 Redy forto kepe hyr day.
Sho traisted wele on Sir Gawayn, *trusted*
That no knyght sold cum him ogayn; *against*
Sho hopid thare was no knyght lifand, *thought*
In batail that might with him stand.

3395 Al a sevenight dayes bidene *taken together (i.e., a week)*
Wald noght Sir Gawayn be sene,
Bot in ane other toun he lay;
For he wald cum at the day
Als aventerous into the place, *adventurous*

3400 So that no man sold se his face;
The armes he bare war noght his awyn,
For he wald noght in court be knawyn.
Syr Ywayn and his damysell
In the town toke thaire hostell;

3405 And thare he held him prevely, *kept himself secretly*
So that none sold him ascry. *inform upon*
Had thai dwelt langer by a day,
Than had sho lorn hir land for ay.
Sir Ywain rested thare that nyght,

3410 And on the morn he gan hym dyght; *prepare*
On slepe left thai his lyowne *Asleep*
And wan tham wightly out of toun.
It was hir wil and als hys awyn
At cum to court als knyght unknawyn. *To*

3415   Sone obout the prime of day
Sir Gawayn fra thethin thare he lay, *thence*
Hies him fast into the felde
Wele armyd with spere and shelde;
No man knew him, les ne more,

3420 Bot sho that he sold fight fore.

171

The elder sister to court come
Unto the king at ask hir dome.   *judgment*
Sho said, "I am cumen with my knyght
Al redy to defend my right.
3425   This day was us set sesowne,   *appointed time*
And I am here al redy bowne;
And sen this es the last day,
Gifes dome and lates us wend oure way.   *Give judgment*
My sister has al sydes soght,
3430   Bot, wele I wate, here cums sho noght;
For, sertainly, sho findes nane,
That dar the batail undertane
This day for hir forto fyght
Forto reve fra me my right.   *rob*
3435   Now have I wele wonnen my land
Withowten dint of knightes hand.
What so my sister ever has mynt,   *claimed*
Al hir part now tel I tynt: *I proclaim lost*
Al es myne to sell and gyf,
3440   Als a wreche ay sal sho lyf.   *beggar forever shall she live*
Tharfore, Sir King, sen it es swa,
Gifes yowre dome and lat us ga."   *judgment*
    The king said, "Maiden, think noght lang."   *(i.e., don't presume)*
(Wele he wist sho had the wrang.)   *wrong*
3445   "Damysel, it es the assyse,   *custom*
Whils sityng es of the justise,
The dome nedes thou most habide;   *await*
For par aventure it may bityde,
Thi sister sal cum al bi tyme,
3450   For it es litil passed prime."   *dawn*
When the king had tald this scill,   *reasoned with them*
Thai saw cum rideand over a hyll
The yonger sister and hir knyght;
The way to town thai toke ful right.
3455   (On Ywains bed his liown lay,
And thai had stollen fra him oway.)
The elder maiden made il chere,
When thai to court cumen were.
The king withdrogh his jugement,   *withheld*

172

3460	For wele he trowed in his entent	*believed in his heart*
	That the yonger sister had the right,	
	And that sho sold cum with sum knyght;	
	Himself knew hyr wele inogh.	
	When he hir saw, ful fast he logh;	*laughed*
3465	Him liked it wele in his hert,	
	That he saw hir so in quert.	*in good spirits*
	Into the court sho toke the way,	
	And to the king thus gan sho say,	
	"God that governs alkin thing,	
3470	The save and se, Syr Arthure the Kyng,	
	And al the knyghtes that langes to the,	*belong*
	And also al thi mery menye.	
	Unto yowre court, sir, have I broght	
	An unkouth knyght that ye knaw noght;	*unknown*
3475	He sais that sothly for my sake	
	This batayl wil he undertake;	
	And he haves yit in other land	
	Ful felle dedes under hand;	*many*
	Bot al he leves, God do him mede,	
3480	Forto help me in my nede."	
	Hir elder sister stode hyr by,	
	And tyl hyr sayd sho hastily:	
	"For Hys luf that lens us life,	
	Gif me my right withouten strife,	
3485	And lat no men tharfore be slayn."	
	The elder sister sayd ogayn:	
	"Thi right es noght, for al es myne,	
	And I wil have yt mawgré thine.	*in spite of*
	Tharfore, if thou preche al day,	
3490	Here sal thou no thing bere oway."	
	The yonger mayden to hir says,	
	"Sister, thou ert ful curtays,	
	And gret dole es it forto se,	
	Slike two knightes als thai be,	
3495	For us sal put thamself to spill.	*in jeopardy*
	Tharefore now, if it be thi will,	
	Of thi gude wil to me thou gif	
	Sumthing that I may on lif."	*exist on*

173

	The elder said, "So mot I the,	
3500	Who so es ferd, I rede thai fle.	*If you're so afraid, I advise you to flee*
	Thou getes right noght, withowten fail,	
	Bot if thou win yt thurgh batail."	*Except that you*
	The yonger said, "Sen thou wil swa,	
	To the grace of God here I me ta;	*entrust*
3505	And Lord als He es maste of myght,	
	He send his socore to that knyght	
	That thus in dede of charité	
	This day antres hys lif for me."	*hazards*
	The twa knightes come bifor the king	
3510	And thare was sone ful grete gedering;	*assembly*
	For ilka man that walk might,	
	Hasted sone to se that syght.	
	Of tham this was a selly case,	*For; strange*
	That nowther wist what other wase;	*knew who; was*
3515	Ful grete luf was bitwix tham twa,	
	And now er aither other fa;	*each other's foe*
	Ne the king kowth tham noght knaw,	
	For thai wald noght thaire faces shew.	
	If owther of tham had other sene,	
3520	Grete luf had bene tham bitwene;	
	Now was this a grete selly	*marvel*
	That trew luf and so grete envy,	
	Als bitwix tham twa was than,	
	Might bath at anes be in a man.	
3525	The knightes for thase maidens love	
	Aither til other kast a glove,	
	And wele armed with spere and shelde	
	Thai riden both forth to the felde;	
	Thai stroke thaire stedes that war kene;	
3530	Litel luf was tham bitwene.	
	Ful grevosly bigan that gamyn,	
	With stalworth speres strake thai samen.	*together*
	And thai had anes togeder spoken,	*If; once*
	Had thare bene no speres broken.	
3535	Bot in that time bitid it swa,	
	That aither of tham wald other sla.	
	Thai drow swerdes and swang obout,	

174

	To dele dyntes had thai no dout.	*fear*
	Thaire sheldes war shiferd and helms rifen,	*splintered; helmets split*
3540	Ful stalworth strakes war thare gifen.	
	Bath on bak and brestes thare	
	War bath wounded wonder sare;	
	In many stedes might men ken	*places; see*
	The blode out of thaire bodies ren.	*run*
3545	On helmes thai gaf slike strakes kene	
	That the riche stanes al bidene	*gems everywhere (on their armor)*
	And other gere that was ful gude,	
	Was overcoverd al in blode.	
	Thaire helmes war evel brusten bath,	*wretchedly broken*
3550	And thai also war wonder wrath.	
	Thaire hauberkes als war al totorn	
	Both bihind and also byforn;	
	Thaire sheldes lay sheverd on the ground.	*broken*
	Thai rested than a litil stound	
3555	Forto tak thaire ande tham till,	*breath*
	And that was with thaire bother will.	*the will of them both*
	Bot ful lang rested thai noght,	
	Til aither of tham on other soght;	
	A stronge stowre was tham bitwene,	
3560	Harder had men never sene.	
	The king and other that thare ware,	
	Said that thai saw never are	*before*
	So nobil knightes in no place	
	So lang fight bot by Goddes grace.	
3565	Barons, knightes, squiers, and knaves	
	Said, "It es no man that haves	
	So mekil tresore ne nobillay,	*princely wealth*
	That might tham quite thaire dede this day."	
	Thir wordes herd the knyghtes twa;	*These*
3570	It made tham forto be more thra.	*reluctant to stop*
	Knightes went obout gude wane	*in great numbers*
	To mak the two sisters at ane:	*at one*
	Bot the elder was so unkinde,	
	In hir thai might no mercy finde;	
3575	And the right that the yonger hase,	
	Puttes sho in the kinges grace.	

175

The king himself and als the quene
And other knightes al bidene
And al that saw that dede that day,
3580 Held al with the yonger may;   *maiden*
And to the king al thai bisoght,
Whether the elder wald or noght,
That he sold evin the landes dele   *evenly; divide*
And gif the yonger damysele   *give*
3585 The half or els sum porciowne,
That sho mai have to warisowne,   *as reward*
And part the two knightes intwyn.   *in two*
"For, sertis," thai said, "it war grete syn,
That owther of tham sold other sla,
3590 For in the werld es noght swilk twa.
When other knightes," said thai, "sold sese,
Thamself wald noght asent to pese."
Al that ever saw that batayl,
Of thaire might had grete mervayl.
3595 Thai saw never under the hevyn
Twa knightes that war copled so evyn.   *matched*
Of al the folk was none so wise,
That wist whether sold have the prise;   *which of the two should*
For thai saw never so stalworth stoure,   *battle*
3600 Ful dere boght thai that honowre.
Grete wonder had Sir Gawayn,
What he was that faght him ogain;
And Sir Ywain had grete ferly,
Wha stode ogayns him so stifly.
3605 On this wise lasted that fight
Fra midmorn unto mirk night;   *dark*
And by that tyme, I trow, thai twa
War ful weri and sare alswa.
Thai had bled so mekil blode,
3610 It was grete ferly that thai stode;   *wonder*
So sare thai bet on bak and brest,   *beat*
Until the sun was gone to rest;
For nowther of tham wald other spare.
For mirk might thai than na mare,   *dark*
3615 Tharfore to rest thai both tham yelde.

176

	Bot or thai past out of the felde,	*before*
	Bitwix tham two might men se	
	Both mekil joy and grete peté.	
	By speche might no man Gawain knaw,	
3620	So was he hase and spak ful law;	*hoarse*
	And mekil was he out of maght	*might*
	For the strakes that he had laght.	*taken*
	And Sir Ywain was ful wery.	
	Bot thus he spekes and sais in hy:	*quickly*
3625	He said, "Syr, sen us failes light,	*we lack*
	I hope it be no lifand wight,	
	That wil us blame if that we twin.	*part*
	For of al stedes I have bene yn,	*places*
	With no man yit never I met	
3630	That so wele kowth his strakes set;	*could*
	So nobil strakes has thou gifen	
	That my sheld es al toreven."	*split open*
	Sir Gawayn said, "Sir, sertanly,	
	Thou ert noght so weri als I;	
3635	For if we langer fightand were,	
	I trow I might do the no dere.	*injury*
	Thou ert no thing in my det	
	Of strakes that I on the set."	
	Sir Ywain said, "In Cristes name,	
3640	Sai me what thou hat at hame."	*are called*
	He said, "Sen thou my name wil here	
	And covaites to wit what it were,	
	My name in this land mani wote;	*know*
	I hat Gawayn, the King son Lote."	*am called*
3645	Than was Sir Ywayn sore agast;	
	His swerde fra him he kast.	
	He ferd right als he wald wede,	*become mad*
	And sone he stirt down of his stede.	*leaps*
	He said, "Here es a fowl mischance	
3650	For defaut of conisance.	*recognition*
	A, sir," he said, "had I the sene,	
	Than had here no batel bene;	
	I had me yolden to the als tite,	*yielded myself; quickly*
	Als worthi war for descumfite."	

177

3655	"What man ertou?" said Sir Gawain.	
	"Syr," he said, "I hat Ywayne,	*am called*
	That lufes the more by se and sand	
	Than any man that es lifand,	
	For mani dedes that thou me did,	
3660	And curtaysi ye have me kyd.	*shown me*
	Tharfore, sir, now in this stoure	*contest*
	I sal do the this honowre:	
	I grant that thou has me overcumen	
	And by strenkyth in batayl nomen."	*taken*
3665	Sir Gawayn answerd als curtays:	
	"Thau sal noght do, sir, als thou sais;	
	This honowre sal noght be myne,	
	Bot, sertes, it aw wele at be thine;	*ought well to be yours*
	I gif it the here withowten hone	*give it to you here; delay*
3670	And grantes that I am undone."	
	Sone thai light, so sais the boke,	*dismounted*
	And aither other in armes toke	
	And kissed so ful fele sithe;	*many times*
	Than war thai both glad and blithe.	
3675	In armes so thai stode togeder,	
	Unto the king com ridand theder;	
	And fast he covait forto here	*desired to hear*
	Of thir knightes what thai were,	
	And whi thai made so mekil gamyn,	*they were so happy*
3680	Sen thai had so foghten samyn.	
	Ful hendli than asked the king,	
	Wha had so sone made saghteling	*Who; peace*
	Bitwix tham that had bene so wrath	
	And aither haved done other scath.	*injury*
3685	He said, "I wend ye wald ful fain	
	Aither of thow have other slayn,	
	And now ye er so frendes dere."	
	"Sir King," said Gawain, "Ye sal here.	
	For unknawing and hard grace	*bad fortune*
3690	Thus have we foghten in this place;	
	I am Gawayn, yowre awin nevow,	*nephew*
	And Sir Ywayn faght with me now.	
	When we war nere weri, iwys,	*nearly exhausted, truly*

178

	Mi name he frayned and I his;	*asked*
3695	When we war knawin, sone gan we sese.	
	Bot, sertes, sir, this es no lese,	*lie*
	Had we foghten forth a stownde,	*a minute longer*
	I wote wele I had gone to grounde;	
	By his prowes and his mayne,	
3700	I wate, for soth, I had bene slayne."	
	Thir wordes menged al the mode	*disturbed; heart*
	Of Sir Ywain als he stode;	
	"Sir," he said, "so mot I go,	
	Ye knaw yowreself it es noght so.	
3705	Sir King," he said, "withowten fail,	
	I am overcumen in this batayl."	
	"Nai, sertes," said Gawain, "bot am I."	
	Thus nowther wald have the maistri,	
	Bifore the king gan aither grant,	
3710	That himself was recreant.	*defeated*
	Than the king and hys menye	
	Had bath joy and grete peté;	
	He was ful fayn thai frendes were,	
	And that thai ware so funden infere.	*found*
3715	The kyng said, "Now es wele sene	
	That mekil luf was yow bitwene."	
	He said, "Sir Ywain, welkum home!"	
	For it was lang sen he thare come.	
	He said, "I rede ye both assent	
3720	To do yow in my jujement;	
	And I sal mak so gude ane ende	
	That ye sal both be halden hende."	*held [to be] courteous*
	Thai both assented sone thartill	*thereto*
	To do tham in the kynges will,	
3725	If the maydens wald do so.	
	Than the king bad knyghtes two	
	Wend efter the maydens bath,	*Fetch; both*
	And so thai did ful swith rath.	
	Bifore the kyng when thai war broght	
3730	He tald unto tham als him thoght,	
	"Lystens me now, maydens hende,	
	Yowre grete debate es broght til ende;	

179

So fer forth now es it dreven
That the dome most nedes be gifen,   *judgment must*
3735   And I sal deme yow als I can."   *judge*
The elder sister answerd than:
"Sen ye er king that us sold were,   *protect*
I pray yow do to me na dere."   *injury*
He said, "I wil let for na saw   *neglect; speech*
3740   Forto do the landes law.
Thi yong sister sal have hir right,
For I se wele that thi knyght
Es overcumen in this were."   *conflict*
Thus said he anely hir to fere,   *only; frighten*
3745   And for he wist hir wil ful wele,
That sho wald part with never a dele.
"Sir," sho said, "sen thus es gane,
Now most I, whether I wil or nane,
Al yowre cumandment fufill,
3750   And tharfore dose right als ye will."
The king said, "Thus sal it fall,
Al yowre landes depart I sall.
Thi wil es wrang, that have I knawin.
Now sal thou have noght bot thin awin,
3755   That es the half of al bydene."
Than answerd sho ful tite in tene   *quickly in anger*
And said, "Me think ful grete outrage
To gif hir half myne heritage."
The king said, "For yowre bother esse   *the ease of you both*
3760   In hir land I sal hir sese,   *(put in legal possession of a feudal holding)*
And sho sal hald hir land of the
And to the tharfore mak fewté;   *fealty*
Sho sal the luf als hir lady,
And thou sal kith thi curtaysi,   *show*
3765   Luf hir efter thine avenant,   *honor*
And sho sal be to the tenant."
This land was first, I understand,
That ever was parted in Ingland.
Than said the king, "Withowten fail,
3770   For tha luf of that batayl
Al sisters that sold efter bene

180

Sold part the landes tham bitwene."
  Than said the king to Sir Gawain,
And als he prayed Sir Ywain
3775   Forto unlace thaire riche wede;
And tharto had thai bath grete nede.
Als thai thusgate stod and spak,   *thusly*
The lyown out of the chamber brak.
Als thai thaire armurs sold unlace,
3780   Come he rinand to that place.   *running*
Bot he had, or he come thare,
Soght his mayster whideware;   *far and wide*
And ful mekil joy he made
When he his mayster funden hade.   *found*
3785   On ilka side than might men se,
The folk fast to toun gan fle;
So war thai ferd for the liowne
Whan thai saw him theder bown.
Syr Ywain bad tham cum ogayn
3790   And said, "Lordinges, for sertayn,
Fra this beste I sal yow were,   *protect*
So that he sal do yow no dere.
And, sirs, ye sal wele trow mi sawes; *believe my words*
We er frendes and gude felaws.
3795   He es mine and I am his;
For na tresore I wald him mys."
  When thai saw this was sertain,
Than spak thai al of Sir Ywaine:
"This es the Knight with the Liown,
3800   That es halden of so grete renown.
This ilk knight the geant slogh;
Of dedis he es doghty inogh."
Than said Sir Gawayn sone in hi,   *quickly*
"Me es bitid grete velani;   *come to*
3805   I cri the mercy, Sir Ywayne,
That I have trispast the ogayn. *trespassed against you*
Thou helped mi syster in hir nede;
Evil have I quit the now thi mede.
Thou anterd thi life for luf of me;   *risked*
3810   And als mi sister tald of the,

181

Thou said that we ful fele dawes   *days*
Had bene frendes and gude felawes.
Bot wha it was ne wist I noght.
Sethen have I had ful mekil thoght,
3815 And yit for al that I do can,
I cowth never here of na man,
That me coth tell toure ne town
Of the Knight with the Liown."
When thai had unlaced thaire wede,
3820 Al the folk toke ful gode hede,
How that beste his bales to bete   *beast; suffering to abate*
Likked his maister both hend and fete.   *Licked*
Al the men grete mervail hade
Of the mirth the lyown made.
3825 When the knightes war broght to rest,
The king gert cum sone of the best   *brought immediately*
Surgiens that ever war sene
Forto hele tham both bidene.
    Sone so thai war hale and sownd,   *As soon as; healthy*
3830 Sir Ywayn hies him fast to found.   *hastens quickly to set out*
Luf was so in his hert fest,   *Love; steadfast in his heart*
Night ne day haved he no rest,
Bot he get grace of his lady,   *Unless*
He most go wode or for luf dy.
3835 Ful preveli forth gan he wende   *secretly*
Out of the court fra ilka frende.
He rides right unto the well,
And thare he thinkes forto dwell.
His gode lyon went with him ay,
3840 He wald noght part fro him oway.   *away*
He kest water opon the stane:
The storm rase ful sone onane,
The thoner grisely gan outbrest;   *thunder*
Him thoght als al the grete forest
3845 And al that was obout the well
Sold have sonken into hell.
    The lady was in mekyl dout,
For al the kastel walles obout
Quoke so fast that men might think

3850   That al into the erth sold synk.
    Thai trembled fast, both boure and hall,
    Als thai unto the grund sold fall.
    Was never in this mydlerde   *earth*
    In no kastell folk so ferde.   *afraid*
3855   Bot wha it was wele wist Lunet;   *knew*
    Sho said, "Now er we hard byset;
    Madame, I ne wate what us es best,
    For here now may we have no rest.
    Ful wele I wate ye have no knight,
3860   That dar wende to yowre wel and fight
    With him that cumes yow to asaile;
    And, if he have here no batayle
    Ne findes none yow to defend,
    Yowre lose bese lorn withouten end."   *renoun will be lost forever*
3865   The lady said sho wald be dede;
    "Dere Lunet, what es thi rede?   *advice*
    Wirk I wil by thi kounsail,
    For I ne wate noght what mai avail."
    "Madame," sho said, "I wald ful fayn
3870   Kownsail yow if it might gayn.
    Bot in this case it war mystere   *necessary*
    To have a wiser kownsaylere."   *counselor*
    And by desait than gan sho say,   *wile*
    "Madame, par chance this ilk day
3875   Sum of yowre knightes mai cum hame
    And yow defend of al this shame."
    "A," sho said, "Lunet, lat be;
    Speke namore of my menye;
    For wele I wate, so God me mend,
3880   I have na knight me mai defend.
    Tharfore my kownsail bus the be,   *it is necessary for you to be*
    And I wil wirk al efter the,
    And tharfore help at al thi myght."
    "Madame," sho said, "had we that knyght,
3885   That es so curtais and avenant   *honorable*
    And has slane the grete geant,
    And als that the thre knightes slogh,
    Of him ye myght be trist inogh.   *In; have confidence enough*

Bot forthermar, madame, I wate,

3890   He and his lady er at debate

And has bene so ful many day;

And als I herd hym selvyn say,   *heard him say himself*

He wald bileve with no lady   *remain with*

Bot on this kownand utterly,   *agreement*

3895   That thai wald mak sertayn ath   *oath*

To do thaire might and kunyng bath

Trewly both by day and naght

To mak him and hys lady saght."   *reconciled*

    The lady answerd sone hir tyll,

3900   "That wil I do with ful gode will;

Unto the here mi trowth I plight

That I sal tharto do mi might."

Sho said, "Madame, be ye noght wrath,

I most nedes have of yow an ath,   *oath*

3905   So that I mai be sertayn."

The lady said, "That will I fayn."

Lunet than riche relikes toke,

The chalis and the mes-boke;

On knese the lady down hir set

3910   (Wit ye wele, than liked Lunet),

Hir hand opon the boke sho laid,

And Lunet althus to hir said,   *thusly*

"Madame," sho said, "Thou salt swere here

That thou sal do thi powere

3915   Both dai and night opon al wise

Withouten anikyns fayntise   *any kind of*

To saghtel the Knyght with the Liown   *reconcile*

And his lady of grete renowne,

So that no faut be funden in the."

3920   Sho said, "I grant, it sal so be."

Than was Lunet wele paid of this;   *well pleased*

The boke sho gert hir lady kys.   *made*

    Sone a palfray sho bistrade,

And on hir way fast forth sho rade.

3925   The next way ful sone sho nome,

Until sho to the well come.

Sir Ywain sat under the thorn,

184

And his lyoun lay him byforn.
Sho knew him wele by his lioun,
3930 And hastily sho lighted downe;
And als sone als he Lunet sagh,
In his hert than list him lagh.   *laugh*
Mekil mirth was when thai met,
Aither other ful faire has gret.
3935 Sho said, "I love grete God in trone
That I have yow fun so sone,   *found*
And tithandes tel I yow biforn;
Other sal my lady be manesworn   *forsworn*
On relikes and bi bokes brade,
3940 Or els ye twa er frendes made."
Sir Ywain than was wonder glad
For the tithandes that he had;
He thanked hir ful fele sith
That sho wald him slike gudenes kith,   *show*
3945 And sho him thanked mekill mare
For the dedes that war done are.   *formerly*
So ather was in other det,
That both thaire travail was wele set.
He sais, "Talde thou hir oght my name?"
3950 Sho said, "Nay, than war I to blame.
Thi name sho sal noght wit for me,
Til ye have kyssed and saghteld be."   *reconciled*
        Than rade thai forth toward the town,
And with tham ran the gude lyoun.
3955 When thai come to the castel gate,
Al went thai in thareat.
Thai spak na word to na man born
Of al the folk thai fand byforn.
Als sone so the lady herd sayn,
3960 Hir damisel was cumen ogayn
And als the liown and the knight,
Than in hert sho was ful lyght;
Scho covait ever of al thing
Of him to have knawlageing.
3965 Sir Ywain sone on knese him set,
When he with the lady met.

185

Lunet said to the lady sone,
"Take up the knight, madame, have done!
And, als covenand bituix us was,
3970 Makes his pese fast or he pas."   *before he goes forth*
Than did the ladi him up rise;
"Sir," sho said, "opon al wise,
I wil me pain in al thing
Forto mak thi saghtelyng
3975 Bitwix the and thi lady bryght."
"Medame," said Lunet, "That es right,
For nane bot ye has that powere.
Al the soth now sal ye here.
Madame," sho said, "es noght at layn,   *nothing to conceal*
3980 This es my lord Sir Ywaine.
Swilk luf God bitwix yow send,
That may last to yowre lives end."
     Than went the lady fer obak,   *aback*
And lang sho stode or that sho spak.
3985 Sho said, "How es this, damysele?
I wend thou sold be to me lele,   *loyal*
That makes me, whether I wil or noght,
Luf tham that me wa has wroght,
So that me bus be forsworn   *I must be*
3990 Or luf tham that wald I war lorn.   *them who wished*
Bot, whether it torn to wele or ill,
That I have said, I sal fulfill."
Wit ye wele, than Sir Ywaine
Of the wordes was ful fayne.
3995 "Madame," he said, "I have miswroght,
And that I have ful dere boght.   *dearly paid for*
Grete foly I did, the soth to say,
When that I past my terme-day;
And, sertes, wha so had so bityd,
4000 Thai sold have done right als I dyd.
Bot I sal never thorgh Goddes grace
At mi might do more trispase;
And what man so wil mercy crave,
By Goddes law he sal it have."
4005 Than sho asented saghteling to mak;   *peace*

And sone in arms he gan hir tak
And kissed hir ful oft sith:
Was he never are so blith.
   Now has Sir Ywain ending made
4010   Of al the sorows that he hade.
Ful lely lufed he ever hys whyfe   *wife*
And sho him als hyr owin life;
That lasted to thaire lives ende.
And trew Lunet, the maiden hende,
4015   Was honord ever with ald and ying
And lifed at hir owin likyng.
Of alkins thing sho has maystri,
Next the lord and the lady.
Al honord hir in toure and toun.
4020   Thus the Knyght with the Liown
Es turned now to Syr Ywayn
And has his lordship al ogayn;
And so Sir Ywain and his wive
In joy and blis thai led thaire live.
4025   So did Lunet and the liown
Until that ded haves dreven tham down.
   Of tham na mare have I herd tell
Nowther in rumance ne in spell.   *tale*
Bot Jhesu Criste for his grete grace
4030   In hevyn-blis grante us a place
To bide in, if his wills be.
Amen, amen, par charité.

Ywain and Gawayn thus makes endyng
God grant us all hys dere blyssing.
            Amen.

[Abbreviations: MS = BL Cotton Galba E. ix. R = Joseph Ritson's *Ancient Engleish Metrical Romancees* (1802). S = Gustav Schleich, *Ywain and Gawain* (1887). F&H = French and Hale, *Middle English Metrical Romances* (1964). EETS = Albert B. Friedman and Norman T. Harrington, *Ywain and Gawain* (1964). Mills = Everyman edition. Full references to these works appears in the Select Bibliography, after the Introduction to this romance.]

Title. *Ywain and Gawain* was probably the poet's intended title, since he makes specific, internal references to the poem this way; he refers, for example, to the audience in line 4 as those who "harkens Ywayne and Gawayne." The poem is clearly about the adventures of Ywain, not Gawain, and EETS speculates that the name "Gawain" was added for audience appeal, he being the more popular and better known of the two knights. Ywain appears in several Arthurian works, as early as the sixth-century *Book of Taliesin*, which contains three panegyrics to him. He is best known, of course, in Chrétien's *Yvain*, but can also be found in the comic thirteenth-century Welsh *Dream of Rhonabwy*, where he and Arthur play at chess. Also the thirteenth-century Welsh *Owain* includes rudiments of Chrétien and the English poet's story of the knight who kills a woman's husband and then marries her, only to lose her and regain her once again.

1   There is a tear at the top of MS, and a brown stain extends from the title down through the first few lines of the text. A large capital letter, trimmed in red and blue extends down four lines into the text.

6   *Tharfore listens a lytel stownde* indicates that this poem, like *Sir Perceval*, belongs to the minstrel tradition, where the bard must settle his audience before he can begin his tale. Such a request for attention is noticeably absent from Chrétien's courtly romance.

9   *sayes*. Taglicht notes that the spelling is *says, sais* everywhere else in the text and that the scribe spells -*s* suffixes with great consistency: "1) Words ending in a stressed diphthong or /i:/ or /u:/ take -*es*, e.g. *praies* 2329, *sawes* 83, *sewes* 3053, *flies* 94, *lyes* 986, *browes* 261. Except: *says*, and *dais: lays* 2791 . . . . 2) Words ending in any other stressed vowel take -*se*, the -*e* marking the length

of the preceding vowel, e.g. *fase* 1534, *gase* 146, *dose* 143, *trese* 2965, *sese* 1899. 3) Disyllabic words ending in *l, r, n, m,* and stressed on the first syllable always remain disyllabic; the ending is normally *-s,* e.g. *girdels* 1401, *fingers* 300, *listens* 6, *Adams* 1052; rarely *-es,* e.g. *shuldres* 424. 4) Words ending in a plosive consonant always take *-es* regardless of the position of the stress, e.g. *landes* 958, *takes* 3563, *getes* 2986, *wodes* 1446, *lesinges* 151, *hauberkes* 649, *covaites* 3642, *herlotes* 2404. Except: *wirships* 1572" (*NM,* p. 641).

16 *Witsononday.* See *Sir Perceval,* note to line 393.

17 *es* is written above the line. EETS notes that the English poet has changed Chrétien's "Carduel in Gales" to Cardiff in Wales, probably assuming Chrétien's geography here to have been inaccurate. Although Cardiff is not as rich in Arthurian tradition as other localities in Wales, it was the departure point for several of the king's adventures.

33 *bitwene.* MS: *bitwne;* R's emendation.

35 The concern with "trowthe," at once the basis for all feudal society and the bond between individuals, echoes throughout the poem: failure to keep one's vows brings shame and ultimately, destruction. Yet as the poem will reveal, one must make one's vows judiciously, for truth and justice must be aligned, and careless promises can lead to ruin. See Gayle Hamilton (1976).

47 MS is split at the top of the page, and a brown stain extends through line 58 on the outer edge. This line begins with a large red capital letter "A," presumably due to another hand.

53 *slepe.* A brown stain on the manuscript obliterates the word. R's emendation.

55 ff. *Sir Dedyne* is a puzzle. A knight whose name bears this spelling appears nowhere else in the Arthurian canon. Chrétien's spelling of the name is "Didonez," and EETS suggests that the English poet was actually referring to Sir Dodynas "the Saueage," who was killed by Lancelot in a tournament (p. 111). However, if the poet were aware of the prose *Tristan* (mid-thirteenth century), he might have had in mind Sir Dinadan, whose amused skepticism toward codes of chivalry would have worked well in this context. *Sir Segramore* is a knight of the Round Table who appears in Chrétien's *Perceval,* the prose *Tristan,* and Froissart's *Meliador.* He was one of the last to be killed by Mordred

in Arthur's final battle. According to the Vulgate, he is the nephew of the Emperor of Constantinople and has a mysterious illness that makes him the object of Kay's contempt. For Kay, see note to lines 261–63 of *Sir Perceval*.

58   *Colgrevance* is Ywain's cousin, who appears in several of the Prose Vulgate romances and briefly in Malory.

68 ff.   Kay's attitude towards Colgrevance's display of manners is probably due to the medieval notion that one's outward grace reflected one's inward grace, or that "manners maketh the man." Kay's failure to rise immediately upon the queen's entrance has put him at a disadvantage in courtesy, or so he believes.

79   *fayntise*. EETS glosses as "guile or deceit"; but Taglicht argues sensibly for "sluggishness" on the basis of the French *peresce* (Chrétien, line 80).

80   *Ne us denyd noght forto rise*. MS: *Ne for us denyd noght forto rise*. F&H's emendation, which improves the meter and avoids the awkward *for/forto* repetition. Eyeskip may be at work from the beginning of the previous line; or the *for* may reflect an awkward attempt to follow Chrétien's *Por ce que nos ne deignames*, as F&H suggest (p. 488). EETS follows F&H. Taglicht defends MS reading, however, calling the emendation unnecessary and likewise citing the French source to which the MS is more close. Taglicht glosses the unemended meaning as "Nor because we did not deign to rise."

84   *despise*. S emends to *despised*.

93   *manes*. EETS glosses the sense as "grieves," as if the word derived from *moan*. Taglicht suggests that it is a contracted form of *manace* (*NM*, p. 642). Mills glosses as "upsets."

94   MS is split here, obliterating the word that R supplies as *flies*. Followed by S, F&H, EETS, and Mills.

98   *brok*. Colgrevance compares the disagreeable Kay to a malodorous badger. The expression is proverbial.

100–15   A brown stain on MS obscures the beginning of these lines. Most editors follow R's readings, though in line 103, instead of *Bot of*, as in R, S, F&H, and EETS,

Taglicht reads, "Bot ofthink that I bygan," and glosses the sense as "But am sorry that I began" (*NM*, p. 642).

135   *me*. Added above the line in another hand.

149   An initial capital letter "H" in blue.

157   The abrupt change in topography, from civilization to the wild woods, often signals the reader to expect the "marvelous."

186   The *MED* translates "burde" as "shield," but EETS suggests that "burde" is a calque from Chrétien's *table*, with the sense of a "sheet of metal," hence a "gong." Taglicht questions the gloss and prefers "shield." Unless we are to believe that one would smite a shield to summon one's attendants, the EETS explanation makes better sense. Originally the "burd" may have been associated with the magic spring as part of a rite to conjure storms, but neither Chrétien nor the English poet seems to have clearly understood this connection (EETS, pp. 113–14). Mills glosses *burde* as "panel," but a panel, likely to have been of wood, would have been battered by a hammer's strong blow.

187   EETS notes the missing relative pronoun, observing numerous other instances (e.g. lines 256, 1068, 1981, 3076–78, 3154).

244   Critics have suggested that the Giant Herdsman, who appears in several romances, can be seen as a foil for Ywain, who will meet up with him in line 612. But just *how* he operates in this regard is an open debate. Doob suggests that, being outwardly ugly, he retains his rationality, as his domination over the beasts implies, while Ywain, at this point in his life, is both "morally ugly" and truly "irrational" (pp. 147–48). Wilson, however, sees in the Herdsman's domination over the animals a "monstrousness" which his "hideous animal features" reflect, a dominance at odds with Ywain's subsequent magnanimous relationship with his own beast (pp. 71–72).

253–54 S reverses these two lines.

309   *al torent*. MS: *alto rent*. Taglicht notes similar formations in MS 823 (*alto drogh*), 934 (*alto breke*), 2619 (*alto rent*), 3551 (*alto torn*), and 3632 (*alto reven*). The forms *torent*, *todrogh*, etc. appear nowhere in MS.

339   Storm-making springs can be found in early classical literature (Pausanias and Pliny, for example), and were often cited by travellers to the East into the Middle Ages and beyond. The presence of anything "unclean" or foreign to the well that stirred the waters was likely to bring about a disturbance. In the West, such writers as Geoffrey of Tours and Nennius narrated accounts of these springs, some of them reputedly found in Wales (George L. Hamilton, "Storm-Making Springs: Rings of Invisibility and Protection — Studies in the Sources of the *Yvain* of Chrétien de Troyes," *Romanic Review* 2 [1911], 355–75).

354   Taglicht emends to *groved*.

403   A red capital "S" here.

436   *bitide*. MS: *bite*. So in R, S, and F&H, who gloss the sense as "for fear worse might befall me." Emendation suggested by E. Kolbing in *English Studies* 24 (1897), 146, and followed by EETS and Mills. F. Holthausen suggests *abide* (*Anglia* 14 [1891–92]), 319.

439   A blue capital Þ here.

457   A red initial letter "N."

470   *karcas of Saynt Martyne*. F&H gloss: "Meaning a flitch of dried beef." EETS notes that Martinmas is a time of slaughtering and suggests that since Saint Martin was noted for his temperance, he is being contrasted here with the heavy drinker who boasts and brags. Kay, true to form, has no use for Ywain's brave words; he implies that Ywain is more a drunkard than a butcher or man of action.

478   *leve at ilke frende*. Kay's scurrilous innuendo is that if Ywain does undertake the quest he had better say goodbye to everyone now, since he will not come back.

482   *say I bad*. Taglicht glosses: "say I told you to" and challenges EETS's "predicted" for *bad*, which he takes to be a preterite for *bede* ("offer") and notes that the text does not confuse *bede* with *bid*, from OE *biddan* (*NM*, p. 643). Mills reads: *say, "I bad!"* and glosses *bad* as "am staying." I follow EETS, which makes good sense to me.

483   A blue initial Þ.

485   *withyn.* MS *with thu.*

509   A red initial capital "A."

522   Arthur's father, Uther Pendragon ("head dragon" or "foremost leader"), appears in Geoffrey of Monmouth's *Historia*, where his London court, his association with Merlin, and Arthur's enchanted birth are described.

526   *barn.* Taglicht, noting that MS shows no sign of *er > ar*, suggests that *barn* may be a variant of *baron* (*NM*, p. 643).

525   It is no accident that Arthur chooses to set out on Saint John's Eve, for that day, June 23, coincided with midsummer's eve and its pagan celebrations. "Elves and fairies were abroad," an opportune time for marvels (EETS, p.116).

559   *karl of Kaymes kyn.* EETS notes that "according to tradition monsters, elves, giants, and spirits of hell were descended from Cain, who was the father of all evil progeny" (pp. 116–17). This, of course, is Grendel's heritage in *Beowulf.* See O. F. Emerson, "Legends of Cain, Especially in Old and Middle English," *PMLA* 21 (1906), 831–929.

575   *palfray.* MS: *palfra.*

585   A blue capital "F."

599   Although the word "sty" or "sti" could refer to a small road or path, it was often used in the Middle Ages to portend the ominous, as in the expressions "prisoun sti" or "helle sti," for the deepest pit of hell (MED, s.v.).

611   A red capital "A."

624   In MS, after *thonor* is the word *hayl*, cancelled by a single line drawn through the middle of the word. EETS without explanation drops the *and* after *thonor*.

649   *On thaire hauberkes.* MS: *Thaire hauberkes.* "[At] thaire hauberkes" first suggested by S; followed by F&H and EETS. S deletes *that* from the line.

664   *folowd.* MS: *folow.* S's emendation.

673   *iwys*. MS: *I wys*, as always in this text. Emendation by S, F&H, and EETS.

686   *Than*. MS: *that*. S's emendation, followed by F&H, EETS, and Mills.

674   Chrétien is very specific in the functioning of the trap: built like a rat trap ("l'arbaleste qui agaite/ le rat"), it had a blade poised to fall at the slightest trigger, and was designed to cut apart anything caught in its path. Beneath the gate are two fulcrums ("trabuchet") connected to the razor-like edge of the portcullis. When activated, these caused the gate to drop, severing anything in its way. Curiously, in light of the English poet's omission of these realistic details, he goes on to treat in a much more naturalistic manner the architectural arrangement of the castle, replacing Chrétien's elaborate fantasy layout.

708   *Here*. The first two letters of this word are obscured by a water stain. R reads *Her*; S and F&H read *Thare*. EETS reads *[He]re* and Mills *Here*.

711   *wate*. EETS glosses as "wait, watch," and places a comma after *wate*, for a rather different reading of the line.

712   *Thai*. MS: *The*. S follows MS. R, F&H, and EETS emend to *Th[ai]*. Mills normalizes to *they*.

737   Magic rings (usually supplied by women) often figure heavily in the story line of medieval romances where they serve to activate the plot and to tie together its loose ends. In this regard, see *Sir Perceval*.

797   "o" in *noght* added above the line.

809   *Sir Ywaine saw*. MS: *Sir saw*. After *Sir* is a faint *Yw* is written above a caret. In the same hand *Ywaine* is written in the margin.

843   *said* added by another hand above the line.

868   *swownyng*; MS: *swownyg*. F&H's emendation, followed by EETS and Mills. R and S emend to *swowyng*.

869   A blue initial capital.

881   *gane*; M: *yane* by another hand over erasure. R's emendation, followed by all.

904	*ful.* MS and R: *fu.* Schleich's emendation.
909	A red initial capital.
915	MS reads *said* above the line in another hand.
931	*Sho kend al.* MS: *Sho al.* R's emendation followed by S, F&H, and EETS. Mills emends to *Sho [wist] al.*
946	The English poet copies this character directly from Chrétien. In both works there is the suggestion that the audience would be familiar with this woman, but no clue to her identify is found in the literature.
959	A blue capital Þ.
987	*thoue.* F&H read MS as *thone*, which they emend to *thou.*
990	*me na mawgré.* Barely legible letters are written above the line after *me.* S reads as *na* and so emends, followed by F&H, EETS, and Mills. R reads as *on.*
998	*bot.* MS: *bo.* R's emendation, followed by all.
1057	*tithyng.* MS: *tithng.* R's emendation.
1059	Another hand has written *him* above the line.
1070	*he* is written above the line.
1072	*Sho* is written out in the left margin.
1133	*he* is written in another hand over erasure.
1146	Salados the Rouse is apparently the English poet's rendering of Chrétien's "Esclados le Ros," a character who does not figure again in the Arthurian legends.
1152	Another hand has written *said* above the line; the "y" of "nay" is written over an indecipherable letter.

1189   A red initial capital.

1254   EETS notes that in the naming of the lady, the English poet has misread a passage in Chrétien: "Prise a Laudine de Landuc/ La dame, qui fu fille au duc/ Laudunet, don an note un law." Mistaking "a Laudine" as one word, he subsequently anglicized it to "Alundyne."

1291   A blue initial capital.

1321   A red capital Þ.

1365   A blue capital "S."

1440   *forto*. MS: *to* is added above the line by another hand.

1449   A red capital initial.

1452 ff. The situation set up by the poet here — the husband's proving himself in "armes" after a happy marriage — is one Chaucer exploits from a female point of view in the Franklin's Tale. In both stories this motif serves to portend trouble.

1539   *ay, whils*. MS: *aywhils*.

1551   A blue capital "S."

1567   Arthur's court tended to move about and one of its seats was Chester. Geoffrey Ashe and others have argued that Chester might have been the "Cair Legion" mentioned in Nennius' *Annales Cambriae*, thus the site of Arthur's ninth battle (*A Guidebook to Arthurian Britain* [London and New York: Longman, 1980], s.v.).

1637   A red capital "S."

1640   MS: *murnig*: R's emendation, followed by others. Madness, following the separation or estrangement from one's beloved, is a part of the courtly code (see, for example, Chaucer's Knight's Tale or "Sir Orfeo"). One may view Ywain as a "Traytur untrew," both to his vow to Alundyne that he will return within the year, and to the real meaning of chivalry. He has been playing at tournaments when he should have been helping the weak and defenseless, and his behavior will subsequently change. But first he must do "penance" in the wild woods. On the other hand, Ywain's frustration may have led to an imbalance of humours, thus associating him with the medieval "wild man" who must gain control of the "beasts" within him. See Anne Hunsaker Hawkins, "Yvain's Madness," *PQ* 71 (1992), 377–97.

1687   *drank*. MS: *drak*. Ritson's emendation.

1700   *ilka*. EETS reads *ilke*.

1709   A blue initial capital.

1713   MS: *A naked man I think I se*. S leaves the line unemended, looking upon *naked* as a substantive (i.e., a "naked man"). R emends to "naked man" and EETS agrees, suggesting that the antecedent "it" in the next line is used here "for a human being regardless of sex." Mills follows R and EETS, as I do too. See resumé of the dispute in EETS.

1745   Taglicht emends *we* to *me*.

1753   Morgan, of course, immediately suggests Morgan le Fay, Arthur's sister, who was believed to have been skilled in medical arts. It is unclear why the English poet refers to her as "he" several times in the following lines. There is no indication in Chrétien that the French poet thought of Morgan as masculine, but Roger Sherman Loomis (*Arthurian Tradition and Chrétien de Troyes* [New York: Octagon Books], 1949, p. 307) cites some evidence that this character's sex was undetermined. Mills emends "He" to "Sho" in line 1755.

1789   A red initial capital.

1823   Text reads *P charite*. R reads as if the abbreviation for "r" is missing in the text, and emends accordingly; followed by S, EETS, and Mills.

1842   Lunet's motive for tossing away the ointment box and then lying to her mistress is obscured in the English poet's work, but not in Chrétien's. There the maiden is told that she must use the precious ointment *only* on the effected part — on Yvain's brow and temples alone, since his brain is causing his madness. Wasting the salve, it is stressed, would not help the knight. In her eagerness to cure

Yvain, however, the maiden deliberately disobeys — thus her ruse to ward off her mistress' anger.

1869   A blue capital "S."

1899   *he*. MS: *the*; R's emendation, followed by S, EETS, and Mills.

1975   A red capital "N."

2055   *obout*. EETS reads *about*, but Taglicht notes that "the form with initial *a*- does not occur in this text" (*NM*, p. 645).

2059   A blue capital "O."

2107   The pronoun "it" is probably used in this instance because Ywain does not know the identity (hence, the sex) of the person in the prison-chapel (EETS).

2136   From barbaric times it was customary in French law for a woman who has accused someone or has been accused herself to be burned at the stake if her husband or champion fails to win the battle fought to exonerate her (EETS).

2181   MS lacks *he*; R's suggestion, followed by S, EETS, and Mills.

2182   This an allusion to Chrétien's *Lancelot* (which that poet was presumably composing simultaneously), although the English poet might not have known it. In the French poem, a strange knight enters Arthur's household and demands to take the queen back to his land where he has imprisoned Arthur's people. If a knight will follow the queen and bring her back, the people will be freed. Kay sets out and then Gawain, although it is Lancelot who will ultimately return her to Caerleon. Chrétien, perhaps advertizing, gives quite a few details. The English poet omits them.

2219   *so* is added above the line by another hand.

2237   *murnyng*. MS: *murnyg*. S's emendation, followed by EETS and Mills.

2249   On giants, see *Sir Perceval*, note to line 1963.

2264   *And*. MS: *In*. S's emendation.

2353   A red capital initial.

2428   Between this line and the next appear the words of the scribe: "here is the myddes of this boke." Since this is not the midpoint of the romance — it is 412 lines past the middle — this remark presents a problem. EETS suggests that the scribe is referring here not only to his own work, but to his copy text as well, and that, since that manuscript was not likely to have been neatly numbered, the scribe of our text simply estimated the number of lines. S hypothesized that the poet carelessly omitted lines here and elsewhere might account for the discrepancy but does not specify which lines have been omitted or why. Neither theory is altogether satisfactory.

2429   A blue capital "S."

2441   *prest*. MS: *prst*. R's emendation, followed by S, EETS, & Mills.

2480   *opon*. MS: *open*. Schleich's emendation, followed by EETS, and Mills.

2522   *foure ogayns tham thre*. The four are Ywain, the lion, God, and justice ("right"), a powerful foursome against the three fiendish accusers.

2523   A red initial capital.

2611   A blue capital Þ.

2645   The rich lady is, of course, Alundyne, who does not recognize Ywain in his battle attire (his visor is over his face) and would not know that her husband would be associated with a lion. It is not yet time for Ywain to make himself known to her.

2662   EETS (citing Ernst Brugger, "Yvain and his Lion," *MP* 38 [1941], 277ff.) notes that it was not unusual in the Middle Ages for a brave knight to be compared to a lion, as in Richard the Lionheart or King William the Lion of Scotland. Doob takes another tack, seeing the lion as a foil for Ywain, and a symbol for what the knight has first lost, then won. His faithfulness to his master contrasts with Ywain's neglect of his wife; his compassion, with Ywain's hedonistic quest for personal glory. The lion's traits are those the knight must learn, and only *after* he learns them can be hailed "the knight with the lyoun" (pp. 150–51). Hawkins ("Yvain's Madness") views the knight's harmonious relationship with the animal as a conquering of his own "inner beasts" and the finding of his identity as a knight who can reconcile the forces and prowess of love.

2676   *len*. Taglicht notes that the MS distinguishes consistently between *len* "grant" (also 2677, 2872, 2875) and *lene* "lend" (737, 1527, 1542, 1824), both from OE *laenan* (*NM*, p. 646).

2683   A red initial capital.

2743   A blue capital "B."

2746   The following story of the lord who died and of his two daughters who used the law to gain their inheritance is found in a number of medieval works — see, for example, *Diu Crone* and *La Mule sans Frein*.

2748   *two* is added above the line in the same hand.

2788   *noght*. MS: *nght*. R's emendation, followed by all.

2798   MS lacks the second *the*. R's emendation, followed by all.

2877   *Lundet*. MS: *Lunded*. R's emendation, followed by all.

2880   *fand*. EETS ignores the rhyme and reads *fond*, but Taglicht notes that that form does not appear in the MS.

2931   A red initial capital.

2935   *said*. Missing in MS. R's emendation, followed by all.

2966   The English poet has taken the episode of the silk maidens entirely from Chrétien, whose own "realistic" details are probably drawn from Sicilian and Oriental sources. See R. A. Hall, "The Silk Factory in Chrétien de Troyes," *MLN* 56 (1941), 418–22.

2995   *noght*. MS: *nght*. R's emendation, followed by all.

3025   I follow Taglicht's gloss here, who notes that the use of *wight* + infinitive in the sense of "capable of" is not noted by the *OED* (*NM*, p. 646), though the usage is common in ME.

3230   *nowther*. MS: *nowthr*. R's emendation, followed by all. It should be noted, however, that the scribe frequently drops *e* from suffixes.

3238   *murnyng*. MS: *Murnyg*. R's emendation, followed by all.

3243   A blue capital "N."

3251   *maiden*. EETS considers the form to be an uninflected plural, but Taglicht suggests the reference may be to *his damysel* in 3237 (see also line 3195) (*NM*, p. 647).

3260   *had* added above the line, same hand.

3289   *saide* added above the line, another hand.

3331   A red capital initial.

3357   *forth er*. EETS reads *forther*. I follow Mills' gloss of *onward*.

3443   A blue capital Þ.

3481   *elder*. MS has *yonger*, written by a later hand over erasure. R's emendation, followed by all. S notes the hint of *l* in the erasure, which he takes to have been part of the original word, *elder*.

3494   *als*. MS: *al*. R's emendation, followed by all.

3509   Chrétien's "incognito battle," between friends, a folkloristic trope, becomes common in subsequent medieval romances, though this is its first appearance in the Arthurian romance (EETS).

3526   *kast a glove*. Throws down the gage, the challenge to a duel.

3567   *nobillay*. I follow Taglicht and Mills' gloss here. EETS suggests "nobility of nature and rank," but see OED *nobley*, sb. 2, which cites this line.

3571   A red initial letter.

3604   *ogayns*. EETS reads *ogaynes*.

3681   A blue capital letter.

3704   *knaw*. MS: *knw*. R's emendation, followed by all.

3767   According to medieval inheritance laws, land should not be divided. Rather, it should pass intact to the eldest son, should there be one. When the heir was a daughter, however, the law was not so precise and two resolutions were possible. First, the land could be held by the eldest daughter as "representative tenent," to whom her sisters would have been answerable according to feudal law. Second, the land could have been "parted," i.e., divided into as many sections as there were daughters to inherit it, and these women would owe fealty to the king. The first solution seems to be comparable to that one found in the poem. (See EETS.)

3769   *withowten*. MS: the second *t* is added above the line in another hand.

3773   A red capital Þ.

3827   *ever*. MS: *over*. R's emendation, followed by all.

3903   *Madame*. MS: *Madana*. R's emendation, followed by all.

3913   *swere here* over erasure: the first *e* of *swere* is added above the line by another hand.

3916   *anikyns*. MS: *akyns*. S's emendation, followed by EETS and Mills. R emends to *alkyns*.

3941   A blue capital initial.

3953   A red capital initial.

4009   A red capital "N."

4033–34 These two lines are scribal and have been added to the MS in the same hand, but in red ink.

Glossary

a *a, any, some; one;* (interj.)

aby *abide, suffer*

akke *oak*

akton *jacket, jerkin*

alkyn *of every kind*

als *as; also*

allan, ane *alone*

alsone *as soon as, instantly, at once*

alswa *also*

althir *very*

amende *remedy (a bad situation)*

appert *impudent*

are *ere, previously, before*

at *at, to, in, by means of; that*

aughte (v.) *ought; possessed, owned;* (n.) *gift, possession*

aw(e)nn *own*

ay *always, ever*

afote *on foot, on his feet*

bacyn *basin*

bade (v.) *bid, persuade, delay; command, taught;* (n.) *hesitation, further ado*

balde *increase*

balde *brave, fearless(ly); confident*

bale *grief, suffering, misfortune*

bande *bound*

bane *destroyer, death, doom*

bann *curse*

bare *boar*

baron *family, nobility*

bathe *both*

bede *offer*

belde *protector*

belyfe *freely, happily*

belyffe *quickly*

bere (v.) *carry; pierce; overthrow;* (n.) *coffin*

beryns *warriors*

bete *remedy, mend*

better *more valuable*

betyde *happen*

bihete *promise, assure*

birde *noble lady, damsel*

bitaughte *entrusted*

bityde *happen*

blake *soot, smoke*

blakke *turn pale*

ble *complexion*

blythe *happy*

body *person*

bole *swelled up*

bon *bane, destiny*

bone *reward*

borde *dining table*

bost *boast*

bot *but, unless, except, before*

bot if *unless*

bote *use, avail*

bother(s) *both*

boure *bower, inner chamber*

203

bown(e) *armed, prepared, bound, ready*

bowsom *willing, obedient, kind*

brade *broad*

brand(e) *sword*

brandes *flames*

(on) brede *far and wide*

bren *burn*

brodire *brother*

brothely *fiercely, violently, vehemently*

browke *lay waste, possess*

brudale *wedding feast*

brynnande *burning*

buske *bush, woods*

busked *made ready, prepared*

byde *bid, sustain, command; take leave of*

bydene *altogether, one and all*

bygone *overwhelmed*

byluffede *beloved*

byrke *birch*

bysoughte *searched for, importuned*

bytaughte *gave*

bythoughte *thought*

calle *invite*

can *know*

carped *spoke*

carpys *debates*

ceté *town, city, enclosure*

chaunged *exchanged*

chere *disposition, state of mind*

clobe-lome *club, weapon*

coste *expense; behavior, distressed*

dare (v.) *hide;* (adj.) *able*

dase *does*

dawe *dawn;* **dawes** days, of old

dede *death; activity*

dele (v.) *deal with;* (n.) *piece, bit*

derne *judge, consider*

dere (n.) *great one, dear; animals;* (v.) *harm, injure*

deren *to inquire, dare; injure, impose*

deris *harm*

dern *secret, concealed, hidden*

derrest *most costly*

dese *dais*

dighte, dyghte *prepared, equipped, dressed, designed; tied*

do *cause*

done *done, caused; put*

doughty *bold, worthy, valiant*

doun caste *taken down*

dose *cause*

draghte *course (of fate)*

drawen *carried away*

drery *sad*

dry *endure*

duelle *dwelle, stay; quash*

dwergh *dwarf*

dyghte *to arm, armed, dressed, prepared*

dyng *strike*

dynned *resounded*

dynttis *blows, strokes*

ee *eye*

eghe, eghne *eye, eyes*

elde *older, more experienced, full grown*

emanges *among*

eme *uncle*

er *before;* (v.) *are*

ertow *are you*

estres *stories*

even *directly*

ever *as even as*

everilkane *everyone*

Glossary

fa *foe*

fade *determined, fated*

fadde *lacking strength; eager for battle*

faire *fair, eloquent*

fande *found, came upon; test strength*

far, fer *at a distance, far*

fare (v.) *go, travel;* (n.) *journey, conduct*

fase *foes*

fast(e) *dance, close together; eagerly, earnestly*

faute *fault*

fayne *joyful, eager*

fayrenes *beauty*

fayntise *guile, deceit*

felawe *person*

fele *many*

felde *field of battle, the joust*

fele *insensitive*

felle, fele (adj.) *fierce, cruel;* (n.) *more*

felly *fiercely*

felt *fetched, took*

fende *fiend*

ferde *fear*

fere (n.) *companion, fellow, equal;* (v.) *terrify, frighten*

(in) fere *together*

feres *fellows*

ferly *at a distance; wonder, marvel*

feste *celebration, banquet*

fet *brought*

filde *field*

fill(en) *to satisfy a desire*

fode *creature; offspring; person*

folde *luxurious*

fole *fool, naif; foal*

foly *foolish*

fonde(n) *try, seek; set out, travel*

for *despite; because of*

forbare *forbade; spared*

forfare *destroy, ruin*

forhevede *forehead*

forlorne *destroyed, utterly lost*

forsake *cease from fighting*

forthe day *late in the morning, late in the day*

forthirmare *farther*

forthirmaste *first*

forthwarde *ahead*

forthy *accordingly, therefore*

forward *agreement, promise*

fostered *brought up*

frayne *seek battle; inquire from, question, ask*

free, fre (adj.) *well-mannered, courteous, gracious;* (n.) *noble person*

freke *knight, man*

frith *forest, woodland*

funden *found*

fyre-iren *steel*

gaffe, gyffe *gave*

gammen, gamen *joy, pleasure, sport, banter*

gan *did*

gare *make*

gase *goes*

gate *way, path; salvation; gaits (steps)*

gayte, gate *goat*

ger(e), gerre (v.) *make, do, cause, equip;* (n.) *things, goods, equipment*

gerys *ways, methods of behavior*

gett, gette *led into, exposed to*

gif (conj.) *if;* (v.) *give*

glade *flow; make glad*

glede *spark*

glyde *walk, move*

gnede *lacking, sparing, stingy; cautious; scarce*

gon *walk, ride, go*

grasse *grassy plot, grass*

graythed *made ready, prepared, arrayed*

graythely *readily, properly*

gree *victory*

gres, gresse *grass, woods*

gret(e) (v.) *greeted; wept;* (n.) *anger*

greves *woods, groves*

grym *horrid creature*

grythe *peace*

gudes *goods*

gyffen a gift *make a pledge*

gyle *trick*

habade, habyde *suffer, stay, await; readily engage in war*

haby *have, abide, suffer*

hailded, haylsede *greeted, saluted*

halde(s) *faithful; fortress*

hale *sound, wholesome, entire*

halely *wholly, entirely*

hals *neck, throat*

hame *home*

happed *cover*

hare *gray*

harmes *calamity*

harnayse *arm (oneself)*

has *concerned*

hat *is called*

hate *hot*

haulle *palace, castle*

hede *head; quality*

hefe *raise, lift*

heghe *lofty, high*

helde *kept*

hele (n.) *health;* (v.) *heal*

hend(e) *gracious, courteous*

hendely *courteously*

hent *seize*

here (v.) *hear;* (n.) *army*

hernyste *armed*

herte *male deer*

heste *vow*

hete *promise*

hete *flames*

hethen *hence*

hevid *head*

highte *was called, was named; command, promise*

hind *female deer*

hode *hood*

holde (v.) *keep;* (n.) *castle*

holtes *woods*

hope *expect, think*

houppe *hope*

hovande *waiting*

hovyde *remained*

"how!" (interj.) *"You!"*

how-gates *however*

hy (n.) *high, noble; haste,* (v.) *hasten*

hynte *received*

ilkane *also, each one*

ilke *same, aforementioned*

in (n.) *household;* (prep.) *in, beside*

infere *together, in company*

innermare *further inside*

inogh *enough, sufficient*

insight *wisdom*

iryn *iron*

iwys *indeed, certainly*

jangleynge *chatter*
justynges *joustings*
kan *know*
kane *can*
kare *sorrow*
kayes *keys*
kechyne *kitchen*
kempe *contestant, warrior*
ken *see, recognize*
kende (n.) *character;* (v.) *knew*
kene *acrimonious; brave, bold*
kenely *daringly*
kepe *put store in*
keste *caste*
kevells *lots*
kevylees *bridles*
kind *offspring; nature*
kiste *chest*
kowth *could, was able*
knave *boy*
knylle *knell*
kynde *nature, natural course of things*
kyth (n.) *words, announcement, news;*
    (prep.) *among my people*
kythe *made known*

lacynge *fastenings*
lange are *earlier*
lare *learning*
late *leave*
lathe *unpleasant, hateful, loathsome*
lavede *to feed liquid to*
law *low*
laykes *sword play*
layne *conceal, hide, lie*
layte *seek*
lef, lefe (n.) *friend, everyone;* (adj.)
    disposed, eager; (v.) *leave*

lele *fair, loyal, faithful*
lele *loyally*
leman *lover*
lende *dwell, arrive*
lere *teach, tell*
lese *lie, lies*
lesse (n.) *common people;* (adj.) *small;*
    (adv.) *scarcely at all*
let(en), lett *surrender, delay, oppose,*
    hinder; allow to pass
lethir *weak, feeble; wicked, bad*
leveande *able, living*
leved *left*
levore *steel spear, far, pole*
lewté *fealty*
list *desired, yearned for*
lome *weapon, penis*
lorne *lose, suffer loss of*
lose *praise, renown*
lothe *injury*
louse *let loose*
lyggand *lying*
lyther *wicked*
lythes *listen*

ma, maa (v.) *make;* (adj.) *more*
Mahown *Mahomet*
maistré (n.) *menacing gestures,*
    conquest; mastery; (v.) *act strongly,*
    act with
maistri *victory, authority*
make (n.) *mate;* (v.) *perform*
mane *man; remembrance; complaint,*
    lamentation, moan
mangeri *feast*
manless *unprotected*
mare (n.) *nobility; female horse;* (adv.)
more

marte *slaughtered animal*

mase *confused, dazed*

mate *dejected, defeated, exhausted*

mawgré (prep.) *despite, notwithstanding;* (n.) *ill will*

mawnger *manger*

may *maiden*

mayne (v.) *rode;* (adj.) *powerful, violent, strong;* (n.) *strength*

maystres *wonders*

mede *reward*

meete, mette *food*

mekill, mekil *much, mighty, large*

menevaire *ermine*

mengede *mingled*

menske *honor*

menye *company, army*

menynge *understanding*

mere *mare*

merkes *thrusts*

mese *dinner, course of a meal*

mesure *moderation*

mete *measure*

mett *measured*

miche *much*

mister *need, be in need of*

mobles *treasures*

mode *mind, heart, set of feelings*

moghte *might, power*

molde *earth, floor*

mon *must*

mone (v.) *remember, reminisce; moan;* (n.) *man; lament*

montenance *space, distance*

more *moor*

most *largest*

moughte *strong, might*

murnand *mourning, grieving*

mynne *less*

mynt *intended, endeavored, aimed*

nakke *neck*

nakyn *not any*

nane *none*

nangatis *in no wise*

nayte *need, require*

nefe *fist*

neghes, neghede *nears, neared*

nere *close*

nerehande *close up*

nome(n) *took; taken, captured*

none *at that time; noon*

nother *other*

nurture, nurtoure *courtesy*

nykkes *refuses*

nynte *ninth*

of *from, at some distance from; off*

ogain(s) *in answer; against*

omell *among, amid*

onane *soon, anon, at once*

one *on, in*

or *ere, before*

ordain *prepare, arrange, plan*

oste *host*

othergates *otherwise*

oughte *properly*

overrynnes *runs over, runs down*

palis *palace, fence of pales, palisade*

pane *lining of garment*

pares *do harm*

parfoy *by my faith*

pase *gait, speed*

paste *gone, departed, passed*

pay(ed) *please(d)*

Glossary

pendid *pertained*

pertis *divides*

pesane *armour to protect upper part of chest and neck*

pese *peace*

Petir! *By Saint Peter!*

pith, pyth *eagerness, strength*

play-fere *sweetheart, playmate*

play, playnge *sport, performance*

playlome *weapon*

pole *marsh*

poustee, powsté *power*

prekande, prikande *riding rapidly*

presande *present*

prese *specified area, crowd*

prest *quickly*

prevé *secret, hidden*

prevee (adj.) *worthy;* (v.) *prove(s)*

prise *prize; value, something worth striving for*

pyn *torment*

quert *health*

qwyk *living, alive*

qwyte *repay*

rade *rode, rode away*

rafe *tore*

rase *rush*

rath(e) *impatient; quickly*

raw(e) row; *turn;* **on rawe** *in turn*

raye *king*

real *royal*

reches *dainties (food), wealth*

recrayhandes *cowards*

rede (n.) *plan, course of action, advice;* (v.) *counsel, plan, advise, demand*

rese(n) *rush*

righte *particulars*

righte(n) *raise*

rist *rest*

rydande *riding*

ryfe *right, correctly*

rynne(n) *run*

rode *set out*

Rode *Cross*

roghte(n) *have concern for, care about*

roke(n) *fall back*

sadde *hard, violent, solemn*

saghteling *reconciliation, agreement, peace*

sal *shall*

sale *hall*

sare *deadly; sore*

sary *sorry, grieved*

say *speak*

schafe *shave*

schende *defeat*

schere *cut*

schewede *showed*

scho *she*

schoke *was shaken*

schone *shoes*

schote, schottyng *to cast (casting) a spear*

seelys, selles *marvels*

seese *sees*

seke *sick*

sekerly *surely, truly*

sekirnes *security*

semely *comely one*

sen (conj.) *since;* (n.) *sense*

sertes *certainly*

sessen *ceased*

sewed *followed*

209

Glossary

seyne *saint*
sho *she*
siche *such*
sith(e) *times, occasions*
skathe *injury; matter of regret*
slaked *laid down*
slee *skillful*
slik(e) *such*
slogh *killed*
sloo *slay*
slone *slain*
slongen *thrown off*
snelle *quickly*
socoure *help, aid, assist*
sogates *thus*
sold(e) *should (be)*
sought *pursued*
soth(e) *truth*
spalde *limbs*
spare *hold back*
sped *hastened*
spedde *been successful*
spoyle *plunder*
sprent *flew, sprang*
sprongen *issued, sprung*
spryng(en) *charging*
stande *withstand*
stane *stone*
stayred *thrust*
stede *warhorse; place*
sterte, stirttes *leaps*
stode *stud*
stoneyde, stonayed *stunned*
stour *battle*
stownde *for a time, for a moment*
stowre *battle, fight*
strang(e) *fine, great, strong*
strekyn *smitten*

strete *path, way*
stroye *destroy*
stryffe *disagreement*
study *meditation, state of reverie*
styffe *strong, powerful*
stynt *hesitate, delay, stop*
stythe *strong*
suffire *be gentle with*
swaa *so*
swayne *knave*
swilk(e) *such*
swire *neck*
swyth(e) *immediately, at once*
sythe *days (time)*
sythen *since (that time)*

ta, tane *taken, judged*
taa *too*
take *come*
take tent *pay attention*
takens *tokens, details*
takynnyng *sign of recognition, token*
tane *the one*
tase *takes*
taughte *showed*
tayte *eagerness*
teche *show*
techyng *upbringing*
telde *camp, pavillion, tent*
tene *vexed, vexation, anger*
thaa *those*
the *thee, you*
thede *that place, country*
thedir *thither*
thee *thrive*
theffe *thief*
ther *where*
thertis *divides*

210

Glossary

thethyn *thence*
thir *these*
tho, thoo *those*
thofe, thogfe *although, as though*
thole *bear, suffer*
thrafe *throve*
thraffe *prosper*
thraw, throw *space of time, while*
thro, throo *those*
throle *suffer, bear*
throo (adj.) *eagerness;* (n.) *anger*
thurgh *throughout*
thusgates *thusly, in this way*
till *unto, to*
tite *quickly*
token *sign*
tone *the one*
too *take*
tother *the second, the other*
travell *deed, effort*
travellande *traveler*
tree *wood*
trenchepayne *bread server*
trow *believe*
tryppe *herd, flock*
tuke *took*
twa *two*
tyde *time*
tyne *lose*
tynt *told; lost, wasted*
tyte *quickly*

uggly *fearful*
umbrere *visor*
unborely *meanly*
uncely *hapless*
uncouthe *foreign*
undertane, undirtane *undertaken*

undir *just below*
undirstande *understand, believe*
unement *ointment*
unfere *infirm*
unhende *clumsy, discourteous*
unkowth *unknown, strange*
unnethes *scarcely, hardly*
unroo *unrest*
unryde *large, numerous*
unsaughte *distraught*
unspoil *despoil, strip of possessions*
untill *until, to*

vencusede *vanquished*
ventale *neck-piece*
vesage *countenance*

wa *woe*
wakened *awakened*
wale *at will*
wande *stick, shaft*
wane (n.) *manners, means; stronghold;* (v.) *goes*
wann *turn; awoke*
wansome *miserable*
wapynes *weapons*
warande *guarantee*
warly *cautiously*
warysoune *reward, treasure*
warre *awake*
wate *know(s)*
wayte, wate *afflict*
wayte *sentinel*
wedde *pledge*
wede *clothing, armor*
welde *wield*
welden *govern, possess*
wele *indeed*

welke *walked*

wend(e) *wend, go, wander; thought, assumed, imagined*

wene *doubt, think*

wened *assumed*

wete *know*

wexe *grew*

whase *whose*

whatkyns *what kind of*

whedire *although, wherefore*

whills *all the while*

whilom *once*

wighte *person, creature*

wightly *boldly, swiftly*

will *desire*

wirchippe *worship*

wirkes *works*

wist(e) *knew*

wit *know*

withy *pliable branch*

wo *bad luck*

wode *(gone) mad; was embedded*

wodde *wilderness*

woke *weak*

wolde *power, possession*

wone (n.) *conduct, custom, course of action, manner, fate;* (v.) *dwell*

wonnes *dwell*

woode-wande *branches*

worthly *worthy, fine*

wote *know*

wreke *avenge*

wrethe *grew angry*

wyche *witch*

wyde-whare *far and wide*

wyghte (adj.) *strong;* (n.) *person*

wynn *enjoy; defeat*

wythen *from whence*

yare *soon*

yede *went (out)*

yelde *yield, pay (for), claim*

yemande *yeomen, guard*

yerne eagerly

yit *yet*

yode *went*

yolde *yielded*

yole *Christmas*

yon, yone *yonder*